Managing International Political Risk

Managing International Political Risk

Edited by

Theodore H. Moran
School of Foreign Service
Georgetown University

BLACKWELL
Business

Michael R. Czinkota, Consulting Editor, North America, Blackwell Series in Business

First published 1998

2 4 6 8 10 9 7 5 3 1

Blackwell Publishers Inc.
350 Main Street
Malden, Massachusetts 02148
USA

Blackwell Publishers Ltd
108 Cowley Road
Oxford OX4 1JF
UK

Library of Congress Cataloging-in-Publication Data

Managing international political risk / edited by Theodore H. Moran.
  p. cm.
  Includes bibliographical references and index.
  ISBN 0-631-20880-1 (alk. paper). – ISBN 0-631-20881-X (pbk. : alk. paper)
  1. Investments, Foreign–Political aspects. 2. International business enterprises–Political aspects. I. Moran, Theodore H., 1943–
HG4538.M348 1998
332.67'3–dc21   98-7600
                                      CIP

British Library Cataloguing in Publication Data

A CIP catalogue record for this book is available from the British Library

Typeset in 10 on 11½ pt Times by Wearset from CRC supplied by the Editor

Printed in Great Britain by MPG Books, Victoria Square, Bodmin, Cornwall

This book is printed on acid-free paper

Contents

III
POLITICAL RISK INSURANCE AS A TOOL TO MANAGE
INTERNATIONAL POLITICAL RISK

Preface

This volume is the outgrowth of a symposium on International Political Risk Management Techniques and the Role of Political Risk Insurance held under the joint auspices of the Multilateral Investment Guarantee Agency of the World Bank Group (MIGA), and of the Karl F. Landegger Program in International Business Diplomacy and the Pew Economic Freedom Fellows Program at the School of Foreign Service, Georgetown University.

MIGA's purpose is to facilitate the flow of foreign investment to developing and transition countries by alleviating investors' concerns about non-commercial risks. MIGA has always interpreted its mandate broadly and, in addition to its well-known investment insurance business, has actively sought to promote investment flows through a variety of other activities and research. This symposium is an outgrowth of those efforts.

The Karl F. Landegger Program in International Business Diplomacy sponsors teaching and research at the intersection of international corporate strategy, public policy, and the conduct of business–government relations. The Pew Economic Freedom Fellows Program, as part of its mission to train leaders from former communist and socialist nations in market economics, develops case studies and course materials that illustrate how foreign direct investment can advance the development prospects of host economies in the developing countries and economies-in-transition.

The objective of this volume is to provide insights into the sources of political risk to international investors, suggest possible tools and techniques for the management of political risk, and offer perspectives on the role of political risk insurance as a part of international investment strategy.

Our shared aim is to help investors better assess and manage the political risks associated with prospective investments because of the benefits to the host countries arising from sound investments. This volume focuses particularly on the challenges associated with foreign direct investment in natural resources and infrastructure.

In so doing, we hope to contribute to removing some of the obstacles that inhibit investors from proceeding with projects that can enhance economic growth and raise living standards in the developing countries and economies-in-transition.

Gerald T. West	Theodore H. Moran
Multilateral Investment	School of Foreign Service
Guarantee Agency	Georgetown University
The World Bank Group	

Introduction:
The Growing Role of Foreign Direct Investment in the Developing Countries

Theodore H. Moran[*]

There has been a dramatic shift over the past decade in the nature of the welcome provided to foreign direct investors in the developing countries and the economies-in-transition, in the magnitude of the response by foreign investors themselves, and in the role that direct investment is playing in the growth of the host countries.

At the same time risks and uncertainties of an extra-commercial nature have not receded, and, in some areas, may be on the increase. The need of international investors and financial institutions for effective tools and strategies to manage risks and uncertainties of an extra-commercial nature remains high.

Three Groups of Questions

This volume explores three broad groups of questions:

First, what are the principal sources of international political risk in the contemporary era? To what extent does the ostensible enthusiasm for the participation of foreign investors in the developing countries and economies-in-transition mask the persistence of old vulnerabilities? What kinds of new vulnerabilities are international companies and financial institutions likely to find most troublesome?

Second, what are the principal tools foreign investors can use to manage international political risk? How can such tools best be integrated into the broader corporate strategy of international investors and financial institutions? How can protection of investors be merged with enhancing the contribution these investors can make to the growth of the recipient economies?

[*]*Theodore H. Moran is the Karl F. Landegger Professor of International Business Diplomacy, School of Foreign Service, Georgetown University.*

Third, what is the particular role of political risk insurance as a tool of investor strategy? How do the roles of public and private political risk insurers differ? Are there complementarities between public and private political risk insurers that can be enhanced and expanded?

The answers to these questions are as important to host country authorities in the developing countries and economies-in-transition, as to the international corporate and financial communities because of the expanding impact that international investors have on their prospects.

To set the scene for the examination of political risk – and of political risk management techniques – it is useful to begin with a brief perspective on the growing role of foreign direct investment in the development process.

The Growing Role of Foreign Direct Investment in The Development Process

From 1990 to 1997, the total of private capital flows to developing countries and economies-in-transition increased fivefold, reaching a level of approximately $256 billion in 1997. These private sources now represent more than four-fifths of all capital inflows to the developing and transitioning world.[1]

The share of foreign direct investment in these movements has more than quintupled over the same period, growing from $24 billion in 1990 to $120 billion in 1997, surpassing all other sources of capital. Official development assistance, in contrast, has averaged $40–50 billion per year, a rapidly shrinking proportion of the total.

The movements of foreign direct investment have been quite unevenly distributed. East Asia and Latin America have been the largest recipients, accounting for some $87 billion in 1997. Since 1992, China has been by far the largest single destination, attracting $37 billion or 31 percent of the total in 1997, although some substantial fraction of this is estimated to represent "round tripping" by domestic investors. The top seven countries have accounted for $71 billion or 65 percent of the total (China, Mexico, Malaysia, Brazil, Indonesia, Thailand, Argentina).

But individual countries elsewhere have improved their draw considerably. These include Hungary and Poland in Eastern Europe, for example: Kazakhstan, Uzbekistan, Azerbaijan in Central Asia, and Vietnam in Southeast Asia. The destination of foreign direct investment is not a static phenomenon.

Foreign direct investment is defined as international corporate operations in which the parent firm exercises control or supervision over the activities of affiliates in multiple countries. It differs from portfolio investment that mutual funds or pension funds (for example) may make in the shares of companies in a foreign stock market in the hope of participating passively, so to speak, in their appreciation. It correlates very imprecisely with the broader category of "capital flows" (even though foreign investment movements do show up in balance of payments statistics), since the actual capital used to carry out corporate operations may be raised locally, or mobilized in a third country, rather than "transferred" from the country of the parent to the location of the investment.

The appropriate way to measure the impact of foreign direct investment is by calculating its contribution to the real economy of the host, rather than merely assessing its behavior as a net financial flow. The gains to the real economy come not just in the form of physical capital formation, but also in the form of human capital development, transfer of technology and of business know-how (managerial skills), and expansion of markets and foreign trade.

Foreign direct investment has a potent role to play in the development prospects of the host countries. Underdevelopment persists when poorer economies are caught in a vicious cycle, in which low productivity generates low wages, which generate low savings, which generate low investment, which reinforces the initial low productivity. Foreign direct investment can turn this vicious cycle of underdevelopment into a virtuous cycle of growth by offering new capital and new avenues for earning foreign exchange to complement local savings, and by supplying inputs of management, marketing, and technology to improve productivity. The result, under reasonably competitive conditions, improves efficiency and enhances the prospects for growth.[2]

There is abundant evidence to support this virtuous cycle of growth arising from the activities of foreign firms.[3] Foreign investors pay higher wages than domestic firms. They exhibit higher levels of productivity. They bring newer and more advanced technology. They respond more rapidly to the opportunities presented by trade liberalization than their purely domestic counterparts.

Foreign direct investors can make a dynamic contribution to the host economy, moreover, that extends much beyond the usual list of valuable ingredients, such as capital, technology, management and marketing expertise, indicated above. In well-structured projects under relatively competitive conditions, they supply a direct link to the cutting edge of most sophisticated processes and best practices in the industry; they upgrade technologies, improve management practices, train workers, and expand marketing networks in an on-going process; they bring technological and human resource improvements into the economy more rapidly than any other avenue of host country acquisition.[4]

Finally, foreign investors provide robust backward linkages into the local economy. In countries that reward domestic as well as foreign investment and that sponsor vigorous programs of indigenous education and skill-training, foreign investors help nurture the expansion of the supplier base, with coaching in production, management, and marketing techniques (including penetration of export markets) for indigenous as well as foreign producers of inputs. Even in industries that are often accused of setting up "screwdriver operations" – such as electronics/computer assembly – there is extensive evidence of spill-overs and externalities that benefit local firms.

The foreign investor activities most frequently referenced in this volume – natural resource and private infrastructure projects – are particularly valuable for the development process. Mining and petroleum operations generate (or save) hard currency revenues; they provide support both to the balance of payments and to the indigenous tax base. Infrastructure projects may produce agglomeration effects:

economies of scope and scale in which economic activities are able to cluster in poles of growth whose components reinforce each other. They are likely to provide social benefits that far outweigh their economic costs.

To be sure, not every foreign investment project enhances the recipient country's prospects for development. Foreign investors can bring negative externalities, such as pollution, or engage in harmful social practices, such as unsafe working conditions. As in the developed world, the contribution of international companies to the local economy is largest within a well-formulated and competently-administered regulatory environment.

Moreover, ill-structured foreign investment projects – in particular, sub-scale projects sheltered from competition in protected local markets – can misallocate resources and generate a negative drag on economic growth.[5] Mandatory joint-venture and/or technology-licensing requirements are likely to result in deployment of older technology and less rapid upgrading of technological, managerial, and quality-control capabilities, and weaker export performance, than projects where the international firms are free to choose their own competitive strategies.

Overall, the expansion of foreign direct investment is positively associated with higher economic growth in the less developed countries and economies-in-transition. And when one examines which way the arrow of causation is pointing – that is, whether higher indigenous growth rates are attracting more investment, or external investment is leading to higher growth – the analysis of changes in foreign direct investment levels and growth rates over time indicates that, while the two variables influence each other simultaneously, there is a clear chain of causality that runs from foreign direct investment to economic growth rather than merely the other way around.

Moreover, foreign direct investment is "patient capital." It has staying power. A large proportion of the movements in international financial markets take the form of transfers of short-term debt instruments and near-money equivalents. In response to economic uncertainties and possible crises these flows can swing from positive to negative in quite short periods of time, exacerbating underlying instabilities. In Latin America in 1993–4 and in Southeast Asia 1997–8 such flows have constituted a substantial drain on local financial markets, on a net basis, with new lending limited to short-term trade-related loans. Shifts of portfolio capital may be slightly less volatile, but abrupt swings in local stock markets illustrate the mobility of portfolio placements as well.

Foreign direct investment, in contrast, is tied to longer term strategies and cannot generally withdraw so quickly. As foreign firms strive to create supplier networks that enhance their position in international markets, they try to align their operations with the fundamental comparative advantages of the countries where they are located. While economic uncertainties and economic mismanagement may indeed lead to a pause in new commitments (and prolonged deterioration could result in the abandonment of some facilities), the economic restructuring that follows a period of financial crisis is quite likely to enhance the international competitiveness of the local subsidiaries of foreign parents and stimulate a new round of investments.

Win-Win Benefits for Home Countries

At the same time, outward investment from the developed countries to the developing countries and economies-in-transition produces win-win outcomes for the home countries, as well as for the recipients of the investment.

In contrast to popular assertions that outward investment "hollows out" the home economy or popular conceptions that outward investment creates "a great sucking sound" of jobs exiting the home economy, outward investment reinforces the competitive position of industries in the home country and in fact increases exports from the home economy.[6]

Comparing the activities in the home country of firms who do invest abroad with those who do not (holding size, R&D intensity, and other characteristics constant), those who engage in international investment exhibit higher levels of exports and higher levels of jobs related to exports than firms who stay at home. The complementarity between outward investment and exports is strong not only for intermediate goods shipped for further processing, but also for exports of finished products from the home country. The expansion of outward investment appears to create a magnet for exports from the home country across regions and across kinds of products.

As a consequence, therefore, outward investment not only leads to more robust export activity than if the home country firms were somehow artificially inhibited from moving some of their operations abroad, but outward investment also improves the composition of good jobs/bad jobs in the home economy, since export-related jobs offer higher wages and benefits than non-export-related jobs.

Overall, outward investment generates profits for the home country firms, intermediate goods and services that may be available to home country producers, final goods and services that may be available to home country consumers, and export-based jobs for home country workers.[7]

Obstacles to Foreign Direct Investment in the Developing Countries and Economies-in-Transition

What are the obstacles to the continuation and enlargement of the role that foreign direct investment can play in the developing world and economies-in-transition, and what can be done to speed further flows?

The greatest stimulus to foreign direct investment lies in progress on the part of host countries and would-be hosts in the developing countries and economies-in-transition to "get the fundamentals right"; namely, to pursue sensible macroeconomic policies in the fiscal and monetary sphere, with appropriate microeconomic policies that reward both domestic and foreign investment, while building reliable legal and other commercial institutions.

"Getting the fundamentals right" on macro and microeconomic policies should be accompanied by vigorous progress in trade liberalization, on the part of richer and poorer countries alike.

But the list of obstacles to enhancing the movement of foreign direct investors does not end there. As the next section of this volume points out, there is a further need to deal with persistent issues of international political risk.

What are the sources of political risk in the contemporary era? What lessons can be derived about managing international political risk in the natural resource and infrastructure sectors? What is the particular role of political risk insurance as a tool in managing international political risk?

These are the questions to which the rest of this volume is addressed. There are three sections, corresponding to each of these three questions, with papers by experienced practitioners that draw on the presentations and dialogue at the MIGA/Georgetown Symposium described in the Preface. I have provided an Overview to each section that offers background, summarizes some of the more salient points in the papers, and raises issues and questions for further discussion and examination.

Notes

[1] These and subsequent statistics come from the World Bank, *Global Development Finance* (Washington, DC: The World Bank, 1998).

[2] Malcolm Gillis, Dwight H. Perkins, Michael Roemer, and Donald R. Snodgrass, *Economics of Development* (New York: W. W. Norton & Company, 1996, 4th Edition).

[3] Magnus Blomstrom and Ari Kokko, *How Foreign Investment Affects Host Countries* (Washington, DC: The World Bank, International Economics Department, International Trade Division, March 1997).

[4] Theodore H. Moran, *Foreign Direct Investment and Development: The New Policy Agenda for Developing Countries and Economies-in-Transition* (Washington, DC: Institute for International Economics, 1998).

[5] Dennis J. Encarnation and Louis T. Wells, Jr., "Evaluating Foreign Investment," in Theodore H. Moran (ed.), *Investing in Development: New Roles for Private Capital?* (Washington, DC: Overseas Development Council, 1986), pp. 61–86.

[6] For a summary of empirical studies of this phenomenon, see Robert E. Lipsey, *Outward Direct Investment and the U.S. Economy* (Cambridge, MA: National Bureau of Economic Research, reprint no. 2020, 1995).

[7] Theodore H. Moran, *Foreign Direct Investment and Good Jobs/Bad Jobs: The Impact of Outward Investment and Inward Investment on Jobs and Wages* (New York: Council on Foreign Relations, 1998).

I
The Changing Nature of Political Risk

Theodore H. Moran

Overview

The climate in which foreign direct investment projects are launched has changed dramatically over the past decade. In nearly every country, a rhetoric of welcome has replaced the ambiance of suspicion and not infrequent hostility found in some countries in earlier periods.

Beneath the rhetoric, most host countries have taken actions and adopted policies that provide some substantive underpinning to the change in tone. Between 1990 and 1997, more than 65 countries introduced changes into the regulations they applied to foreign direct investors; of some 599 such changes, 575 pointed to greater liberalization or promotion of foreign firm activity.[1]

To what extent does this change in attitude mean that some of the old political risks faced by international investors are disappearing? Are new political risks arising? Are there new versions of old threats for which foreign investors need protection?

Old and New Sources of Political Risk

In the first paper in this section, Louis T. Wells, Jr., Herbert F. Johnson Professor of International Management at the Harvard Business School, defines political risks as threats to profitability that are the result of forces external to the industry and which involve some sort of governmental action or inaction. As a first approximation, political risks can be distinguished from commercial uncertainties that arise from changes in economic conditions, such as cost, demand, or extent of competition in the marketplace. They can also be distinguished from acts of nature like fire, earthquakes, floods, and from unexpected accidents or thefts arising in the normal course of business.

To the extent that political actions in a particular host country can affect economic conditions within an industry, or increase the likelihood of fires, accidents, and thefts, the distinctions inevitably begin to blur. Similarly, to the extent that economic miscalculations on the part of a particular set of host authorities weaken or interrupt their ability to meet commitments they have promised to foreign investors, political and economic risk overlap. Finally, to the extent that the motive for a hostile act toward foreigners may be attributed to political, or work-place, or environmental grievances, the specification of political as opposed to commercial or economic causation may be somewhat arbitrary.

The conceptual difficulty of isolating political risks will reappear as a theme throughout this volume.

Some of the traditional sources of political risk seem to be clearly on the wane. The threat of nationalization and expropriation that dominated past decades has declined precipitously. In 1975 there were 83 cases of expropriation. From 1981 to 1992, by one estimation, there were no more than 11 such cases.[2]

But other traditional sources of political risk have not disappeared, including war, civil disturbances, and the continuing emergence of independence movements. The end of the Cold War, Wells points out, has given increasing prominence to ethnic and religious tensions. Old fashioned economic nationalism may be triggered by the inequalities and austerities that the more liberal approach to international trade and investment bring.

At the same time, argues Wells, new sources of risk are emerging. Stronger local business interests may wish to enter what used to be the relatively secure spheres of foreign investor activity, posing a new threat if they use political connections to procure favorable treatment or preference over foreign firms. The domains where foreign and local companies predominate increasingly interpenetrate each other. Local legal systems, or even bilateral treaties promising "national treatment," seldom provide reliable protection against discrimination.

The spread of democracy opens foreign investors to popular criticism, especially when regimes change. The decentralization of power may have the same effect, pushing local debate about policies toward foreign investors in a direction at variance to central government preferences. Local authorities may care more about tolls or revenues associated with infrastructure projects, for example; central authorities may worry about the country's image in international capital markets.

Contemporary mangers, moreover, may be less well prepared to deal with political risks than their predecessors of two decades ago. Many of these managers, Wells asserts, come from the ranks of deal markers, whose bonuses depend upon closing international investment negotiations successfully in the present, rather than worrying about changes that may not emerge for a number of years in the future.

To this list of political risks, Sandy Markwick, Manager, Political and Security Risk Analysis, Control Risks Group, adds the dangers posed by corruption: on the one hand, foreign investors have to face the dangers of unfair awarding of contracts when corruption plays a role; and, on the other hand, foreign investors have to face unfair criticism in the awarding of contracts even when corruption plays no role whatsoever.

The expanding presence of organized crime in some countries, Markwick points out, can lead to intimidation, shake-downs, and systematic theft and fraud.

At the same time, pressure from NGOs (Non-Governmental Organizations) on issues such as human rights and the environment, he argues, complicate the traditional commercial considerations of international companies, especially when backed by boycotts, selective purchasing, and other pressures on the part of states and municipalities in the developed world.

Finally, the growing use of sanctions as a tool of foreign policy – whether toward Cuba, Libya, Iran, or Burma – circumscribes the commercial activities of international companies and not infrequently leaves them stranded in the middle as different governments in the industrial world issue conflicting directives for them to follow.

The Quantification of Political Risk Assessment

How can international corporate strategists assess this array of old and new political risks?

William Irwin of Chevron Overseas Petroleum Inc. argues that political risks such as these can be quantified and built into a probabilistic business model. The central task is to identify which variables in the business model can be influenced through political action. Then, asserts Irwin, through interviewing experienced individuals and experts within the company, within peer companies, and outsiders in the public and private sectors, one can specify the high, low and mid-range values of the political risk variables.

The next step is to perform a sensitivity analysis, integrating the expected value of each of the variables, and generating a graphical representation of the impact of changes in the most sensitive variables. The outcomes may not be symmetric: there may be more up-side potential, than down-side, or vice versa.

Finally, the corporate strategist, according to Irwin, can incorporate the political risk assessment into a decision tree that represents the chronology of choices through the course of the investment process and operating life of the project.

Irwin's approach to quantifying political risk is part of a tradition of political risk assessment that has been vigorously debated by specialists on political risk since before the fall of the Shah of Iran some two decades ago. The arguments about the extent to which political risks can be subjected to quantitative analysis will be examined in further detail at the end of this Section.

Prior to that, one particularly persistent danger to some of the largest international investments – called the "obsolescing bargain" – requires careful examination.

A Persistent Vulnerability to the Obsolescing Bargain

Within the new environment where international investors operate, one source of risk that has bedeviled corporate strategists for more than three decades remains firmly embedded for some types of investment projects, namely, the threat of the obsolescing bargain.

The obsolescing bargain refers to the vulnerability of firms with large fixed investments to find the terms of their operating agreements changed, or renegotiated, once their operations are in place and have proved successful. This vulnerability will pervade the analysis in subsequent chapters. The dynamics of the obsolescing bargain merit more detailed exploration here, at the outset.

As Wells notes, the idea of the obsolescing bargain grew from the effort of Raymond Vernon to understand the evolution of relations between host governments and foreign investors in the developing world in dynamic terms.[3]

Early attempts to model the investor/government relationship in the less developed countries relied on the idea of bilateral monopoly: host governments controlled the conditions of access, foreign investors controlled the capital, management, and technology needed to bring an operation to successful fruition. Each side was likely to structure the investment agreement to capture any rents for itself.

But this bilateral monopoly, argued Vernon, was too static. It ignored the role that risk and uncertainty played in conveying bargaining power to one side or the other: when risk and uncertainty were high (before an investment project was launched), the foreign firm had the power to demand terms that incorporated a premium for that risk and uncertainty; when risk and uncertainty had dissipated (after an investment project was successfully launched), the host authorities who did not want to continue paying for initial risk and uncertainty had the power to adjust terms to eliminate the premium. The investor/host relationship therefore was likely to become rather unstable, with the possibility of abrupt swings in contractual outcomes.

Empirically, investment projects with certain characteristics appeared particularly exposed to the obsolescing bargain.[4] Projects involving large fixed investments suffered a "hostage effect"; they could not credibly threaten to withdraw. Projects with stable technology could not use the ability to withhold the most recent upgrades to reinforce their bargaining position. Projects that produced commodity-like (undifferentiated) products could not use control over brand-name recognition to ward off having their investment agreements squeezed by host authorities.

Projects with large fixed investments, stable technology, and undifferentiated products – in particular natural resource and private infrastructure projects – therefore find themselves faced with an inherent "structural vulnerability" to the dynamics of the obsolescing bargain. In the past, they have been notable targets for confiscation, expropriation, and other forms of host government ownership. More ominously, for the present era of privatization, they have been particularly exposed to changes in tax rates and tariff structures that may call into question the viability of undertaking such operations in the first place.

At first glance, one might assume that the phenomenon of the obsolescing bargain would be a thing of the past. Much of the damage done to foreign investors in earlier periods was accompanied by anti-multinational corporation rhetoric that is much less prominent today.

Perhaps, if the thrust of economic nationalism embodied in the renegotiation of investment contracts were to represent nothing more than what some economists have referred to as the search for "psychic gratification" – an ideological or otherwise non-rational manifestation of what Charles Kindleberger once called "the peasant, the populist, the mercantilist, or the nationalist which each of us harbors in his breast" – there might be grounds for hoping that it would never reappear again.

But what the obsolescing bargain model reveals is a certain quasi-"rational" dimension to the loosening and tightening of the terms of investment that underlie the emotional and/or ideological content of any particular host/investor relationship.

Foreign investors must arrange terms that compensate themselves and their financial backers for the initial risk and uncertainty; they must also arrange compensation structures that allow successful projects to pay for unsuccessful projects, winners to pay for losers. Host governments are unlikely to find it in their interest to let foreign investors be compensated for initial risk and uncertainty indefinitely; successor authorities, in particular, are likely to find political as well as economic reasons to renegotiate large, prominent foreign investment contracts.

The "structural vulnerability" of international investors in the petroleum, mining, pipeline, and other infrastructure sectors is not likely therefore to be a transient phenomenon. As Linda F. Powers, Senior Vice President, Enron International, and Timothy J. Faber, Managing Director for the Americas, GE Capital, point out in the next Section, host authorities in the developing countries and economies-in-transition continue to assume an instinctive "responsibility" to manage the returns to foreigners over the life cycle of highly visible and sensitive infrastructure and natural resource projects.

What kinds of actions can investors in particularly exposed sectors take to mitigate the possibility of political risk associated with the renegotiation of investment agreements? Many of the conventional investor responses fall short of providing meaningful relief.

The Inadequacy of Conventional Investor Responses to the "Obsolescing Bargain"

One common-sense response has been for international corporations and their financial backers to raise the hurdle rate before such vulnerable projects are approved, and to front-load the benefits for the external investors.

But the challenge for international investors in such exposed sectors does not lie in obtaining yet more generous opening terms. It lies in maintaining the stability of such opening terms over longer periods of time. Insisting upon even more favorable terms at the beginning may in fact just help trigger an adverse reaction later on.

A second common-sense response has been for international corporations and their financial backers to adopt a portfolio approach to project investing, counting upon the diversification of project sites to provide a basis for self-insuring against political risks in any given one.

But if all of the individual projects have similar characteristics – large fixed costs, stable technology, undifferentiated products – and hence suffer the same "structural vulnerability," the protection that comes from a diversified portfolio may prove illusory. The self-insurer may unwittingly be subjecting himself to systemic risk.

Perhaps more promising, in addressing the problem of "structural vulnerability," has been a third route – the growing use of international project finance, perhaps backed by multilateral guarantees and political risk insurance, to help ensure the stability of investment agreements in natural resource and private infrastructure ventures.

This approach, weaving together non-recourse financing, multilateral guarantees, and political risk insurance, will be explored in some detail in the next two sections of this volume.

Wells, Markwick, and Irwin provide sophisticated analyses of the complexities of assessing international political risk, and offer some interesting suggestions about methods to help mitigate political risks. Prominent among these is the judicious selection of partners in the host country to help shield the foreign investor.

Questions and Concerns for the Future

Three of the most controversial questions raised in the presentations by Wells, Markwick, and Irwin concern whether political risks can be quantified, how considerations of political risk can be integrated into international corporate strategy, and whether local partners can provide protection against political risks in the host country.

First, to what extent can political risk assessment be subjected to quantitative analysis, as asserted by William Irwin?

Attempts to quantify political risk have taken several forms.[5]

There have been efforts to use "objective" indicators, often economic, such as changes in host country growth rates, inflation rates, income disparities to predict political outcomes (changes in government, changes in governmental policies) directly.

There have been efforts to use expert panels to make subjective estimates of the relationships between such variables and political outcomes.

Both have been the subject of considerable contention, with some investors and financial institutions finding quantitative methods quite helpful in assessing political risk and others rejecting such an approach.

More widely accepted have been attempts to try to make systematic comparisons between the assumptions and predictions of outside experts and the assumptions and predictions of internal managers, with the aim of assessing where insiders and outsiders differ (rather than necessarily trying to judge which group might be more "right"). While not pretending to yield authoritative predictions of political outcomes, this exercise may be useful to alert corporate strategists to factors or scenarios that might affect their operations which they may have overlooked or underestimated. This helps guard against distortions, clientitis, over-optimism, or over-pessimism in the formulation of planning options.

Second, related to the debate about quantification, is the question of how objective or subjective estimates of political risk might best be integrated into corporate decision-making?

One approach (the so-called "financial approach") has been to attempt to derive a discount factor for political risk that can be used to adjust the hurdle rate for approving the investment in the first place. This has the appeal of allowing the comparison of multiple potential investments with differing mixes of commercial and political uncertainties.

But, as indicated earlier, this "financial approach" may be misleading for projects where the problem is not the generosity of the opening conditions but rather the fragility of the return profile over time. And, by itself, this approach may simply eliminate from further consideration large numbers of potential high payoff opportunities.

An alternative approach (the so-called "strategic approach") emphasizes the need to search for tools and techniques to spread, offset, or deter hostile actions at particularly sensitive moments over the life of investment agreements. This allows customization of risk management for individual projects, but is less useful for comparing many prospective projects at the same time.

There has been frequent contention between those who focus on financial analysis and hurdle rates and those who try to shape corporate strategic relationships to mitigate political risk. But as the subsequent Sections of this volume show, the two can be used to complement each other.

Third, to what extent can the selection of host country partners be effective in mitigating political risk?

"One common and long-standing recommendation for reducing risk has been that the investor should include a local partner in his project," reminds Louis Wells. "The belief is that the local partner will provide some protection against actions that harm the interests of the venture." Host country partners can provide helping in finding indigenous suppliers, in raising local finance, in customizing local products, and in penetrating local markets; host country partners can also warn of local dangers, furnish local camouflage, deflect local criticism, arrange local support in high places.

On the other hand, "the more a project sponsor relies on the connections of a local partner to negotiate special arrangements with the host government outside of transparent bidding or other established selection procedures, the more vulnerable the project will be to charges of favoritism and corruption should the government's attitude toward the project, and its local participants, change," warns Robert Shanks, Partner with Morrison & Foerster, later in this volume (a concern echoed by Wells as well). "Today's well-connected insider can easily become tomorrow's embarrassment if the government administration changes."

Moreover, as Timothy Faber of GE Capital argues, while the establishment of a joint venture may initially align the interests of the foreigner and the local participant, those interests may diverge at a later stage: "now the investor has a liability rather than an asset in the local partner."

The historical record suggests a need for caution about the protection that joint venture relationships can provide. While joint ventures suffered fewer cases of nationalization in earlier periods than wholly owned subsidiaries, the joint venture relationship with a host government-related partner did not offer much comfort from subsequent intervention or contract renegotiation on the part of local authorities.

Moreover, Paul Beamish has found that dissatisfaction and instability are endemic in joint venture relationships in developing countries.[6] In a survey of 66 joint ventures located in 27 less developed countries, Beamish found that 61 percent gave an "unsatisfactory" rating to the partnership. Within this same sample, there was an instability rate of 45 percent after three years of existence. For the subset of joint ventures incorporating government partners, the instability rate was an even higher 56–59 percent.

There may however be some hopeful indications for the future. A consistent finding has been that widespread public ownership of the local affiliate in host countries (rather than partnerships with particular firms and individuals) does help protect foreign investors against adverse treatment.

From this perspective, the expansion of indigenous equity (and debt) markets in developing countries and economies-in-transition – as Linda F. Powers, Senior Vice President of Enron International suggests in the next section – may provide avenues for foreign investors to experiment with protection-through-broad-host-ownership with some reasonable hope of success.

Notes

[1] United Nations, *World Investment Report 1997* (New York: United Nations Conference on Trade and Development, 1997).

[2] Michael S. Minor, "The Demise of Expropriation as an Instrument of LDC Policy 1980–1992," *Journal of International Business Studies*, vol. 25, no. 1 (first quarter 1994).

[3] Raymond Vernon, *Sovereignty at Bay* (New York: Basic Books, 1971).

[4] For a survey of the evidence on how international investors with different industry/project characteristics have designed strategies to offset political risk, see Theodore H. Moran, "Mining Companies, Economic Nationalism, and Third World Development in the 1990s," in John E. Tilton (ed.), *Mineral Wealth and Economic Development* (Washington, DC: Resources for the Future, 1992), pp. 19–38.

[5] Cf. Jose de la Torre, "Forecasting Political Risks for International Operations," *International Journal of Forecasting*, no. 4 (1988), pp. 221–241; James E. Austin and David B. Yoffie, "Political Forecasting as a Management Tool," *Journal of Forecasting*, no. 3 (1984), pp. 395–408; Stephen J. Kobrin, *Managing Political Risk Assessment: Strategic Response to Environmental Change* (Berkeley, CA: University of California Press, 1982).

[6] Paul W. Beamish, *Multinational Joint Ventures in Developing Countries* (London: Routledge, 1988).

1
God and Fair Competition: Does the Foreign Direct Investor Face Still Other Risks in Emerging Markets?

Louis T. Wells, Jr.[*]

In spite of the warm welcome that most Third World countries now extend to foreign direct investors, that investment remains risky.

Risk, of course, is nothing new to foreign investors. In fact, much foreign investment is itself a response to risk – the risk that a multinational competitor will preempt a low-cost source, that a local firm will capture an export market held by the multinational, and so on. Moreover, investors are always threatened by new technology or a better marketing gimmick from competitors; and any investor must worry about natural disasters, such as earthquake, fire, or flood. But these are "commercial" risks and "acts of God."[1] The focus of this paper is on "political" risks that investors face in developing countries: those risks that are principally the result of forces external to the industry and which involve some sort of government action or, occasionally, inaction.[2]

Much of the existing literature on political risk in the developing countries is outdated. It has long focused on expropriation. In the decades of the 60s and 70s expropriation was indeed a striking and prominent risk and, to the pleasure of academics, measurable.[3] To be sure, expropriation was never the sole political risk faced by investors. War and civil disturbances have always posed a threat.[4] Other frequently encountered risks were changes in contract, imposition of price controls, and shifts in economic policy that resulted in inconvertibility of earnings and overvalued currencies. Although expropriation seems virtually to have disappeared – one author could identify only 11 cases from 1981 to 1992, while he identified 83 alone in 1975[5] – numerous experiences of foreign investors in developing countries suggest that noncommercial risk is still to be reckoned with. Yet, the literature has done little to address the kinds of risks that current investors face.

Three recent examples illustrate today's risks:

[*]Louis T. Wells, Jr. is the Herbert F. Johnson Professor of International Management, Graduate School of Business Administration, Harvard University.

1. In a well-publicized 1995 case, the newly elected government of the State of Maharashtra in India unilaterally canceled the contract for an electric power generation plant to be built and owned by a consortium led by Enron Corporation of the United States. Even after new negotiations led to a revised deal, local press continued to criticize the arrangement as being too generous for the foreign investor. It was far from clear that the renegotiation of the $2.8 billion project ended non-commercial risk.

2. In 1996 British Petroleum was faced with the consequences of an announcement by the government of Indonesia that the tariff on imported ethylene used to produce polyethylene would rise from 0 to 20 percent.[6] British Petroleum held 51 percent of PT Peni, a joint venture in Indonesia to produce polyethylene from ethylene. Just before the tariff hike on its major input, it had refused to pay the above-world-market prices demanded for ethylene manufactured locally by Chandra Asri, a cracker in which one of the president's sons held substantial equity.[7] The government decision had followed months of sometimes acerbic public debate among ministers about protecting Chandra Asri. The result of the new tariff was a reduction in the effective protection (imported polyethylene itself was subject to a 40 percent duty[8]) for the manufacture of polyethylene, a contract to buy ethylene at above-world-market prices from Chandra Asri, and a shift of profits from British Petroleum's affiliate into Chandra Asri.[9] The future looked bleaker for Peni, since the government had announced a scheduled reduction in the polyethylene tariff (and the ethylene tariff) to 10 percent by 2003, as part of its strategy of liberalizing trade policy.[10]

3. In 1989, Conzinc Riotinto Australia and other owners were forced to close their huge open pit copper mine on Bougainville, in Papua New Guinea. The rebels of a secessionist movement in Bougainvillea, whose population is ethnically different from the mainlanders, had blown up power-line towers and ambushed workers.[11]

In spite of many such examples of problems with their investments in developing countries, managers have tended to become lackadaisical in their evaluations of risk in the developing countries.

Why the New Optimism?

The new optimism on the part of managers has its basis in the turn-around in attitude toward foreign investors in the developing countries. Scores of countries that once railed against foreign investment – while accepting it when it was essential – have created investment promotion agencies whose sole task is to attract investors; many have disbanded their screening agencies, or dramatically simplified the hurdles to would-be investors.

The newly favorable attitudes on the part of host governments are the result of a number of changes. First, most other sources of foreign capital have virtually dried up, and domestic savings have not increased to fund growth expectations. Gone are the easy loans from commercial banks that were available when international banks were awash with petro-dollars. Foreign aid has become increasingly scarce. Although portfolio funds are growing, they are believed to threaten stability much more than direct investment. Second, government officials once doubted their own competence in dealing with foreign firms. Today's officials have been trained abroad and no longer fear the manipulations of the clever foreign business manager. They can speak the same lingo and understand some of the complexities of transfer prices, royalties, debt-to-equity ratios, and so on. Third, currently fashionable growth strategies emphasize exports. Since foreign firms appear to control many of the desirable export markets, their role is important in making the new strategies work. Fourth, those growth strategies have emphasized the private sector and have also led to changes in trade and other policies that make the interests of the private investor – foreign or domestic – more congruent with the national interests.[12] Finally, multilateral financial institutions press countries to be more open to foreign direct investment.

International agreements have also comforted the foreign investor. While agreements fall far short of the GATT for Foreign Investment proposed 25 years ago by Goldberg and Kindleberger,[13] they do provide some increased security for the investor. In addition to a network of hundreds of bilateral investment treaties, several regional trade agreements give some assurance on foreign investment within regions. NAFTA contains extensive protection for investors, for example; and a set of non-binding principles on investment has been accepted by the APEC economies. Further, whether a regional trade agreement covers foreign investment or not, once trade barriers begin to fall the member countries almost inevitably compete to attract foreign firms to their sites in order to serve the regional market. This competition makes investors feel more comfortable.

Investors are also reassured by some prospects for broader international agreement on foreign investment. The OECD has set out to negotiate an investment agreement; although developing countries may not join at the outset, current attitudes suggest that they might eventually become signatories.[14] Even though the Uruguay Round focused on trade, the resulting agreement expanded coverage to deal with some foreign investment matters. The extent of WTO protection remains untested, but there are hints of impact. For example, in 1996 when the Indonesian government introduced measures to favor a prospective producer of a national car over foreign firms already in the country, both the American Automobile Manufacturers' Association and the Japanese Trade Ministry pressed their government to take Indonesia before the WTO; their claim was that the policies discriminate against other producers.[15] The threat itself probably served to constrain Indonesian policies. Moreover, PT Peni, mentioned earlier, could feel reasonably secure that the tariff on its input would not exceed the rate at which Indonesia had "bound" its petrochemical tariffs under the Uruguay Round.[16]

Although the new favorable attitudes of host governments are genuine – I have yet to see government officials enter an arrangement which they thought at the time would be unstable – many of the factors that led to expropriations in the past have not changed as much as it might appear. First, nationalism, and the accompanying concern about foreign ownership, do not seem to diminish with development. Bucking the trend to welcome foreign investors with open arms, in 1988 the United

States itself introduced controls, through the Exon-Florio Act, over certain foreign acquisitions. Second, in their eagerness to promote reform, multilateral institutions and national aid organizations have certainly oversold many countries on their prospects of attracting foreign investment. In fact, foreign direct investment has added up to only about three percent of the gross fixed capital formation in developing countries.[17] Even that number is a misleading indicator for the bulk of the developing world, since the ten largest recipients accounted for almost 80 percent of the investment.[18] As the inevitable disappointment and frustration set in, nationalism is likely to re-emerge in some countries. Finally, changes that are occurring in the developing countries increase the likelihood that the foreign investor will be made a scapegoat. Industrialization brings pollution; economic liberalization, it can be argued, brings inequality. Since foreign investors are associated with industrialization and liberalization, the foreigner will be blamed for problems.

In sum, although there are good reasons for optimism on the part of investors, the old risks have not entirely disappeared. Moreover, a number of changes in the developing world suggest new risks.

Changes in the Developing Countries

The developing countries represents a disparate group of countries. It is dangerous to lump together places that are as different as Ghana, Indonesia, and Korea. Yet, in the past 10 to 15 years some common trends have swept through the developing countries and affected the risks faced by foreign investors.

Development Strategy

Perhaps the least frequently recognized, but most pervasive, non-commercial risk for the foreign investor comes from a change in development strategy by the host country.

Many foreign investments were undertaken in the 60s, 70s, and early 80s, when the prevailing development strategy in the developing countries was based on import substitution. Policies included high import tariffs, restrictive quotas, and licensing of competition to induce investors to build plants to serve the local market. Even though the market might not be large enough to justify an efficient plant, small, inefficient plants could be very profitable.

In the 1980s, however, a new consensus arose that led to drastic changes in development strategy. Dozens of developing countries have reduced their import barriers and eliminated licensing of production capacity. Investors who had built plants that depended on protection have seen their returns plummet, unless they undertook substantial investments to make facilities competitive in the world market. Rare were the investors who foresaw this shift which would so dramatically affect their overseas operations.

At one time, increased protection for the upstream supplier to PT Peni would have led to higher tariffs on downstream protection, as well. But with Indonesia's recent shift away from import substitution toward a focus on competition and exports, a further increase in tariffs on downstream products would be unacceptable. Indeed, downstream protection was scheduled to decline in the future. The foreign owners were being squeezed on both sides, costs of inputs and prices for output.

As fashions in development strategy have changed, so have fashions in management of the economy. Especially in combination with today's more open market strategies, these changes can provide serious problems for foreign (or local, for that matter) firms. Traditional policies for macroeconomic management have long been understood, as have the risks associated with them. Many investors have known, for example, that high inflation rates might lead governments to tighten monetary and fiscal policy, with the unfortunate outcome that local markets shrink, at least temporarily. But few investors were prepared for the fashion of the early 90s of fighting inflation by allowing the real exchange rate to appreciate – as illustrated by Argentina and Mexico. Until the 1995 crash of the Mexican peso, the International Monetary Fund was pressing some other countries to follow similar policies to squeeze out inflation. With low protection, firms manufacturing in countries with appreciating currencies typically found themselves swamped with imports and uncompetitive on export markets;[19] this, even though their plants might be world-scale and efficient.

Stronger Local Business

Perhaps the most difficult new risk for multinational managers to evaluate arises from the growing influence of powerful local businesses that want to enter what used to be the rather secure domains of foreign investors. The story of PT Peni/Chandra Asri was triggered by just such a change.

Two or three decades ago, in most countries of the developing world foreign investors had little to fear from local private firms. Local investors could not assemble the capital required to enter most of the businesses that were of interest to foreigners. In Asia and Latin America, however, a few private local businesses have grown to the point that they can now muster the resources to challenge the multinational. As private local firms have moved into industries that were once the domain of foreign firms,[20] they have used their political connections to demand favorable treatment that places them at an advantage over existing or prospective foreign investors.

Of course, rich local enterprises are the inevitable and desirable result of development. But the ability to assemble large sums of capital has often accrued only to politically influential investors. Investors with the needed funds are likely to have accumulated them under earlier policies of import substitution, licenses, and restrictions on foreign investment. Licenses and protection, and the associated monopoly rents went to the influential. Similarly, many countries required foreign investors to have local partners. As a result, a few influential local businessmen secured a source of wealth by serving as more-or-less silent partners with foreign enterprise. Influence yielded money; in turn, money from licenses and joint ventures yielded more political influence.[21]

Local businesses have used this influence to press for changes in government policy that will give them advantages in activities that had been the domain of foreign investors. Influence is especially important in countries where "property rights" are poorly developed – that is, in the developing countries and in the economies-in-transition. The resulting policies affect foreign firms that might compete with the local firm, but also those which can provide markets for the output of the domestic investor – as did PT Peni for Chandra Asri – or materials that are needed for its production. In the case of PT Peni, that pressure was quite open. In other cases, it may be more subtle. A reluctant firm may find licenses revoked or new ones difficult to get, it may face inspections that reveal fictitious or petty violations of regulations, and so on.[22] In the Philippines, local firms intervene to block successful bids of foreign firms for large projects.[23]

Strong private enterprises have a long history in some of the more industrialized developing countries. For decades, there have been large and influential privately owned manufacturing firms in Korea, Taiwan, Argentina, Mexico, and Brazil, for example. In the early stages of industrialization, such local businesses typically considered foreign investors as providing opportunities – as customers or as partners. Foreigners were viewed as potential competitors for powerful local firm only at the fuzzy boundaries of their respective domains.

In the past, domestic firms defended their sectors from foreign encroachment in ways that posed little risk to multinationals. The first line of defense by local business was to use its influence to exclude foreigners from entering certain markets. Exclusion was feasible because of the rather tight controls that most developing countries exercised over incoming foreign investment. In Korea and India,[24] for example, certain industries were clearly reserved for the large business houses. Foreign participation was limited largely to licensing arrangements in those industries. More often, potential investors were not given quite such a clear signal. Rather, they had to apply for permission to invest. Although the typical agency charged with accepting or rejecting foreign investors purported to make its decision according to some kind of objective economic analysis, many seemed more responsive to political influence than to the narrow technical analysis recommended by economists. Decisions on foreigners' applications were delayed to give time to local investors to organize opposition. If they were sufficiently influential, they could mount a successful campaign to have applications rejected. Although foreign investors objected to the process, at least the "no" came before investors had placed large sums of money at risk.

Newly fashionable economic strategies have led to the demise of this approach to foreign investment in many countries. Governments have been pushed by competition with other countries (or by multilateral lenders or investors' home countries) into dropping ad hoc screening processes. Thus, Korea's investment approval process has been largely dismantled. Turkey approves a wide range of investors automatically. Indonesia's process remains, but rejections are rare. And so on around the developing world. The switch has meant that investors now face the risks associated with powerful private interests after they have invested their capital.

In the past, powerful domestic firms did have a second line of defense, if foreign direct investment made it through the screening process. In the occasional encounters between local business and foreign firms that struggled over the same sector, the usual solution was some kind of alliance. The high tariffs or restrictive quotas of import substitution strategies meant that there could be sufficient profits for all. In the Chandra Asri case, both enterprises could have been protected; they might even have merged into a vertically integrated business. The alliance between foreign and local firm was often pressed by government, under the influence of local firms. In India, for example, a foreign firm would face restrictions on expansion until it included an Indian private firm in its ownership.[25] Similarly, in Brazil alliances between local and foreign business were the outcome of conflict at the edges of each group's domain.[26] The alliances posed little threat to the foreigner. As Evans put it at the end of the 1970s, referring to Brazil: "the idea of dislodging foreign firms from their dominant position had all but disappeared."[27] But economic liberalization in the developing countries has limited alliances as a solution to conflict with local enterprise, just as it has weakened the controls over incoming investment. Falling protection has meant the end to rents large enough to satisfy both parties.

In the past, some foreign investors had another kind of local firm to contend with: the state-owned enterprise. But state ownership was concentrated in certain sectors, especially mining, plantations, and infrastructure. Often the goal of the government in establishing such enterprises was to capture certain sectors for local investment which would otherwise have been held by foreigners. State ownership was common in steel, for example, where technology was easy to come by, but local firms could not amass the sums of capital required for the business. In some cases, state-owned firms were built to learn a business in which foreigners were already dominant, with the goal of eventually replacing them. State-owned enterprises were built, for example, in petroleum and hard rock mining eventually to capture these industries from foreigners.

Although state-owned enterprises were the object of government favor, their domains were generally obvious – often spelled out in legislation, or even in the constitutions of some countries[28] – and their influence reasonably predictable. State firms limited foreign investors, but investors had learned to evaluate risks of this kind explicitly or intuitively.

The overall pattern was a set of rather clear domains. State-owned enterprises dominated industries characterized by large, lumpy investments, long-term returns, and readily attainable technology. State firms, or private firms tied in with state firms, controlled local raw materials that could be monopolized and some mature large-scale industries. Private local firms acting alone were largely in industries characterized by intense competition and resulting low returns. Multinationals dominated industries where technology (including managerial skills) was important, universally applicable, rapidly changing, and not obtainable on the open market. At the borders of domains, alliances were more typical than conflicts.[29] Such clearly demarcated domains have collapsed with the growth of rich domestic firms and with the new development strategies.

It is important to note that the new-found power of local private firms is, in most countries, not connected with a renewal of anti-foreign sentiments. Powerful private enterprises may even include foreign partners. Thus, Chandra Asri, which sought PT Peni as a customer, incorporates Japanese interests among its investors.[30] Moreover, the targets of these influential enterprises need not be foreign. If a poorly connected local enterprise stands in the way of one of the newly powerful firms, it too may face damaging government policies. Nevertheless, the threatened enterprise is more often than not foreign, since foreigners are especially strong in the sectors where there are monopoly rents and thus where influential local firms want to operate. With anti-foreign sentiments at least temporarily unpopular, rather than railing against foreign influence, domestic firms now generally appeal to the newly popular ideology of private sector development. In a place like Indonesia, they sometimes justify their demands for a favored position by appealing to ethnic issues. Thus, the Indonesian president explains that his children must be successful to demonstrate that ethnic Indonesians, and not just the ethnic Chinese, can progress in business.

Especially frustrating for foreign investors are the kinds of policies that are used in the interest of the new challengers. Even in the more successful developing countries, concepts of property rights differ from those that are often assumed in the United States. As a result, developing country governments show little hesitancy to single out one firm in an industry for special treatment. This stands in contrast to the United States, where firms in a similar class expect similar treatment.[31] In France and Italy, where more discrimination is accepted, such discrimination must nevertheless be widely seen to be in the national interest. Yet, in the developing world – democratic countries and authoritarian alike – extensive property rights enforced with non-discriminatory policies are rare. The foreign investor can expect little protection from the local legal system, or from bilateral treaties promising "national treatment." In fact, discrimination is "national treatment."

Spread of Democracy

From some points of view, one of the most encouraging trends in the developing countries is the spread of democratic government. Yet, while the rise of multi-party democracy decreases certain risks for investors, it can increase others.

In countries where opposition parties are relatively free, attacks on foreign investment provide an appealing way to challenge the government in power. In democratic India, it was the opposition Shiv Sena and Bharatiya Janata parties that led the attack on Enron's power project. Papua New Guinea's democratic central government no doubt felt more constrained in cracking down on the rebels who closed the Bougainvillea copper mine than would most authoritarian regimes.

Although democracy – or simply increased tolerance of opposition – often leads to more open attacks on foreign investment, it can also provide some protection against arbitrary policies such as the tariff increases that faced BP in Indonesia. In a more democratic country, opposition parties would almost certainly have pounced on the tariff increase as a tool to shift profits into the hands of the president's family.

Still, protection of investors in the fledgling democracies of the developing countries is quite weak. Even in the democratic developing countries, improvements in property rights have generally lagged behind other changes. When questions about policy with respect to foreign investment are very complex and thus difficult for opposition parties to turn into popular issues, the government in power is subject to considerable private influence.

While democratic governments may increase risk, authoritarian regimes provide some protection for the foreign investor. The authoritarian regime is likely to use its power to suppress any opposition's attempt to criticize its deals with foreign investors. In authoritarian Indonesia, for example, attempts in parliament to question the terms of a power project (Paiton I) similar to Enron's in India soon petered out, as the government made it clear that the deal was not to be the subject of controversy.

But the partial protection from controversy granted by an authoritarian regime does not guarantee safety. First, investors are faced with the threats posed by individuals close to the regime, as the Chandra Asri case illustrates. Second, the inevitable changes in authoritarian regimes are often accompanied by criticism of the outgoing government. To discredit the past regime, the new one attacks past deals made with foreign investors as resulting from corruption or incompetence, or both. With regime change, old deals may be renegotiated, or domestic partners close to the outgoing regime may find their assets taken over and their foreign partners squeezed.

Weak States

A long-standing fear on the part of a foreign investor was that the host government would take a sudden turn to the left. In fact, this kind of shift was the focus of those who tried to forecast country risk. The efforts to forecast were warranted, since such changes were often accompanied by wholesale nationalizations of foreign investment. Even though the collapse of Communist regimes has sharply reduced the fears that governments of the radical left will come to power in the developing countries, extremist movements, usually very nationalistic, have not disappeared. There is little doubt where foreign investors would stand in a fundamentalist Islamic Algeria, for example. Moreover, civil wars and other domestic disorder (including organized crime) appear to be on the rise. At the extreme, they are associated with total regime collapse.

Civil wars and rebellions are not new to foreign investors. In fact, potential income from foreigners' projects have often provided an economic incentive for break-away movements, in Katanga and Biafra, for example. The social changes wrought by large projects in remote areas, as in Irian Jaya and Bougainvillea, have also fueled independence movements. In the process, foreign investors in countries where the state's authority is weak may find their properties unusable, as happened to Bougainvillea Copper.

In many cases, civil wars and rebellions affect only peripheral areas of a country, where the only foreign investors are petroleum, mining, or plantation companies, or their service units. On the other hand, when disturbances lead to regime collapse, all investors suffer. Although foreign investors had little exposure in Somalia, both Americans and Europeans had substantial investments in Liberia – in iron ore mining and rubber growing, in particular, but also in banking and petroleum refining. With the collapse of order, activities on the part of virtually all foreign investors ground to a halt.

While the Cold War raged, the rivalry between the super-powers placed some limits on civil wars and regime collapses. At the height of the Cold War, fearful of the implications of a power vacuum, one or the other of the super-powers would probably have prevented the collapse of government in places like Somalia and Liberia. The end of the Cold War has, it seems, reduced fears on the part of the United States of the consequences for global stability; one brake on conflict has faded.

Predicting political turmoil has always been difficult. Ethnic tensions and weak government were obvious in Liberia, for example, for a decade before the regime fell apart. There could have been little question that the risk was high for investors, although the timing of major change was very uncertain. Moreover, the risks of independence movements should be apparent when huge projects are undertaken in remote areas that are ethnically different from the rest of the population. The native population of Bougainvillea and Irian Jaya, for example, differ from the groups that control government. And weak central governments are an invitation to rebellions. It should be no surprise that guerrillas in Colombia, for example, harass foreign oil companies in remote areas where the government has little capacity to exercise authority.[32]

Decentralization of Power

Along with liberalization of the economy, another current fashion in development policy is to decentralize government. Giving more power to local jurisdictions is proposed as a way of defusing the tensions between the center and the periphery, often as a tool to calm ethnic differences. At the moment talk about decentralization exceeds action, but the possibility of further decentralization ought to enter investors' analysis of risk. Although the evidence is not yet in, decentralization may, in fact, succeed in lowering the chances of civil war, and stronger regional governments sometimes offer opportunities to the investor beyond that of peace. On the other hand, regional governments pose special threats.

Where regional governments compete to attract foreign investors, decentralization has meant more favorable deals for investors. Thus, the government of Ho Chi Minh City (formerly Saigon) has struggled with the central government to gain jurisdiction over foreign investment in its region, largely in order to make it easier for investors to come to the city. It has mounted its own investment promotion programs, and has shown more willingness than the central government to adjust policies to respond to the concerns of investors. Similarly in China some regional governments are more accommodating to foreign investors than is the central government. Although few regional governments can totally avoid central government control, in fact in many countries the multinational has benefited from competition among local entities for foreign investment – whether that competition is among the US states or regional governments in the developing world.

Regional governments do not, however, always compete to attract foreign investment. On occasion, they pose a greater barrier to investment, and more harassment of existing investors, than does the central government. In Indonesia, for example, foreign investors typically complain about obstacles at the regional level; local governments in Indonesia do little to attract foreign firms.

When regional or other subunits of government act against a foreign investor, they are less constrained than the central government, since they care little about the broad impact of their steps. Thus, the Thai Expressway and Rapid Transit Authority demonstrated little concern about the effect on the investment climate of its dispute with foreign investors over a Bangkok toll road in 1993.[33] Its interests were quite specific and narrow – the charges for toll and the distribution of the revenue. Similarly, the government of the State of Maharashtra in India showed little worry about the possibility that its dispute with Enron would slow other foreign investments in India. The investment climate was a federal problem, not one for the state.

Forecasting the attitude of regional governments or other subunits of government is difficult. Where foreign investment is mostly for projects for which location is determined by sources of raw materials or location of markets, local government may be more of a barrier than a help. Provinces typically do not compete for copper mines, toll roads, or power plants, since location is determined by materials or markets. Where investors have choices about location, competition is more likely. Thus, the regions of China and the former Saigon compete for light manufacturing for export markets. More important, the structure of local government matters. In Indonesia, for example, local government is less representative of local interests than in some other countries. With officials appointed from the center, with little local tax base, and with career paths of bureaucrats not concentrated at the local government, regional units are less likely to push for local economic interests. With few strong ties to the local community, Indonesian local officials appear to view foreign investment largely as a source of bribes. On the other hand, in countries where careers of local officials are built locally, some perception of regional economic interests is likely to determine the stance of local government.

International Disputes

Foreign investors can also become embroiled in international disputes. The simplest and most predictable international disputes are those over borders. Tensions over oil and gas around the Spratly Islands should be no surprise.[34] A look at a few maps indicates that neighboring countries have different ideas as to where their borders lie: with China, Malaysia, the Philippines, Taiwan, and Vietnam all laying claim to the area. But tensions were minor until the islands were deemed economically attractive and the 200-mile economic zone principle was accepted. Now both China and Vietnam have awarded contracts to American companies for overlapping areas.[35]

More difficult to predict are other international disputes. Almost any kind of international conflict can affect foreign investment. For example, investors and prospective investors in China have faced problems as China and the United States clashed over human rights, intellectual property, and sale of nuclear technology to Pakistan. Chrysler's plans to expand its jeep plant to small-car production and General Motors' efforts to build an engine plant in Shanghai seemed hostage to US threats on trade.[36] Similarly, beginning in 1996, non-US investors faced US sanctions if their Cuban activities involved properties previously owned by corporations with US shareholders.

Border disputes and issues of human rights, intellectual property, and so on have been with the investor for a long time. However, like civil disturbances, during the Cold War conflicts were generally suppressed by the Western industrialized countries, which feared that actions against offending governments might be an additional pressure driving those governments into the Communist camp. With the end of the Cold War, the hesitancy on the part of developing countries' governments to act has declined.

Investors are not defenseless. In most cases, international agreements provide investors with a degree of protection against international disputes, but appeal to them is costly and prolonged. If China were a member of the WTO, for example, the United States would be subject to discipline if it were to impose trade restrictions on Chinese products without the authorization of the WTO. China would presumably appeal to the WTO, rather than threaten US investors. In the case of Cuba, targets of US sanctions were threatening in the summer of 1996 to appeal to the WTO. No one expected quick resolution, however.

Management and the New Risks

Most managers of multinational enterprises are ill equipped to deal with the shifting risks that they face in emerging markets. They need both analytical tools and organizations that can estimate and respond to risk. Many multinationals are weak on both counts.

In the 1970s some firms – especially in petroleum and banking – built internal units to undertake political risk analysis.[37] In recent years, due to dissatisfaction and budget cutting, many of these groups have been disbanded. In fact, most were not very helpful in the first place. Staffed with political scientists and ex-State Department and CIA personnel, they were weak in business analysis. They might know what was going on in a remote country, but they were ill prepared when it came to translating facts and projections into implications for the firm and recommendations for management decisions. General country briefings – at which they were good – were increasingly pushed to the back burner by top management as managers found themselves too busy to listen to broad generalizations that did not include relevant action recommendations.

The firms that built internal units to analyze political risks were those with extensive operations in the developing countries. Many had experienced first hand the nationalizations of the 1960s and 1970s and the loan defaults of the 1980s. But today's investors in the developing countries include many firms with little experience outside the industrialized countries. Power generating companies are, for example, jumping directly from regional US markets to the developing world. Indeed, a number of investors in infrastructure are not even experienced in the industry at home. Similarly, with stagnant markets or intense competition in Europe and Japan, manufacturing companies are venturing rapidly beyond these sites to the potentially large markets of India, China, Indonesia, and Brazil for major projects before they have extensive experience in smaller investments in the developing countries.

Without experience with the expropriations of the past (even some experienced companies appear to know little of their own history), and faced with eager host countries, managers in these firms succumb to the enthusiasm of "investment champions" within the enterprise who push their pet projects. In fact, managers are often rewarded for closing "deals," with no adjustment for the risks that these deals carry.[38] Not unusual is a current bonus based on the net present value of the discounted cash flow in forecasts. Since risks turn into events far down the road, these managers are likely to be in other positions when problems eventually arise. There is no incentive for them to focus on dangers; and in-house analysts whose job it is to examine risk are viewed as enemies.

Similarly, top management becomes committed early to their favorite sites. Many are the stories from analysts whose warnings fall on deaf ears as top management responds that the investments must go ahead for "strategic reasons." The arguments behind those "strategic reasons" and similar buzzwords are rarely spelled out in convincing argument.

Finally, many managers continue to believe certain myths, although the available evidence suggests that they are simply not true. In particular, managers have always hoped that host countries would be constrained in their treatment of investors already in the country because of the negative impact that ill treatment would have on prospective new investors. When foreign investment was viewed suspiciously anyway, this shield seemed rather thin.[39] But, with the new turn toward foreign investment, managers are even more confident that governments will not act in ways that will frighten off future investors. Yet, actions against one investor seem to have little long-term effect on other investors. Indonesia's announcement of the new tariff on ethylene and its national car policy both generated widespread criticism by other potential investors. The head of the Asia-Pacific region for one US multinational was quoted as saying: "We would think much harder about doing anything in Indonesia now," following the announcement of the national car deal.[40] But in spite of the rhetoric, foreign investment in Indonesia continues to climb. Other power negotiations in India did slow as the fate of Enron's project in Maharashtra lay in the balance; but deals with foreign firms for generating capacity in India quickly picked up steam again, after the renegotiation seemed over. Moreover, sanctions from home countries gather little support even from other investors. Their fear of the impact on general attitudes in the country toward foreign investment outweighs their fear that allowing the government to win in one case increases the chance of an attack on them.

In sum, once a proposed investment reaches a certain stage in many firms, no one wants to hear of risks – neither the "deal makers," whose bonuses are threatened, nor top management which has become deeply committed. Myths and buzzwords justify their confidence, and faith is placed in the hopes that safety will come because of the damage that government attack would cause to the general investment climate. The risks remain.

Old Tools

Even in the new climate, the old ways of thinking about non-commercial risk have not lost their utility. With a few adjustments, they still provide a useful starting point for analysis.

Perhaps the most powerful framework for thinking about noncommercial risk has been "the obsolescing bargain" model.[41] The model starts with a simple principle: governments prefer local investors to foreign investors. This preference is manifested especially strongly in politically sensitive sectors. Foreigners are allowed, albeit reluctantly, even in these sectors if the benefits they bring convincingly outweigh the economic and political costs associated with foreign ownership. But, once those benefits are no longer apparent, the risk for the foreign investor climbs.

In this calculus, the benefits of foreign investment include particularly capital, technology, and access to foreign markets. The foreigner has been tolerated in projects that require large amounts of capital, since local business could not amass the sums required. Or, if he brings technology that is not easily available on an open market. Or, if the foreigner controls export markets that would not be accessible without foreign participation.

Important to the analysis is the fact that the perceived contributions of the foreigner can extend over long periods in some projects; in others, the continued presence of the foreigner may not be essential, since the benefits are transferred upon investment or soon thereafter, and remain in the country whether or not the foreigner stays. Plants in high-technology industries, for example, are likely to be the recipients of continuing new inputs of know-how over decades, if they remain foreign owned. Similarly, when foreign firms offer access to foreign markets because of their reputation for quality or regular, timely delivery, their continued presence is essential if the exports are to be maintained. In such cases, the investor remains secure, except in the face of really dramatic upheaval. In contrast, benefits from the continued presence of the foreigner decline sharply soon after investment in certain mining, plantation, and infrastructure projects. The foreign investor's contribution consists largely of capital provided at the outset and, perhaps, some design and management know-how. That capital comprises mainly immovable assets – often trees, pavement, rails, or a big hole in the ground. Once the investment is in place, the design has been done and the necessary simple management skills are captured quickly by locals.

When the benefits of continued foreign presence have declined, governments are pressed to focus on the costs – by their own concerns or by opposition groups.

Payments of dividends abroad look particularly burdensome because, unlike debt, they seem to have no terminal date. In addition, the fact is discovered that some of the deals struck for infrastructure and privatization may not be so great for the host country. As the perception of the net gains shifts, governments can be under great pressure to eliminate the costs of foreign presence – or at least to squeeze the investor's earnings so that the drain on the economy is reduced.

When the balance has tilted, conflicts are often triggered because of some perceived slight: the claim that the foreigner is underpaying workers;[42] the reluctance of the investor to expand to meet the demand that the government forecasts; the recognition that the foreigner has been granted a monopoly position, and the belief that he is exploiting it;[43] and so on.

The danger for investors has been viewed as especially great if the project is large and politically sensitive; this means especially investments with an element of monopoly, projects that extract natural resources, investments in infrastructure, and projects in a "strategic" manufacturing industry.

Even when the presence of a foreign firm is still important to a country, an early investor may suffer as the number of foreigners offering similar resources expands in a maturing industry. With more alternative investors to provide technology, capital, or markets, governments seek better deals than they could negotiate with early investors who were in a strong bargaining position. Alternatively, with new options government might renegotiate deals with the original investor – under threat of switching to another investor.[44] Thus, in 1977, as more firms had relevant computer technology, India was willing to press IBM to take in local equity, and accept the likelihood that IBM would leave rather than renegotiate; India was confident that it could rely on other investors because the number of potential suppliers of know-how had increased since IBM had established its subsidiary in India.[45]

Not surprisingly, in light of the obsolescing bargain model, nationalizations have tended to come in waves as the foreign presence in particular industries has become less important. During the late 60s and early 70s, for example, the weakening of control over downstream markets by international mining firms led host governments to act. As Eastern Bloc and other state-owned smelters provided alternative customers, major private aluminum companies began to lose control over their bauxite mines. As petroleum markets opened in the 1970s, oil firms were particularly likely to lose their producing facilities. These takeovers and renegotiations simply echoed earlier takeovers of electric power, telephone, and tram system investments throughout the developing world.

The practical implications of the obsolescing bargain model for risk evaluation have been clear: an investor should first determine whether his continued presence is essential and whether the project is politically sensitive. The wise investor also asks whether the number of suppliers of the know-how is likely to increase soon, so that other firms might offer deals that would undercut the original one.

The use of the obsolescing bargain model has been complemented by efforts to classify host countries. In most cases, the goal has been to identify in advance those countries that are particularly likely to act against all foreign investors, rather than against investors in particular industries or in special circumstances. The usual assumption that underlies that analysis is that radical regime change results in action against foreign investors. Indeed, such changes, usually to the left, as in Cuba, Tanzania, Algeria, Chile, and Nicaragua, have accounted for many expropriations. Yet, the success of forecasting timing of regime changes has hardly been sufficiently accurate to help in investment decisions.[46]

Although the old approaches have provided useful ways of thinking about non-commercial risk, the changes in the developing countries suggest more complexity in the political process that leads to action against foreign investors. And they suggest the growing importance of some kinds of risk that are not easily captured in the obsolescing bargain model and classical country analysis.

Can An Investor Still Identify Risky Projects?

Management's lackadaisical attitude toward risk may be appropriate if the risk of a particular project simply cannot be estimated. Yet, I have suggested that there are tools that allow some risk assessment. Moreover, for a few risks, insurance is available. On top of that, there are actions that can reduce risk where it is inherently large.

The obsolescing bargain model, I have claimed, still suggests that certain businesses are more risky than others. The lack of control over export markets or a continuing input of technology or capital can spell trouble. Yet, the model is stronger with some adjustments. For example, the political sensitivity of the industry is less important today in determining risk, since the threat has shifted from government acting on its own to include actions initiated by private firms. A local private firm responds to earnings potential, not politics, in its choice of targets. Thus, political sensitivity matters less than the financial interests of locally influential firms. And no longer can a foreign firm feel secure because entry into its industry requires large sums of capital, since local investors in many developing countries can now assemble the funds for most industries. On the other hand, serious challenges are still unlikely where a very small number of foreign firms control technology or access to foreign markets. Yet, even these firms may face pressure from influential local customers or suppliers, if not from local competitors. Thus, a new level of analysis of the local private sector should be a part of the examination of risk.

Political sensitivity does, of course, matter in some cases. It is likely, for example, that investment in electric generating projects is still safer than investment in distribution, where the foreigner is more visible to consumers and is more likely to be blamed for price hikes or for capacity shortages.

Changes in developing countries suggest that "industry" is not the only variable relevant to an analysis of non-commercial risk today. For example, with more authority in regional governments, location seems to matter more than in the past, almost regardless of the industry. Thus the location of Enron in Maharashtra was as important as the fact that the investment was in power generation. The state election that led to a local coalition government of nationalist parties soon initiated the attack on Enron. In attacking Enron's deal, the parties drew national attention to their claim that the country's dominant political party was selling out India's interest for personal bribes. Similarly, it seems that the concern of the Thai Expressway and Rapid Transit Authority with revenue and the public reaction to toll rates was as important as the welcoming attitude that the central government extended to foreign investors, when it came to conflict over the Bangkok toll road. Thus, political analysis must go beyond the central government.

In fact, as in the past some risks are more "country" risks than "industry" risks. Changes in development strategy or macroeconomic policy, for example, affect a wide range of industries. But the impact of broad policy shifts varies according to the orientation of the investment. Changes in protection or in exchange rate policy affect exporting firms particularly sharply. And firms producing non-tradables for the domestic market are least likely to be affected. The wise investor is aware of trends in development strategies and the directions of movement in potential investment sites.

In sum, the manager need not be at sea when it comes to analyzing non-commercial risk. An understanding of the old tools and the recent trends can provide a great deal of help to the analyst. But management has to expand the analysis. Equally, the manager must be willing to listen to those who identify risks, and to take protective steps when risks are high.

Can One Insure Against Risk?

Faced with substantial risk, the foreign investor can, on occasion, protect against risk either by purchasing insurance of one form or another or by spreading resources across a larger number of projects.

Buy Insurance as Protection

Investment insurance is sometimes available from home-country agencies. For US firms, for example, the Overseas Private Investment Corporation (OPIC) sells insurance for investments in a large number of host countries. In addition, investment insurance can be obtained from the Multilateral Investment Guarantee Agency (MIGA), a part of the World Bank Group, and from private insurance companies.[47] OPIC and MIGA cover investments only in countries where guarantee treaties have been concluded with host governments. The treaties themselves bind host governments in ways that probably reduce the risk of the events against which insurance is provided.[48]

Investment insurance is limited in another important way: in spite of some experimental insurance contracts, investment insurance is available primarily to cover the risks of discrete events whose impact is measurable. These include expropriation, war and civil unrest, and currency inconvertibility.[49] Many of the more subtle risks of today – reduced protection, favors for competitors, and so on – are not covered. In addition, MIGA will protect against losses from breach or repudiation of contract, but the investor must be able to "invoke an arbitration clause in the underlying contract, and obtain an award for damages." Failure of the host government to pay will trigger the claim against MIGA.[50] Insurance against breach or repudiation of contract is, not surprisingly, generally the most expensive of the insurance offerings, with base rates of 0.8 percent to 1.25 percent annually of the amount covered.

Costs of insurance have fallen in recent years. But this should not be surprising or comforting, since available insurance tends to cover risks of the past, not the risks that dominate today's investment. Although there have been various experiments with insurance against changes in contractual terms, they have not solved the major problems. Among the difficulties with today's risks are determining exactly what the entering contract was, especially when much was implied rather than written; determining when an insured event has occurred; and measuring the amount of the damages. As a result, much risk is still not the subject of investment insurance policies, and insurance is unlikely to develop in the near future to cover events that are difficult to identify and where the sizes of the resulting losses are very hard to measure.

The development of more sophisticated derivatives markets has opened up the possibility for an additional kind of insurance. Risks of changes in fuel prices, for example, can now be insured through forward and options markets for gas. Similarly, futures markets have developed to cover currencies of a number of developing countries. But forward, options, and swap markets are used primarily to insure against currency risks over fairly short periods or for specific risks where the amounts at stake are easily quantified. They are used for covering short-term accounts payable and accounts receivable, and sometimes for the currency risks associated with long-term debt. The costs, the limited markets, and the uncertainty about the size of exposure have meant that currency markets have not been commonly used to cover other long-term risks, such as the risk that a plant's profits will fall because of a long-term appreciation in the host country's real exchange rate. And, of course these markets are not relevant for risks of expropriation, changes in contract, and pressures from local private firms.

Enter International Alliances

Another approach to risk management is to spread resources over a larger number of projects. Although the risk of some loss may increase, the risk of a really large loss declines. One approach has been to share investment with other firms in the industry. Aluminum and petroleum companies long invested jointly in large lumpy projects to spread a firm's limited resources over a larger number of projects.

Although infrastructure investments are frequently undertaken by consortia, the interests of the parties can be quite different. Equipment suppliers, for example, may be interested primarily in the short run, since they are likely to capture profits through supplying the project and will usually be paid early. Suppliers of fuel are likely to be in the project for the long haul, but the profits captured from fuel sales will make them less concerned about renegotiations or price controls that reduce profits of the enterprise as a whole. Lenders will care about changes in arrangements only to the extent that those changes threaten debt service by drastically reducing cash flow. On the other hand, equity holders are likely to be the first hit by changes in terms or by government takeovers. With the different interests, it is hardly surprising that the assembly of consortia is a time consuming process; internal conflict may emerge in the future as members respond differently to threats.

Can an Investor Reduce the Risk in a Given Project?

The investor cannot always choose projects or countries where the risk is low, nor can he insure against all risks. But there are steps that the investor can take to reduce the risks in a given project. The experience of investors suggests the following:

Make Money in Related Operations

When the core investment is risky, an investor can sometimes reduce overall risk if he can make a substantial part of his profits in another part of the value-added chain or in related operations. For example, Enron might have chosen to capture a substantial part of its profits in the supply of fuel for the Indian power plant. One supposes that this was a part of its objective in establishing itself as the supplier of fuel, probably from its operations in Qatar, in the agreement that followed the revisions demanded by the Indians. Similarly to railroad investors in 19th-century America who earned a substantial portion of their profits from the land rights that they obtained alongside their rail lines, Gordon Wu chose to make money on services connected with toll roads in China.[51] If the core project is squeezed, peripheral activities may assure adequate returns.[52]

Joint Venture with a Local Partner

One common and long-standing recommendation for reducing risk has been that the investor should include a local partner in his project. The belief is that the local partner will provide some protection against actions that harm the interests of the venture. Of course, joint venture partners serve other roles. Most important is the market knowledge or access that they bring. Sometimes they control raw materials and are essential to assure access. If they contribute financial assets, they may even help in spreading risks for the foreign firm.

Some doubts about the effectiveness of local partners in protecting against non-commercial risk were raised long ago, in a study that concluded that joint ventures were more likely to be expropriated than wholly-foreign subsidiaries.[53] Even British Petroleum, in the case of Chandra Asri, had included a son of the president as a partner in its PT Peni plant. Nevertheless, the joint venture was squeezed in favor of the supplier, in which another son of the president held shares. In spite of the example, the findings of the earlier study on joint ventures and expropriation may be misleading. It is likely that joint ventures have been more frequent in industries where risk was already highest. The conclusion may reflect only the initial risk, rather than any increase in risk that comes from participation of a local partner. Yet, regime change can turn a once attractive partner into a liability. Who knows how the sons of Indonesia's current president will be viewed by the next president?

Avoid Blame Associated with Privatization

Today, many investments are again being made in infrastructure in the developing countries, in spite of the industry's rocky history.[54] Many of the investments are in privatized assets of previously state-owned firms, or they supplement infrastructure that has been operated by the state in the past.

Especially in environments of rapid inflation, governments of developing countries have rarely raised prices for electricity, transportation, and other infrastructure sufficiently to offset general price increases. As a result, to make privatization attractive, prices must increase sharply. The price increases, if undertaken by the foreign investor, are likely to be politically sensitive and increase the risk for the investor. Probably less risky is to favor projects where consumer and industrial prices are not below those required for profitability: even if the increases have been made in preparation for privatization. The wise investor might insist that the price increases be made before he takes over.

Prepare for Regulation

Governments are almost always compelled to regulate prices in industries characterized by natural monopoly, or where the government has created monopolies. In infrastructure, however, regulation has usually been undertaken informally as long as infrastructure was owned by the government. With privatization, the informal mechanisms collapse. A few governments have planned ahead and built regulatory bodies before foreign private investment has entered. In most cases, however, regulatory procedures are established at best while privatization is taking place; often, afterwards.[55] As a result, most investors have little idea of what the approach to regulation will be before they commit funds; even more rarely do they have any history on which they can draw for projections.

On occasion, the investor can influence the form of regulation, if he avoids the temptation of resisting its inevitable introduction. The wise investor probably seeks to have regulation in place before he invests;[56] failing that, he will at least support the introduction and attempt to influence it toward transparency and rationality.

Design the Financial Structure to Minimize Risk

Host countries have a strong record of honoring foreign debt, even after foreign-owned projects have been nationalized. In Indonesia, when Indosat was being nationalized, the government was even careful to notify creditors that the obligations of the enterprise would be honored, as the government acquired the equity.[57]

The record for honoring debt from parents and other affiliates seems almost as strong as that of debt from independent financial institutions. As a result, a financial structure that depends heavily on debt may provide more security than one with a lower debt: equity ratio. Although tax and other considerations should enter into the determination of the financial structure, so should an analysis of the impact of various structures on noncommercial risk.

Involve Strong International Interests

Some reduction in risk may derive from the participation of a range of parties in a venture. If the interests of a number of parties are affected by action against the investors, then, the argument goes, those parties can bring additional pressures to bear on the host government to secure the original arrangements.

A strong case for the usefulness of involvement of a number of developed countries emerged from the experience of copper mining in Chile.[58] The American copper companies were able to pursue their interests in European courts because of the network of international delegations. In that case of a radical (although elected) regime change, multi-nation involvement did not in the end secure investors' properties, but in a less radical change it might well have discouraged government action.

More recently, managers have focused on involving multilateral financial institutions in their investments, in particular World Bank affiliates.[59] The underlying assumption is that countries that are willing to take action against private investors will be more hesitant if the interests of those institutions are affected. The World Bank and the Inter-American Development Bank, for example, would defend their interests by imposing sanctions on an offending country. The participation has often taken the form of direct loans and equity holdings by the multilaterals; more recently, participation by multilaterals has been sought in funds set up to pool money for investment in developing countries. A former World Bank official, Moeen Qureshi, one of the organizers of such a fund, explained that its ties to multilateral institutions can reduce the risk that a host country will not honor its commitments to private investors.[60]

Participation of multilateral organizations in the financing of foreign investments may well give host governments second thoughts about actions that will affect the interests of investors. On the other hand, the protection will probably be less than expected. First, to the extent that the funds from multilaterals are in the form of debt, actions that squeeze equity holders but leave enough cash flow to service debt may not generate a response from multilateral institutions; this is especially the case given the record of host governments in honoring debt. Even when the multilateral institutions hold equity, their equity stakes are generally very small. Second, some of the actions short of expropriation are sufficiently subtle and gradual that they are unlikely to trigger a reaction. In fact, the presence of multilateral organizations may encourage exactly those kinds of actions, rather than the old-style expropriations. Finally, the power of the multilateral institutions to issue viable threats is declining as the funding they provide makes up an ever smaller portion of the external resources going to developing countries. For fiscal year 1995–6, for example, the World Bank's net disbursements to developing countries were considerably less than its reported loans of $21.4 billion; each of the regional multilateral institutions accounted for significantly smaller flows. In contrast, in 1995 some $170 billion of private money moved to the same group of countries.[61]

Seek a Defensible Process for Negotiating Entry

Investors state a preference for transparency in government regulation, and they support competitive markets in principle. Yet, when they negotiate arrangements for foreign investments in the developing countries, they often negotiate in secrecy and engage in bargaining processes that are not competitive. When they do so, they leave themselves open to charges of "sweetheart deals," corruption, and unreasonable terms. Enron's project in India, for example, was negotiated without competing bids, under a "fast track" arrangement. Opposition parties in the state of Maharashtra were thus able to charge that Enron had struck a deal that was too favorable for the company, and that it had obtained this deal by bribing officials. Without competitive bidding, and with a great deal of secrecy surrounding the negotiations, an investor is prone to face problems if it is called on to defend its arrangements. On the other hand, the risk of charges being widely believed are reduced when contracts are obtained through competitive bidding and when the process is reasonably transparent.

Look for Innovative Forms of Agreement

The experiences of petroleum and mining companies offer other lessons in risk reduction. As their bargaining positions weakened, they turned to innovative forms of contracts to reduce the political sensitivity of their investments or to encourage delays in changes in their agreements.

One of the innovations was to separate ownership from control and earnings. Ownership is a politically sensitive issue, especially when natural resources are involved, when monopolies have been granted, or when the general public is affected by the delivery of a basic service. For mining and petroleum, service and production sharing contracts evolved as ways of leaving nominal ownership in the hands of host country nationals, while the foreign investor retained the rights to control decisions that were important to him and to capture sufficient earnings to justify the investment. Further, production sharing contracts called for payment "in kind," seeming to avoid some of the foreign exchange costs associated with the transfer of dividends abroad.

Another element of innovation in mining agreements was to build change into the agreements. The goal was to recognize the need for change as bargains obsolesced, but to build in a schedule so that governments would be less tempted to act as soon as they recognized that change could be made. Even when governments face great pressure to make changes in the arrangements, they may delay action if the contract calls for the change to occur automatically in a reasonably short period of time. On the other hand, if the agreement fails to provide for change or postpones change for too long, the government may act immediately.[62] Still another approach has been to abandon long-term agreements for those issues where general legislation is adequate. Many minerals investors, for example, have decided that operating under general tax legislation provides more stability than do contractual arrangements that purport to fix tax regimes for decades. In spite of this experience, some recent infrastructure agreements attempt to bind terms for 20 or 30 years, an invitation for renegotiation.

Certain innovations have, however, been introduced into infrastructure through "build, operate, and transfer" (BOT) and "build, own, operate, and transfer" (BOOT) arrangements. A number of power contracts include provisions for changes in pricing over time. Paiton I in Indonesia begins with very high unit charges for electricity and schedules reductions after the first six years. The justification is probably based on the needs in the early years for cash flow for debt service. But the reduction will kick in at a time when the odds have increased that the deal will be subject to questions. In spite of these examples, innovation outside the petroleum and mining industries has not yet caught up.

Seek Sensible Methods of Dispute Settlement

Where large sums of money are involved, foreign investors often seek methods of settling disputes outside the courts and legal systems of their host countries. Thus, some investment agreements call for international arbitration through, say, the International Center for the Settlement of Investment Disputes (ICSID). Agreements are sometimes subject to laws of other countries. But, methods of dispute settlement that entail costs so high that they are unlikely to be used provide little protection for the investor. On the other hand, reasonable mechanisms may reduce the risk of government intervention.

Although demands for settlement outside the host country imply distrust of the local legal system, host countries sometimes understand the investor's concern and agree to submit disputes to outside rules and procedures. In fact, such provisions can prove useful. Enron, for example, in its conflict in India threatened to draw on the provisions in its agreement for arbitration in London.

Although many agreements provide for international arbitration, few agreements provide for methods of settling disputes that are too minor to justify the expense and the likely souring of relations that are associated with major arbitrations. The result is that both parties are hesitant to use the specified dispute settlement mechanisms for small disagreements, and are unable to deal with issues in a way that both parties trust. A few mining agreements have been innovative in seeking alternative methods of settling disputes so that the choices reflect the seriousness of the issue. And the parties to a dispute do not fear initiating the settlement mechanism, if they feel aggrieved. Similar gradations for settlement of different kinds of disputes might be appropriate in other industries.

Will the Investor's Home Government Provide Help?

Investors hope that the threat of intervention from their home governments will deter unfavorable action on the part of host countries. Although the days of US marines landing to protect investors have passed (unless, perhaps, US oil supplies are threatened), the United States does appear to offer some protection. The terms of the Generalized System of Preferences call for withdrawal of benefits from a host country if the properties of a US investor are taken without prompt and adequate compensation. The Hickenlooper Amendment calls for the withholding of US aid from countries that act similarly, while the Gonzales Amendment demands that US representatives in multilateral financial institutions vote against loans to offending countries.

Yet, US words speak louder than its actions; and host governments have learned this. The actions under the Hickenlooper and Gonzales amendments can be delayed if the president deems that delay is in the national interest. As a result, only very rarely have they been implemented.

The US government sometimes issues statements of concern about threats to US investors. When the Indian state of Maharashtra began to investigate the Enron deal, the US government reacted with an announcement from the Department of Energy:

> Failure to honor the agreements between the project partners and the various Indian governments will jeopardize not only the Dabhol Project but also the other private power projects being proposed for international financing.

The US announcement seems only to have provided oxygen to the fires of nationalism. *The Hindustan Times* declared: "it is time that the West realized that India is not a banana republic which has to dance to the tune of the multinationals." The state government announced the cancellation of the contract two months and one day after the US government warning.

Other foreign investors in offending countries rarely push for strong actions to defend their colleagues, fearing that their own government relations will sour as a result of strong home-country actions. Further, in the case of the United States, actions to defend its investors have often run up against other foreign policy objectives that may be damaged by confrontation.

Although the United States (and the governments of other industrial countries) have been hesitant to take strong unilateral action against host governments, it seems that they may be less reluctant when they are backed by international agreements. Given the role that international agreements can play in reducing risk, investors might well be served by devoting effort to understanding their provisions and the political constraints that governments face in enforcing them. Furthermore, investor support for specialized agreements, such as on transfer pricing, might well be in the interest of investors and they might gain by encouraging the conclusion of such agreements at least among sets of countries.

The Risk–Return Trade-off

Insurance, risk reduction, and help from home governments can go only so far. In the end, investors must accept a certain amount of risk, if returns are to be earned. Yet, the relationship between risk and return is not simple. Managers are taught to think of high risk as requiring high returns. Where risks are high, the argument goes, investors will not tread unless the expected returns are also high. Yet, in the case of foreign investment, the causal link between risk and returns is complex. Investors might demand a high return because commercial risks are high or because they believe that they face large non-commercial risk. Whatever the reason that investors seek high returns, if those returns materialize they may themselves increase the risk of the investment. Governments can be pushed, by their own calculations, by the pressure of opposition, or by local private firms envying those returns to respond with steps that reduce the costs of foreign investment to the economy or which shift profits to local investors. Thus, the unfortunate paradox: the investor who seeks high returns to offset high risk may, in so doing, increase the risk.

Notes

[1] See, for example, Raymond Vernon, "Organizational and Institutional Responses to International Risk," in Richard Herring (ed.), *Managing International Risk* (New York: Cambridge University Press, 1983), pp. 191–216.

[2] A rather exhaustive list of risks appears in Jeffrey D. Simon, "A Theoretical Perspective on Political Risk," *Journal of International Business Studies* (Winter 1984), pp. 123–43.

[3] Prominent in this literature has been the work of Stephen Kobrin. See, for example, his "Expropriation as an Attempt to Control Foreign Firms in LDCs: Trends from 1960 to 1979," *International Studies Quarterly*, no. 29 (1985), pp. 329–48. See also Robert G. Hawkins, Norman Mintz, and Michael Provissiero, "Government Takeovers of US Foreign Affiliates," *Journal of International Business Studies* (Spring 1976), pp. 3–15; David A. Jodice, "Sources of Change in Third World Regimes for Foreign Direct Investment: 1968–1987," *International Organization* (Spring 1980), pp. 176–206.

[4] In a 1982 book, Kobrin reported a survey in which managers identified civil disorder and expropriation as the two most important risks in developing countries. Stephen J. Kobrin, *Managing Political Risks Assessment: Strategic Response to Environmental Change* (Berkeley: University of California Press, 1982), p. 118.

[5] See Michael S. Minor, "The Demise of Expropriation as an Instrument of LDC Policy, 1980–1992," *Journal of International Business Studies*, vol. 25, no. 1 (first quarter 1994), p. 180.

[6] The imports were also subject to a 5 percent surcharge.

[7] In fact, the government had been quite explicit in its intent. The Minister of Industry announced that the tariff was intended to encourage local ethylene consumers to make long-term contracts with Chandra Asri. Once those commitments had been made, the tariff might again be lowered, allowing BP's affiliate to import without tariffs that portion of the ethylene that Chandra Asri could not provide. See "Standardization of Chemical Industry Tariffs Sought," *The Jakarta Post* (July 2, 1996).

[8] Actually, a 20 percent tariff plus 20 percent surcharge. See "Chandra Asri Gets 25 percent Import Tariff Protection," *The Jakarta Post* (June 10, 1996), p. 10.

[9] PT Peni retained some protection, but the impact on profits of the new tariff was suggested by the 11 percent fall in the price of the publicly traded shares of Tri Polyta, a convertor of propylene, when it was faced with a similar tariff decision to force it to buy from Chandra Asri. See "You Were Saying?" *Far Eastern Economic Review* (February 29, 1996), p. 53.

[10] See "Costly Chemicals," *The Jakarta Post* (June 11, 1996), p. 4.

[11] See "Chaotic Paradise: An Audacious Rebel in Papua New Guinea Shakes Copper Market," *The Wall Street Journal* (January 3, 1990).

[12] The role of protection in leading to investments that are profitable for the investor but not economically beneficial to the host country is clearly demonstrated in Dennis J. Encarnation and Louis T. Wells, "Evaluating Foreign Investment," in Theodore H. Moran (ed.), *Investing in Development: New Roles for Private Capital?* (New Brunswick, NJ: Transaction Books, 1986), pp. 61–86. Reduction in import protection sharply increases the probability that private and national interests will coincide.

[13] Paul M. Goldberg and Charles P. Kindleberger, "Toward a GATT for Investment: A Proposal for Supervision of the International Corporation," *Law and Policy in International Business*, vol. 2, no. 2 (Summer 1970), pp. 295–325.

[14] Optimistically, Monty Graham proposes global agreement within the GATT/WTO framework. See Edward M. Graham, *Global Corporations and National Government* (Washington, DC: Institute for International Economics, 1996).

[15] See "Tunky Visits US to Explain Trade, Industry Policies," *The Jakarta Post* (June 8, 1996), p. 8.

[16] The bound rate was 40 percent, higher than the actual rate.

[17] Figure for 1986 to 1990, from Annex Table 5, United Nations Conference on Trade and Development, Division on Transnational Corporations and Investment, *World Investment Report 1995* (New York: United Nations, 1995). As low as it is, the figure seems to include ploughed back earnings as well as new inflows.

[18] Ibid, Table 1.3, p. 12.

[19] The problems recently faced by manufacturing firms parallel those faced in the oil producing countries in the 1970s and early 1980s. The appreciation of real exchange rates was not a conscious policy on the part of such countries, but the so-called "Dutch Disease" was similar in its impact on manufacturing firms. But without the recent emphasis on open markets, the result was not always disaster for the firm; tariff or quota protection could be increased or capital subsidized to assure that the manufacturer survived.

[20] For a particularly clear statement of "domains" of different types of investors, see Peter Evans, *Dependent Development: The Alliance of Multinational, State, and Local Capital in Brazil* (Princeton: Princeton University Press, 1979), p. 284.

[21] Evans, op. cit., pp. 299–300 and pp. 309–14, refers to Mexico and Nigeria to illustrate wealth from joint venture requirements, but many businessmen in other developing countries got their start in the same way.

[22] *The Economist* reported a more subtle case: Giordano's (a Hong Kong-based clothing firm) faced problems with licenses in China that were, it seems, caused by an influential local firm. See "Business in Hong Kong: The China Line," *The Economist* (June 15, 1996), p. 58.

[23] "Investing in the Philippines: The Perils of Being a Foreigner," *The Economist* (September 7, 1996), p. 62. The foreign investors were Hong Kong and Malaysian.

[24] For the influence of private Indian industrialists on admissions policy, see Dennis J. Encarnation, *Dislodging Multinationals: India's Strategy in Comparative Perspective* (Ithaca: Cornell University Press, 1989), pp. 8 and 190, in particular.

[25] See Dennis J. Encarnation, *Dislodging Multinationals: India's Strategy in Comparative Perspective* (Ithaca: Cornell University Press, 1989), p. 160.

[26] Evans, op. cit.

[27] Evans, op. cit., p. 127.

[28] See, for example, the constitution of Indonesia, which reserves certain sectors to state control. Although recently the government has re-interpreted the provision, at one time state control was interpreted as state ownership. In fact, one of the charges against ITT in the late 70s was that its ownership of Indosat was unconstitutional. Similarly, Mexico has struggled with the constitutional implications of privatization of petroleum and petrochemical chemical activities.

[29] Evans, op. cit., p. 284.

[30] Similarly, when one of the Indonesian president's sons, Hutomo Mandala Putra (Tommy), challenged the existing automobile producers – mostly Japanese – by deciding to produce a "national car" and obtaining exemption from the duties and excise taxes that other producers had to bear, the partner in the enterprise was the Korean Kia Motors Corporation. See "Bimantara's Request for Car Policy Review Refused," *The Jakarta Post* (June 6, 1996), p. 8.

[31] Of course, even in the United States there are exceptions; yet, the principle of equal treatment for firms in similar situations is broadly agreed, even though practice may occasionally differ.

[32] See Diana Jean Schemo, "Oil Companies Buy own Army to Tame Colombia's Rebels," *The New York Times* (August 22, 1996), p. 1.

[33] For a brief summary of the case, see Louis T. Wells and Eric S. Gleason, "Is Foreign Infrastructure Investment Risky?" *Harvard Business Review* (September/October 1995), p. 46.

[34] See "Risk and Return," *The Economist* (April 27, 1996), p. 66.

[35] Ibid. In another example, this time as a "forecast," the risks for private investors of a proposed dam in Laos are described in "Dam Risky," *The Economist* (July 27, 1996), p. 62.

[36] Velisarios Kattoulas, "US Car Giants Rev up after China Trade Deal," *The Reuter Asia-Pacific Business Report* (June 18, 1996).

[37] See Braince Mascarenhas and Ole Christian Sand, "Country-risk Assessment Systems in Banks: Patterns and Performance," *Journal of International Business Studies* (Spring 1985), pp. 19–35; and R. J. Rummel and David A. Heenan, "How Multinationals Analyze Political Risk," *Harvard Business Review* (January/February 1978), p. 69.

[38] There is plenty of evidence to suggest that government negotiators are similarly driven to close "deals," with little attention to the long-term implications.

[39] For an early effort to dispel this myth, see P. Juhl, "Economically Rational Design of Developing Countries' Expropriation Policies toward Foreign Investment," *Management International Review*, vol. 25, no. 2.

[40] See Henny Sender, "Confidence Booster: Indonesian Power Project Secures Quick Financing," *Far Eastern Economic Review* (April 11, 1996).

[41] See Chapter 2 of Raymond Vernon, *Sovereignty at Bay: The Multinational Spread of US Enterprise* (New York: Basic Books, 1971).

[42] This cause has been cited for takeovers of mining and plantation investments.

[43] The latter two have been common in infrastructure take-overs. For example, both played an important role in the purchase by the Indonesian government of ITT's Indosat subsidiary in the late 1970s.

[44] Of course, the changed bargaining power of the host government as the choice of investors expanded has been reflected in the terms under which new investors establish their operations, as well. See, for example, Nathan Fagre and Louis T. Wells, "Bargaining Power of Multinationals and Host Governments," *Journal of International Business Studies*, no. 9 (Fall 1982), pp. 9–23.

[45] For a full account of IBM's experience at this time in India, see Joseph M. Grieco, *Between Dependency & Autonomy: India's Experience with the Computer Industry* (Berkeley: University of California Press, 1984).

[46] The literature on country risk analysis includes James E. Austin and David B. Yoffie, "Political Forecasting as a Management Tool," *Journal of Forecasting*, no. 3 (1984), pp. 395–408; Jose de la Torre, "Forecasting Political Risks for International Operations," *International Journal of Forecasting*, no. 4 (1988), pp. 221–41. Dan Haendel and Gerald T. West, with Robert G. Meadow, *Overseas Investment and Political Risk* (Philadelphia: Foreign Policy Research Institute, 1975). For hindsight into inaccuracy, see R. S. Rummel and David R. Heenan, "How Multinationals Analyze Political Risk," *Harvard Business Review* (January/February 1978), pp. 62–71. The authors assign a .85 probability to sharp political unrest in Indonesia. An investor who followed the implicit advice would have missed 18 years of astounding growth with political stability. Interestingly, the forecast was made in the year that Indonesia undertook the last nationalization for 18 years. Thomas E. Krayenbuehl, *Country Risk: Assessment and Monitoring* (Cambridge: Woodhead-Faulker, 1985); Briance Mascarenhas and Ole Christian, "Country-Risk Assessment Systems in Banks: Patterns and Performance," *Journal of International Business Studies* (Spring 1985), pp. 19–35; Jeffrey D. Simon, "Political Risk Forecasting," *Futures* (April 1985), pp. 133–47; Frederick J. Truitt, "Expropriation of Foreign Investment: A Summary of the post World War II Experience of American and British Investors in Less Developed Countries," *Journal of International Business Studies* (Fall 1970), pp. 27–34; and Pierre Wack, "Scenarios: Shooting the Rapids," *Harvard Business Review* (November/December 1985), pp. 139–50. A review of approaches appears in Chapter 9 of David K. Eiteman and Arthur I. Stonehill, *Multinational Business Finance* (Reading, MA: Addison Wesley, 1986, 4th edition).

[47] See Robert Svensk, "The Role of Private Sector Insurance," in Fariborz Ghadar, Stephen J. Kobrin, and Theodore H. Moran (eds.), *Managing International Political Risk: Strategies and Technologies* (Washington: Ghadar Associates, 1983), pp. 114–17.

[48] Gerald T. West, "The Utility of Public Political Insurance as a Risk Transfer Mechanism," in Ghadar, Kobrin, and Moran, op. cit., pp. 118–39.

[49] The coverage is, however, limited by MIGA to $50 million for a single project. See Paul Lewis, "World Bank Fund to Help Poor Countries," *The New York Times* (August 3, 1996), p. 36.

[50] "Investment Guarantee Guide," MIGA, n.d.

[51] "How It Was in America," *The Economist* (May 25, 1996), p. 66.

[52] Perversely, it can happen that the peripheral activities are the subject of the squeeze. There is some evidence that PT Peni was purchasing at least some of its ethylene from a BP-owned cracker in Malaysia. BP as a whole might well attribute to Peni the contribution from ethylene sales in the Indonesia investment.

[53] See David G. Bradley, "Managing Against Expropriation," *Harvard Business Review* (July/August, 1977), pp. 75–83.

[54] See Louis T. Wells and Eric S. Gleason, "Is Foreign Infrastructure Investment Still Risky?" *Harvard Business Review* (September/October 1995), pp. 4–12.

[55] For an excellent treatment of the issues, see Bernard Tenenbaum, "Regulation: What the Prime Minister Needs to Know," *The Electricity Journal* (March 1966), pp. 28–36.

[56] The absence of any regulatory mechanism to control the prices that Indosat could charge for its telecommunications services in Indonesia and the guarantees against such a mechanism in the agreement with ITT were important reasons for the nationalization of Indosat in 1980. See unfinished book manuscript on this nationalization by Rafiq Ahmed, Tulane University.

[57] A short report of the nationalization appears in Louis T. Wells, "Is Foreign Infrastructure Investment Still Risky?" *Harvard Business Review* (September/October 1995), p. 8.

[58] Theodore H. Moran, "Transnational Strategies of Protection and Defense by Multinational Corporations: Spreading the Risk and Raising the Cost of Nationalization in Natural Resources," *International Organization*, vol. 27 (Spring 1973), pp. 158–66.

[59] For early attention to this approach, see Christian H. Walser, "Multilateral Institutions and Political Risk: Deterrence, Co-Financing, and Compensation," in Fariborz Ghadar, Stephen I. Kobrin, and Theodore H. Moran (eds.), *Managing International Political Risk: Strategies and Techniques* (Washington, DC: Ghadar and Associates, 1983), pp. 71–9.

[60] Lloyd Bentsen, former Secretary of the Treasury in the United States, and some former officials of multilateral institutions joined to establish the fund for Latin American infrastructure. Reported, along with a description of the fund and its sponsors, in Jeff Gerth, "In Post-Cold-War Washington, Development is a Hot Business," *The New York Times* (May 25, 1996), pp. 1 and 6.

[61] See "All of a Sudden Every Banker is a World Banker," *The Economist* (July 27, 1996), p. 61.

[62] The Peruvian Marcona agreement allowed for 50 percent state participation in 1982, 30 years after the agreement was signed. This was viewed as being too far in the future by the Socialist government of the early 1970s.

2
Trends in Political Risk for Corporate Investors

Sandy Markwick[*]

Profound changes in the global investment climate and the political shifts on which they are based have led to changes in the nature and extent of political risks faced by firms investing worldwide in the 1990s. Free markets increasingly have taken root in the developing world and ideology has given way to pragmatism. Meanwhile, there has been a parallel spread of elected civilian governments. Authoritarian military regimes and single-party states now stand out as notable exceptions.

Louis Wells discusses many of the fundamental trends in political risk. Companies no longer fear the outright expropriation of business assets that occurred in the 1960s and 1970s. Instead, political risks in the 1990s involve more subtle forms of official interference – inconsistent enforcement of rules or contract renegotiations – which can nevertheless be highly detrimental to an investment.

Several key trends lie behind government interference in foreign investments in the 1990s. Stronger domestic business groups in emerging markets, as well as representing an increase in commercial competition, also fuel political risks to investment projects. Powerful local groups can protect vested interests using informal structures and relationships that are not available to foreign investors who in contrast may have to rely on weak institutional safeguards. Wells highlights democracy's double-edged sword for investors: greater accountability on the one hand while increasing the scope for opposition parties to criticize foreign corporations as a means to attack incumbent governments. Furthermore, decentralization means that regional politics has taken on a new significance than when power was to a greater extent concentrated in the hands of a national executive.

---

[*] *Sandy Markwick is Manager, Political and Security Risk Analysis, Control Risks Group.*

I will focus on four other important areas of risk which have an increased significance in the 1990s and which complement Wells's analysis: corruption; organized crime; the increased accountability demanded of transnational corporations; and US sanctions.

The paper in each case suggests some of the varied strategies that companies can adopt to mitigate contemporary political risks and concludes with a discussion of how to assess exposure to political risk.

Institutional Weakness and Unclear Rules

The great strides made in economic reform in emerging markets generally have not been fully matched by a commensurate development of institutions. Checks and balances to executive power – bureaucracies, judiciaries, political parties, and legislatures – are less effective in emerging markets than they are in the advanced democracies of North America and Western Europe. This leads to excessive powers in the hands of presidents who enjoy greater freedom from accountability and a greater degree of discretion than in political systems with a clear separation of powers.

If economic reforms are easily imposed by powerful presidents they can also, in theory at least, be just as easily reversed. With the benefits of macroeconomic improvements yet to trickle down significantly to the developing world's poor and political stability not assured, presidents may be inclined to resort to limited intervention in investments under popular pressure.

Executive power to circumvent legislatures to issue executive decrees tends to produce duplicate and contradictory laws. Powerful leaders with discretionary powers to change laws or enforce them arbitrarily lead to unclear or unstable rules and regulations for business. Business requires institutional safeguards, not weak legislation even if it backs foreign investment.

In Kazakhstan, for example, President Nursultan Nazarbaev's use of decrees contradicts Kazak law in a bid to attract foreign investment. Foreign companies who invest under a cloud of irregularity cannot be confident that the same arbitrariness will not be applied to their detriment in the future. A functioning legal system that is "more than a wall decoration" is required.[1]

The use of decrees to augment legislation leads to confusion as shown by legal uncertainties facing Argentina's two telephone monopolies Telecom (owned by France Telecom and Italy's Stet) and Telefonica Argentina (owned by Telefonica of Spain and Citibank Equity). A presidential decree in January 1997 restructured telephone rates (raising the cost of local calls while reducing long-distance rates) but subsequent court decisions have, by turns, supported and rejected the move.

Meanwhile, companies cannot necessarily rely on the courts to clear up ambiguities in investment regulations or disputes should they arise. The law in many emerging markets is, to varying degrees, slow, inefficient, and politicized. Seeking partnership can be an effective way of doing business in unfamiliar markets and of mitigating risk in the process. However, ambiguous legal frameworks and a lack of transparency in government make it easier for local firms to resort to unorthodox techniques to exclude foreign rivals should a partnership go sour.

In Russia, for example, foreign investors complain of an elite group of favored businessmen who enjoy privileged connections to government. US investment banker Boris Jordan was stripped of his multi-entry visa in 1997 blaming unscrupulous, but influential, rivals of Oneximbank with which Jordan has an association.[2]

Mitigating institutional inadequacies are the following:

- Institutional uncertainty will make companies less willing to risk large-scale investments and may make them more inclined to seek a quicker return.
- The prospect of lengthy and expensive litigation means that business often avoids the court system where possible. Business may take advantage of independent arbitration mechanisms provided by, for example, Chambers of Commerce, sectoral organizations and the UN.
- Legal inadequacies may make private contracts in an anonymous market place an unattractive option. Instead, business focuses on "personal" transactions with people drawn from a limited pool of trusted partners. Lengthy business courtships that last for months before contracts are signed are often attributed to cultural differences. But they stem also from sound material logic. If the courts cannot be relied upon to provide independent judgement in the event of disputes with business partners, it is important to feel comfortable with a partner to reduce the chances of disagreements arising in the first place.
- Companies should back up their personal contacts with partner companies with thorough due diligence to determine, for example, a potential partner's financial standing, reputation and political connections.
- Companies should cultivate good relations with officials independently of a joint venture partner. Contacts should be at least as senior as those maintained by the potential partner.

Corruption

One of the key implications for business of poorly functioning or underdeveloped institutions is corruption. Demands for bribes from senior officials and politicians to win contracts ("grand" corruption) and to lower level officials to facilitate bureaucratic processes ("petty" corruption) constitute an obstacle to business and a genuine political risk to investors.

Costs of corruption can be much higher than the financial burden of "grease payments." Companies may lose commercial opportunities unless they pay large-scale bribes to public officials. Alternatively, revelations of bribe payments – something that becomes more likely as democracy allows opposition parties and the press to operate more freely – may subsequently undermine a company's position.

Local competitors or opposition groups in emerging markets will place foreign adversaries under the microscope in a bid to discover any misdemeanors or questionable practices which they can then use as ammunition against an investor.

Opponents of Enron's Dabhol power project in Maharashtra state in India used circumstantial evidence of corruption to fuel their campaign. The project had been negotiated behind closed doors leading opponents to make unproven allegations of corruption.

Corruption is, of course, nothing new to business operating around the world. However, there is evidence that corruption has increased. Structural adjustment policies in the developing world have led to cuts in public sector pay; low paid officials are more prone to accept or demand bribes. Meanwhile, the spread of free markets to former strict command economies in Eastern Europe, the former Soviet Union and China has opened up new pastures for both investment and corruption.

Furthermore, some privatizations have been subject to corruption and a lack of transparency, though in the long term reducing the role of the state in the economy should restrict the ability of bureaucrats and public officials to exchange information, favors and government contracts in return for bribes. A US Commerce Department official recently reported that since 1994 the government had learned of significant allegations of bribery involving foreign firms in 139 contracts valued at $64 million.

A further change which increases the significance of corruption can be found in global attitudes. Multilateral organizations increasingly view corruption, not as an effective means of "oiling the machine" or of filling gaps left by the absence of functioning tax-raising institutions but, instead, as an obstacle to development. International initiatives to tackle corruption are gaining momentum. In November 1997, the OECD approved a treaty to criminalize the payment of foreign officials by companies. The World Bank and IMF are taking steps to remove corruption linked to their own programmes. Furthermore, the International Chamber of Commerce has drawn up a new advisory code and the UN passed a declaration in December 1996 obliging signatories to criminalize transnational bribery of public officials and make it an extraditable offence.

Large multinational corporations are already highly sensitive about their reputations. Now, and still more so in the future if international initiatives are given "teeth," there are likely to be real penalties for being found out. The US companies have faced these issues since the 1970s and the passage of the Foreign Corrupt Practices Act (FCPA) – now, it seems, changes in the rest of the world may level the playing field for US corporations.

Strategies Against Corruption

What are the practical steps that companies can take when faced with corrupt officials? Blanket advice to "just say no" smacks of naivety and may, from time to time, be unrealistic. The distinction between "grand" and "petty" corruption is an important one; offering accommodation to a customs official in a company's port facility so that the official does his job more efficiently is, most would agree (including US law), qualitatively different from paying an official to win a government tender.

Nevertheless, as a general rule "just say no" is recommended. A short-term problem might be solved by a bribe, but the potential long-term costs will probably be much higher. A company that pays once may be approached for more at a later date. Also, a company by paying bribes companies may incur the wrath of other domestic groups who could gain access to power at a later date.

Here, the FCPA may serve a useful purpose for US companies who can give a polite rebuff citing the US law. Colgate-Palmolive has claimed success with this approach in China.[3] A corporate code of ethics, properly implemented with careful compliance procedures should back up a "just say no" approach. Record-keeping procedures should apply to overseas affiliates, agents, consultants, and other middlemen and "facilitators" who should be carefully chosen and kept under firm control.

Furthermore, companies can lobby host governments to ensure transparency and legitimately report corruption committed by other firms if they think they have been unfairly deprived of a contract.

In addition, companies which invest in development projects in local communities can point to these in the event of an approach for a bribe from local officials. It will be more difficult for local individuals to undermine a company's operation if it has the support of the local community.

Organized Crime

Weak institutions also partly explain the growth of organized crime in Eastern Europe and the former Soviet Union. The geographic spread and power of criminal groups in new emerging markets means it constitutes a qualitatively new risk for business. There are an estimated 6,000 criminal gangs operating throughout Russia made up of around 100,000 individuals.

The threat from organized crime groups takes a variety of forms. Extortion from protection rackets is the most common problem for western businesses in Russia who are targeted by criminal gangs because of their access to hard currency. It is reported that 70 percent of firms in the Russian Federation pay extortion demands. In June 1995, a Russian-American oil joint venture received a demand for $25,000 per month; the company subsequently left Russia. Threats to back up extortion demands can range in seriousness from nuisance telephone calls to bombings and murder. Samsung of Korea had premises bombed twice in 1994. A German household equipment company had its warehouse burnt down. Demands in Moscow average $5,000. Alternatively, mafia-linked business groups may attempt to intimidate competitors with threats. Crime groups may undertake sophisticated research into a company's finances including collecting detailed data from tax authorities, banks and information available only from company employees. The information is used both to gain access inside a company and to determine an appropriate level of demand.

Theft is another principal threat from organized crime groups and particularly affects manufacturers. Criminal gangs organize theft rings or "sponsor" fraud by management or workers within a company. Entrenched management structures persist from the Soviet era when managers considered factory product their own.

Strategies Against Risks from Organized Crime

Investments in emerging markets where organized crime poses a serious threat to business should be undertaken by trusted people with local political and cultural knowledge and language skills. Understanding the local environment is fundamental to the choice of management team. Companies need to familiarize themselves with the local operating environment. What is the significance of the operation to the local community? What are the hidden agendas?

Companies investing in existing operations should carry out an independent due diligence to establish the reputation of local management; their involvement (or otherwise) in fraud; the mechanisms for fraud and theft; and the extent of influence of political and criminal groups.

Strong management control of financial and accounting procedures need to be established. Physical security maybe be needed in the face of threats; the existing security at an operation may be part of a fraud and may need to be overhauled. Pro-active policies to encourage support for a project locally will disarm attempts to stir up anti-foreign sentiment.

International Pressure Group Scrutiny of Business

One of the growing challenges facing companies investing globally in the 1990s falls broadly into the area of community relations and corporate responsibility. Public opinion is more educated and sensitive to the importance of environmental protection and Non-Governmental Organizations (NGOs) and campaign pressure groups have grown in influence. Failure to adopt international standards in environmental protection and labor can lead to public opposition to a company's activities which may encourage host government interference in investments.

Additionally, the same neglect of the environment and labor standards, or association with governments accused of human rights violations, can lead to direct pressure group campaigns targeting those companies involved. Traditional definitions of political risk typically are confined to non-commercial forces involving government action or inaction. However, companies do not just risk official government action if they neglect community concerns or limit corporate responsibility. They also face disruption to the smooth operation of their business from the actions of campaign groups acting independently of governments.

NGOs recognize that in the global context of a diminishing role for the state, international corporations are ever more important. Accordingly, the focus of NGOs has shifted towards greater scrutiny of international companies to ensure they also demonstrate greater responsibility.[4]

Satellite communications bring images to worldwide audiences with maximum impact while computer networks allow pressure groups to co-ordinate activities and spread information globally.[5] NGOs worldwide form a civil society on a global scale and combine central and regional expertise to switch local issues on to an international stage. By publicizing and coordinating sophisticated campaigns through the Internet pressure groups can reach a wide audience and bring the activities of companies in the remotest of areas to the world's attention. Risks, like opportunities, are increasingly global.

Sustained NGO campaigns can consume senior management time; embroil companies in time-consuming litigation; undermine employee morale thereby increasing turnover of staff and reducing the prospects of attracting high-caliber recruits; and lead to official and consumer boycotts.

In April 1996, PepsiCo announced the sale of its 40 percent stake in a joint venture in Myanmar (Myanmar) and finally broke all its investment ties with that country in January 1997. PepsiCo's decision to withdraw came in response to a boycott campaign by an alliance of pressure groups known as the Free Myanmar Campaign (FBC) which organizes opposition to Myanmar's military regime. The boycott had led to the cancellation of a $1 million contract to supply products to Harvard University. Although PepsiCo had considered Myanmar an exciting emerging market and an area where it could steal a march on its competition, the boycott made it clear that the company "had more to lose in the US than it could gain in Southeast Asia."[6]

While boycott campaigns are nothing new, communications technology ensures that they are more effective. Beer manufacturers Heineken and Carlsberg and a list of garment manufacturers including Levi Strauss, Liz Claibourne, and Eddie Bauer have pulled out of Myanmar since 1992.

Manufacturers of consumer goods are particularly vulnerable to boycotts because their products have a higher profile than, for example, capital goods manufacturers. However, campaigners sometimes try to extend the power of the boycott by encouraging city and state administrations in the US to adopt policies of "selective purchasing." At least ten cities in the US as well as the state of Massachusetts passed selective purchasing agreements in 1996 imposing bans on businesses operating in Myanmar. Massachusetts issued a blacklist of some 150 companies with links to Myanmar, including Siemens, Unilever, and BMW.

While Myanmar has been the main target of these campaigns, other campaign groups are attempting similar tactics. Campaigners have proposed selective purchasing agreements to penalize companies operating in Nigeria. New York City council is considering a ban on city government contracts with companies investing in any one of 15 countries that it alleges persecutes Christians, including China, Indonesia, Saudi Arabia, Egypt, and Pakistan. Many of these campaigns can be dismissed as posturing with little chance of achieving an impact, but not all.

Environmental concerns, often closely linked to human rights, most frequently affect oil and mining companies. NGOs in support of the Huaorani Amerindians in Ecuador sued Texaco in a New York court which, although unsuccessful, was costly and time-consuming for the company. Asarco, owners of Southern Peru Copper Corporation (SPCC), has similarly faced court proceedings in the US for its activities in Peru, as has BHP in Melbourne for alleged environmental damage in Papua New Guinea. Increasingly, companies must satisfy project financiers that environmental concerns have been adequately addressed.

Oil and mining companies often operate in remote rural areas which may be the scene of separatist, ethnic, religious, or revolutionary insurgency. It is a delicate balancing act to maintain good relations with security forces which will help ensure protection against political violence while avoiding close identification with those same state forces who may be engaged in a counter-insurgency with little regard for human rights. A British Member of the European Parliament (MEP) publicly accused BP of providing the Colombian army with intelligence identifying individuals linked to guerrilla groups who subsequently "disappeared." Shell has suffered some of the most damaging publicity stemming from its activities in Ogoniland (Nigeria) where it is accused both of contaminating the environment and of complicity of with a repressive regime. Anger towards Shell reached its height following the execution of Ogoni activist Ken Saro-Wiwa in November 1995.

Shell was also the subject of another controversy in 1995 – over its plans to dump the Brent Spar oil installation in the North Sea. The episode illustrates the increasing sophistication of environmentalists. Through a combination of dramatic direct action and savvy use of the media, Greenpeace captured the public imagination. Greenpeace was more adept at setting the agenda and reacting to events than Shell UK. In comparison, Shell's PR campaign appeared "ponderous, sparse, reactive and focused on scientific argument."[7]

In many of these controversies, international companies can claim to operate within the law with the full support and co-operation of their host governments. However, the message of NGOs is that compliance with the law is not enough – particularly when vital environmental issues or human rights are at stake. If a controversy arises it is likely to damage the relationship with the host government which will come under pressure to protect domestic concerns.

Mitigation of Risk Stemming from Pressure Group Politics

In a survey of 51 major European companies conducted by the Industrial Research Bureau (IRB) for Control Risks Group in late 1995, 90 percent of respondents felt that the impact of pressure groups on their operations was significant or would increase over the next five years. However, only 20 percent had formal procedures in place to establish dialogue with NGOs and fewer still to evaluate their impact.

As a minimum requirement, companies need to take NGOs and the issues they champion seriously and apply international standards at the very least in environmental and labor practices.

Companies need to evaluate the potential impact of NGOs on specific projects. Certain questions should be automatically included in a due diligence check-list: is the company operating at the highest international standards in terms of the environment and human rights? Is the host country a human rights "pariah"?; Are the company's activities likely to provoke controversy? Is there an active NGO campaign on any issue related to the proposed venture? If so, how influential is it and what impact will the campaign have on domestic politics in the investor's home country?

Companies have to respond to the challenges posed by a more demanding civil society by explaining their points of view to a consumer audience and their domestic political representatives. Companies must acquire new sensitivities as well as new communication skills to present their cases persuasively and without distortion.

Pressure group campaigns have caused some companies to make an explicit commitment to take issues such as the environment and human rights into account when making overseas investment choices; a recognition that companies might have ethical responsibilities which are broader than merely maximizing shareholder value within the context of laws of the land.

Companies which adopt a pro-active strategy in relations with local communities are less likely to encounter serious problems at a later date. It is noteworthy that Shell, after its negative experiences in Nigeria, is being very active in negotiating with local communities in developing its Camisea gas field in Peru. Strategies to prevent becoming the target of international pressure group campaign go hand in hand with strategies to mitigate political risk in the host country. Companies which sustain their welcome over the long term with local communities and host governments will naturally face reduced political risks. Gaining the "licence to operate" from a local community, not just acceptance in the eyes of the law, will reduce the chances of national or regional government interfering with business operations for political reasons. It will also reduce the prospects of a business becoming the target of an international pressure group campaign.

Companies must determine attitudes within local communities, but this is not achieved by merely liaising with local political representatives. Elections are an imperfect means of articulating popular opinion, particularly in developing countries where a tradition of decentralized elected government may be weak and political power may be highly subject to patronage and elite control.

This democratic disfunction in emerging markets is illustrated by a controversy in the town of Tepotzlan (Mexico) dubbed the "Golf War." A consortium including GE Capital of the US was forced to abandon a project to build a business complex, including a golf course after local inhabitants' anger led to clashes with the police and the death of a protester. Farmers feared the diversion of scarce water resources away from their land to service the business center. Opposition to the development from the community came in spite of the support for the project from the local mayor, a representative of the ruling Institutional Revolutionary Party (PRI).

Companies should enter into a process of genuine local consultation and consensus-building – and not merely for the sake of public image. Effective public participation "must visibly and substantially affect our plans, our project designs, and our actions."[8] The lesson of Tepotzlan is that consultation must not be confined to official channels of authority, but must seek out independent and grass roots attitudes. While such a process adds costs, evidence shows projects which undergo genuine community liaison turn out "demonstrably more acceptable, viable and sustainable."[9]

Furthermore, investments will be more sustainable if the economic benefits of a project are shared broadly within local communities and not limited to national governments or local elites. By simply paying taxes to national governments, companies cannot be sure that the benefits are filtering down to target communities. Companies can more directly benefit communities by providing a high proportion of good jobs for locals, including management positions, and using local suppliers through social expenditure, for example, building schools, providing training, or improving local health care. Public consultation at this stage is vital to ensure that the most effective and useful projects are identified; popular disillusion will soon follow if companies simply throw money at a high-profile project than turns into an unsustainable white elephant. A cautionary note: development projects need to be sensitively handled to avoid being seen as a form of bribery.

Sanctions

US sanctions are a significant risk in the 1990s which deserves more consideration. Sanctions have become a new tool of foreign policy in the US in the 1990s which show that political risk can reside in Washington, DC as well as a host nation where an investment is taking place. US unilateral embargos aims to sanction numerous countries, most prominently Iran, Iraq, Libya, Syria, Sudan, North Korea, Cuba and, since April 1997, Myanmar.

US companies are already banned from operating in Cuba, but the 1996 "Helms-Burton" Act applies sanctions against companies from outside the US who "traffic" in property confiscated from US citizens following the 1959 revolution. Other "extra-territorial" legislation includes the 1996 Iran-Libya Sanctions Act (ILSA) which, in order to discourage Iran and Libya from sponsoring terrorism, bans US companies from investing in there and requires the US to apply sanctions against foreign firms investing large sums in either country's energy sector.

There are serious question over whether such sanctions against non-US companies are enforceable. The US's allies in Europe, Mexico, and Canada are vociferously opposed to attempts to apply legislation to third country companies and are challenging such legislation in the WTO. Despite the problems, US domestic politics and the pursuit of votes may result in further attempts to impose sanctions on other countries.

The sanctions legislation against Iran prevents US companies competing for investment opportunities there; Conoco made the first deal with Iran since the 1979 revolution, but the agreement was canceled by an executive order by President Clinton in 1995. Also, the measure has reduced the number of supply sources available to US companies thereby limiting their flexibility in the marketplace and putting them at a competitive disadvantage vis-a-vis non-US companies.

Non-US companies have been sanctioned for investments in Cuba. The directors of Canadian mining firm Sherritt International were refused entry to the US in accordance with the "Helms-Burton" Act. Italian telephone company Stet is seeking to settle a compensation payment to ITT whose subsidiary was expropriated to form the Cuban phone company. Other firms have withdrawn from investments in Cuba or ruled out investment in the country in the first place because of fears of the implications on its US business. A Canadian mining company ruled out an investment in Cuba even though it did not involve property claimed by US citizens or companies and therefore was not in violation of "Helms-Burton." The company is a major exporter of nickel to the US and was not prepared to risk a wider interpretation of the law in the US.

Strategies to Mitigate Risks from Sanctions

The ways to mitigate risks stemming from US sanctions are limited. Non-US companies who chose to challenge the US's right to sanction them if they invest in Cuba, Iran, or Libya can lobby their home governments to put pressure on the US not to enforce legislation.

Non-US companies who flout sanctions legislation would also be wise to consider the importance of any US investments and exports now and in the future before they proceed. They would also be wise to divest interest in the US first to prevent assets being seized.

The Role of Insurance

Political risk insurance continues to be a useful tool to mitigate risk for investors. Political risk insurance, particularly from the public sector, acts as an effective preventative deterrent against government's interfering with investments. The World Bank's Multilateral Investment Guarantee Agency (MIGA) has never paid out a political risk claim. When disputes arise it has been able to use the political clout of the World Bank to persuade host governments against a particular course of action. Similarly, OPIC has the backing of the US government and the Export Development Corporation (EDC) of Canada. By increasing the range and nationality of interests involved in insuring or financing an investment project, companies will increase the deterrent effect discouraging host government interference.

However, political risk insurance and the financial structure of a deal are only partial responses to political risk. Insurers can only cover investments against those political risks which are quantifiable and provable. The insurance industry by necessity uses a limited definition of the term "political risk" which cannot cover the range of frustrations and obstacles encountered in the complex emerging markets of today. Even where risks are quantifiable and provable, the market cannot always cover the largest investments. Innovation from within the insurance markets may result in coverage for some of today's newer risks, but companies need to complement insurance and financing with the range of strategies listed above in order to fully mitigate political risks.

How to Assess Risk

Thorough project-based political risk analysis is essential for companies to understand the most effective strategies to mitigate risk. Undertaking political risk analysis should not be conducted merely as an after-thought to satisfy minimum due diligence requirements, but instead should be undertaken early as a integrated part of a feasibility study.

Companies need to be aware of political uncertainties and the dynamics within a host country driving politics at national, regional, and local level. However, effective political risk analysis is not just a question of evaluating country risk. Instead, risk assessments must identify the implications of social, political, and economic conditions for each particular project. Proposed projects will have winners and losers in the host country, for example, among landowners, business competitors, politicians, communities, and workforces. The key to analyzing the political risks facing a project is to identify the winners and losers and assess their relative abilities to help or hinder a project, either directly or by influencing a host government.

The attitude of the host government towards an investment will also be influenced by the balance of power between an investor and a host government. For example, a foreign investor initially may be essential as a provider of technology or capital that cannot be provided locally. In these circumstances a host government is more likely to override any domestic objections to a project than if local businesses could equally undertake a project. The unique ability of a foreign investor to conduct a project may not last the lifetime of a project. If the technology required for the project does not change significantly over time it is likely that local businesses will soon acquire the technology which they previously could not offer. Alternatively, if the technology requirement are dynamic, a foreign investor may be one step ahead of local competition and will more likely be able to maintain its strong position vis-a-vis a host government.

Also, the balance of power between a investor and a host government will be affected by the simple law of supply and demand. Is the government offering a scarce opportunity for which foreign companies are falling over themselves for the right to develop? If so, governments will be tough negotiators and will be more tempted to renegotiate contracts at a later date or secure benefits for themselves through unexpected interventions. Consider the comments of Indian Industry Minister Murasoli Maran daring Susuki to pull out of a profitable 15-year joint venture because of a dispute with the government over its choice of a managing director: "there are thousands of people waiting. The Americans are there, the Germans are there... There are several people better than Susuki available in this world."[10] Alternatively, the balance of power will shift to investors where governments compete with other countries to attract limited investment funds.

Some other relevant questions to ask in assessing political risk to a project include the following:

- Did the company win a project as a result of a competitive tender? If not, or if the process was not transparent, a company may be open to accusations that it negotiate behind-closed-doors or bribed officials.
- Does the investment constitute a privatization? An investment may be unpopular if a foreign company buys a state asset, particularly in sensitive industries. Are the terms of the agreement seen as particularly favorable to a foreign investor? Did the investors secure concessions after tough negotiations? These may make the operation more prone to political opposition.

- Did a company receive assistance from well-connected local politicians to secure to bid? If so, how closely associated with that individual is the project and is that person's position secure?
- Is the project seen as providing valuable goods and services that cannot be provided locally?
- Does a project involve a large-scale investment from the outset which would commit a company in the long term? This may weaken a company's negotiating position once the investment has been made in comparison to companies who could simply abandon a project in the knowledge that they cannot lose money yet to be invested.
- Does a contract allow for renegotiation in the event of subsequent changes to market conditions? If a contract becomes less attractive to a host government during the lifetime of a project than is was when it was signed the government might seek renegotiation. If this is not forthcoming, an investment raises risks of unilateral government intervention. As Wells discusses in his conclusion, seeking higher returns may not be the best way to offset risk. Success, in the form of higher returns, may increase risks still further.

Notes

1 Charles Clover, "A worrying emphasis on re-centralization," *Financial Times* (July 23, 1997).
2 Chrystia Freeland, "Banker blames rivals," *Financial Times* (October 14, 1997).
3 Agnieszka Klitch, "Bribery in economies in transition: the Foreign Corrupt Practices Act," *Stanford Journal of International Law*, vol. 32 (Winter 1996).
4 For a full discussion of the pressure group politics and its effect on business see *No Hiding Place – business and the politics of pressure* published by Control Risks Group, 1997.
5 For a discussion of the use of the Internet by pressure groups see John Bray, "A web of influence," *The World Today* (August/September 1997).
6 Bray, op. cit.
7 *No Hiding Place*, op. cit.
8 James Cooney, "Global mining: three priorities in a politically challenging world," Paper presented to Northwest Mining Association's Annual International Convention, December 1995, Spokane, Washington.
9 Ibid.
10 Jonathan Karp, "India alarms multinationals by two investors," *The Wall Street Journal* (September 22, 1997).

3
Political Risk:
A Realistic View Toward Assessment, Quantification, and Mitigation

William T. Irwin[*]

Abstract

The geothermal industry provides one of several opportunities for infrastructure investment in Indonesia. The cultural, regulatory, and business environments in Indonesia have several unique features which should be considered when making an investment decision. These decisions can be made with confidence by understanding the probabilistic nature of risks and their assessment. Good computer tools exist to assess risks, and their outputs provide useful insight towards risk mitigation planning.

Indonesia – Background

Until 1997–8, Indonesia enjoyed rapid and sustained economic growth during the 32-year leadership of President Suharto. The shift towards industrialization and open relations with other nations has yielded a direct benefit to its people. During this growth period, Indonesia has improved its relative standing with regard to quality of life. Statistics indicate that 60 percent of the general population lived below the poverty line in early Repelita I (the five-year planning cycle 1969–73). That figure has dropped to less than 14 percent in the current year. Indonesia's per capita income is now pushing towards $1,000, and the country is now firmly in the middle income group of the global community.[1]

[*]William T. Irwin works for Chevron Overseas Petroleum, Inc. He was formerly with Amoseas Indonesia, Inc.

Prior to 1997–8, several economic indicators show increasing prosperity for the nation. Indonesia enjoyed a 7 percent annual growth rate for its Gross Domestic Product (GDP) for the previous twenty-five years.[2] The relative importance of agriculture has lessened over this period. GDP growth was initially fueled for this OPEC member nation by the oil boom of the late 1970s. National Policy was carefully tailored towards a more diversified economy after the precipitous drop in oil prices in the mid 1980s. This diversification has been largely successful – Indonesia has maintained a double-digit growth rate through the 1980s and into the 90s, while concurrently lessening the dominance of oil and agriculture (figure 3.1).

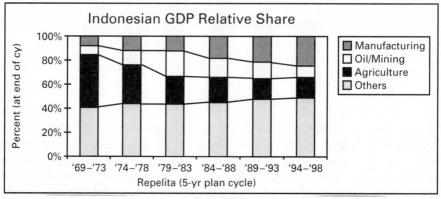

figure 3.1

This GDP growth and the shift away from both agriculture and petroleum is mirrored – or more accurately, catalyzed – by increases in power generating capacity (figure 3.2). Indonesia has realized a 3,300 percent increase in installed power capacity since 1969.[3] Meeting the ever-increasing demand for power is paramount to successfully continuing its double-digit growth.

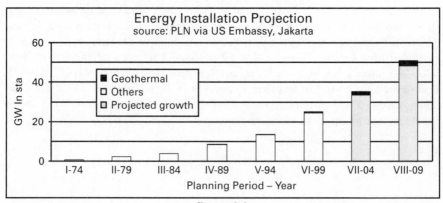

figure 3.2

The Power Market

Even with this wide growth, access to power is limited. Indonesia ranks in the lower echelon of ASEAN members with a 350 kWh per capita power consumption. Efficient development of power is a challenge for the country. As a widely dispersed, archipelago nation, electrical power distribution is difficult. Although Java and Bali are served by an interconnected grid, the other islands are served by much more localized systems. Many smaller areas are powered by small, expensive, diesel-fueled generators.

Reliability concerns mean most big buildings and industries invest in large stand-by generation equipment. Some industries take advantage of captive power, taking sole responsibility for all of their power needs.

The government recognizes the necessity to grow the amount of installed capacity and improve distribution efficiency. The process is obviously capital intensive, and to continue with a fully nationalized power industry would put unacceptable strains on its treasury. In recognition of its need, policies have evolved during this decade to allow foreign investment in power projects.

Geothermal Opportunity

Although an OPEC member nation, only a finite petroleum reserve exists in Indonesia. Some analysts predict Indonesia will become a net oil importer early next century. Efforts are being made to improve the management of internal consumption of petroleum products, thus extending their availability for export.

Indonesia is situated near the metaphorical "Ring of Fire," the chain of volcanos which rings the Pacific from the Americas though Asia. By its position and augmented with other geologic, climatic, and hydrologic factors, this heat is easily "mined" to the surface. Naturally occurring steam reservoirs can be exploited with wells and facilities to generate electrical power. This represents useful, environmentally friendly power production from an indigenous, non-exportable resource. An estimated geothermal potential of nearly 20,000 MW exists across the island nation.[4]

Government policy has evolved to encourage and support geothermal development. Several western nations are entering into contracts with the state power company to invest in the industry. These projects typically include a minority Indonesian partner, often with funding limitations. Although local participation is a prerequisite to entering the business, the local partner can be an invaluable asset with regard to access to officials and interpretation of cultural issues.

Funding the Development

Delays and Costs

Geothermal projects require a 2- to 5-year exploration investment of several tens of millions of dollars to identify and quantify the resource. Financial commitment to power plant construction is taken only after the resource is defined. Various financing schemes are employed through the exploration phase and power plant construction. These are often rolled into non-recourse project financing at the onset of commercial operations. This allows for significant improvements in return at the cost of smaller equity participation.

The decreased participation means profits are shared with the funding institution. For operators driven more by overall net present value, preference may be given to equity financing. This allows a satisfactory rate of return, albeit somewhat smaller, for a greater than three-fold equity increase. In an industry with limited investment opportunity, equity financing is the most reasonable opportunity for companies focusing on cash growth.

Project financing also creates an upward drive on unit development costs. Operators claim that soft costs associated with project financed geothermal projects hover between $400–500 per kW installed. This represents some 20 percent of the overall project cost.[5] (figure 3.3)

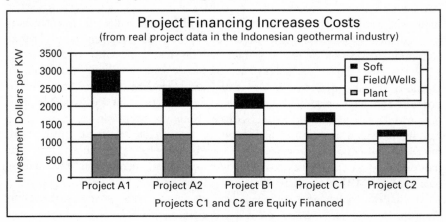

figure 3.3

Project financing also creates schedule delays of at least one year. This is time required to comply with the various levels of certification, assessment, and documentation required by lending organizations.[6] This creates in incredible impact to the economics of a project which is already straining by the time and investment required for exploration and assessment.

These cost and schedule issues which are greatly influenced by project financing are partially responsible for geothermal's price premium in comparison to other power generation projects. More complete utilization of this environmentally friendly, renewable energy source can be enhanced if the finance community introduces efficiencies in its processes.

Political Risk Assessment

Myth and Reality

Simplistically, political risk is nothing more than uncertainties which are seen as possibly more likely to occur in the project than they would be in the business environment from which the investor is accustomed. These risks can take many forms including disruption of equity participation (by dilution or expropriation), forced renegotiation of contracts, forced contracting procedures, avoidance of agreed commitments, revision of regulation, or any political/cultural change which may impact priorities and disrupt your business plans. Obviously, better understanding of changes that may occur in the business environment will allow better decisions.

Sometimes, the amount of risk in an area is less than what "experts" may think. It is important to differentiate between risks and unfortunate realities. Risks are probabilistic by their nature. When a certain condition approaches 100 percent probability of occurring, it becomes a reality. For example, some countries require local participation in all ventures. Often this local partner does not bring investment capital to the project. They are carried, sometimes with less than attractive payback schemes – sometimes with no payback at all. The existence of local participation is, in this case, a reality and not a risk. In fact, it is quite arguable their full equity participation should not be considered a risk also.

Many people look at Indonesia's Busang gold prospect, which was making headlines late 1996 to early 1997, as an example of political risk. Before the fraud was uncovered, the mining community was ecstatic as estimates of the gold reserve increased dramatically. Then the murmuring started as the press began quoting government sources indicating the government should have a piece of the Busang action. Finally, a significant chunk of the project was awarded to a prominent and well-connected businessman. The global uproar was deafening.

But really, it was not too surprising. Whenever the potential profits from a business that exploits a natural resource become increasingly large, the government will always enter the picture and want its share. That is a universal truth. It happened in the United States, when petroleum supply disruptions occurring in the middle 1970s pushed prices up several hundred percent. The oil companies obviously reacted to the huge upswing – so did the government. The oil companies were summoned to Capitol Hill and shown, in dollar form, what the government thought its share of the take should be. That was the conceptual birth of the Windfall Profits Tax, which took up to 70 percent of the incremental profits created by the price upswing.

To take this thought one step further, investors will likely be alone when the business climate falters. The precipitous drop in oil prices which occurred in 1986 devastated the domestic oil industry, which now employs less than half of the people than it did in its heyday – a loss of over 300,000 jobs in a single industry.[7] United States production dropped, and efforts to locate reserves to replace production all but stopped. Dependence on foreign oil passed well over 50 percent by the time of the Gulf War. There was nil government assistance to a crippled industry which lost thousands of irreplaceable experts, while dependence on a vital resource which drives both the economy and quality of life was shifted further beyond American control. Sad, but not surprising. The government will be there when it looks good, but conspicuously absent when times get tough. It is not a risk; it's a reality.

People are quick to point out that it was private Indonesian business, not the government, which latched on to Busang. First we must realize the government/economic culture is quite different in Indonesia. Distribution of wealth to the masses runs in an alternate fashion, but it does run. These prominent businessmen may be considered in a gray area between private citizens and government. Much of their business's incoming revenue is given back directly or indirectly to the community. Sometimes in the form of charitable organizations, sometimes less direct means. For example, the clove monopoly in Indonesia is famous. Indonesians smoke a common kind of cigarette blended with cloves. The east Java factory that makes these cigarettes employs some forty thousand people – the cigarettes are made entirely by hand. If this business was run in a more Western fashion, automation would come in, workers would be cut by 90 percent, operating costs would plummet, and the region would burn at the hands of the suddenly unemployed people who are angry at selfish profit taking.

As the Busang prospect became increasingly attractive, the need for local participation became more important. This should not be a surprise; it should be anticipated. This is simply the nation keeping its share of value of its natural resource.

Quantifying Risk

Good desktop computing tools exist to perform comprehensive probabilistic analysis on project proposals. The first step is to identify all variables which are probabilistic in nature (influenced either politically or other). Each risk component must be expressed in quantifiable terms. For example, expropriation may be expressed as a shortened contract life. If you can't create ways to quantify the risk, it probably is not really a risk.

The second step is to consider each risk, and assign high, low, and expected values. With each value should be a corresponding probability of occurrence, with all probabilities for each risk summing to one. Great care should be given to this effort, for it becomes the foundation of the risk assessment. It is best to identify and poll experts, both inside and outside of your organization, to develop truly realistic and believable values.

The next step is to be sure that the business model is structured to include these components along with other non-risk variables. This is easily done with the standard spreadsheet applications available today. Build the model using the expected values case.

Several off-the-shelf software tools exist which facilitate probabilistic analysis of a business proposal. The user simply loads the high, low, and expected values (along with corresponding probabilities) into the software, and links the business model spreadsheet. Executing the software builds a macro that systematically interrogates the spreadsheet with each value.

The first and simplest exercise is to run a sensitivity analysis. In this case, the software starts with the expected values, then takes one variable and runs the model with both the high- and the low-end values. The resulting high and low economic parameters are then extracted. This process is repeated for each variable nominated. The graphically displayed results demonstrate which variables are most sensitive (figure 3.4). The most sensitive variables are the ones a project developer should focus on – by attempting to minimize downside and catalyze upside potential. In the geothermal industry, we have found that projects are most sensitive (on an IRR basis) to power price and issues affecting capital investment and less sensitive to project life and operating costs. Capital costs fluctuation become slightly less important, while equity participation and project life dramatically increase in importance, for companies that focus on NPV creation for their economic decisions.

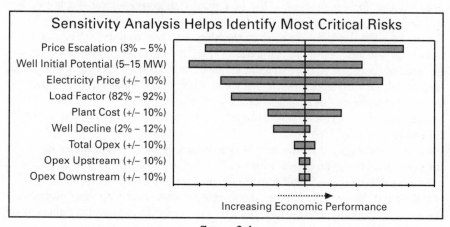

figure 3.4

A second probabilistic analysis tool interrogates the business model spreadsheet to create a cumulative probability curve of the economic performance of the project. Figure 3.5 shows and example of this curve, with cumulative probability measured on the y-axis and the economic parameter (in this case, net present value in $millions) along the x-axis. This allows the analyst to assess the likely economic outcome, plus up- and downside potential of the prospect. The shape of the curve also allows the analyst a useful qualitative assessment of the degree of uncertainty for the prospect.

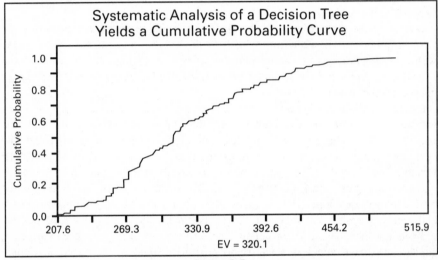

figure 3.5

The initial step in collecting data for a probability curve is to construct a decision tree for the problem. This is a graphical, chronological display of key decisions and uncertainties in the project. A simple decision tree is shown as figure 3.6. The several elements in the decision tree include choice variables, shown as squares, represent variables where the developer has choice (go/no-go, size of investment, etc). Chance variables are those which are out of direct control of the developer, such as various market conditions, are shown as circles. Probabilities (in percents) are also displayed with each possible outcome of the chance variables. Dollar figures are logically displayed to represent investment, etc.

The solution of the decision tree is determined by simply calculating the value for each branch of the choice variable. The value of the Don't Invest choice is easy. Zero dollars invested and zero dollars outcome yields zero net profit.

The Invest branch is a little more complicated. Summing the probability-weighted net profits solves this branch. For example, using the values from figure 3.6:

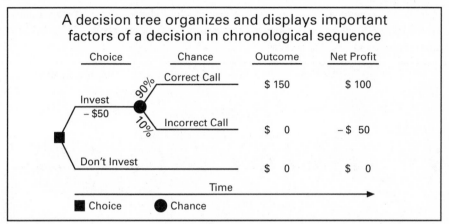

figure 3.6

$$90\% \times (-50+150) + 10\% \times (-50+0) = 85$$

In this case, the value of the Invest branch (85) exceeds the value of the Don't Invest branch (0), so the good decision would be to invest.

Reversing the probabilities (ie: only 10 percent probability of a correct call) would yield a different result. In this case we have:

$$10\% \times (-50+150) + 90\% \times (-50+0) = -35$$

The value of the Invest branch (−35) for this case is less than the value of the Don't Invest branch, so the good decision would be to not participate in the project.

Keep in mind that Decision Analysis does not guarantee success, but merely allows a good decision. The possibility of unfavorable outcome still exists. Through careful selection of probabilities and thorough analysis, proper assessment of risks is possible and the quality of decisions is improved. The developer is still making a risk decision, but perhaps can make the decision with more confidence.

Real investment decisions are much more complicated than the simple example just discussed. Figure 3.7 represents a potential gas project being considered for investment. This example has two choice variables and ten chance variables – these variables, along with several others are included in a business model developed on an off-the-shelf spreadsheet application. The complicated analysis of large decision trees is perfectly suited for computer.

Decision analysis software analyzes the decision tree by systematically interrogating the spreadsheet-based business model against every combination of high, low, and intermediate values (with corresponding probability) for each uncertainty. This requires a significantly larger number of executions than the sensitivity analysis, which sequentially checks high and low ends for one variable only against the expected values of the others. The software returns values for each of the economic parameters requested (say, IRR, NPV, P/I) for each combination.

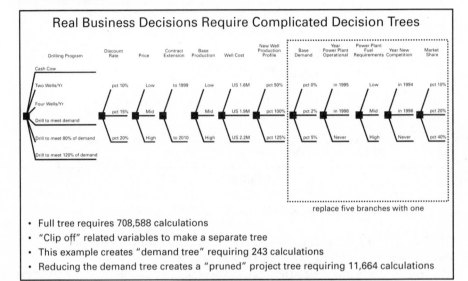

figure 3.7

As all decision trees, the calculation methodology is simple, but very cumbersome due to the sheer number of simple calculations required. The number of calculations made during a decision tree analysis is equal to the product of the number of uncertainties of each variable. For the example shown in figure 3.7, ten variables have three values (say high, low, and expected), one variable has two values, and the initial variable has six values. The number of required calculations would be

$$(3)10 \times (2)1 \times (6)1 = 708,588$$

separate executions of the spreadsheet. Assuming today's computing technology allows each model to be executed in only five seconds, the full distributed assessment of all of these variables would require 984 hours. Imagine how frustrating it would be to discover a careless input error after 41 days of computing.

Obviously this is too much time to wait for output. The size of the decision tree may be "pruned" by removing insensitive variables identified during the sensitivity analysis. The initial step is to ensure that only highly sensitive variables are shown as uncertainties. Another "pruning" technique is to identify several variables which relate to one concept. In the example case above, the last five branches relate to demand. A separate tree of (3)5 = 243 calculations may be run in only 30 minutes, and would create a cumulative probability curve describing the impact of demand, as shown in figure 3.8.

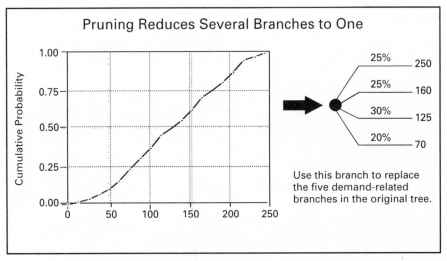

figure 3.8

Analysis of this demand curve could allow, say, a range of four values with corresponding probabilities for demand. This could be built into the remaining five three-valued variables, one six-valued variable, and one two-valued variable to create a tree requiring

$$(4) \times (3)5 \times (6)1 \times (2)1 = 11{,}664 \text{ calculations}$$

Analyzing this pruned tree would require 16 hours at five seconds per calculation. This is still a great deal of time, but much more manageable than 41 days. Obviously, careful effort to use only highly sensitive variables and work to "prune" the tree by combining like variables will mitigate patience-drain and dramatically shorten analysis time.

The shape of the distributed probability curve allows a good qualitative assessment of risk (figure 3.9). A low-risk project is described by a nearly vertical "S" curve, where a high-risk project is described by a much flatter "S" curve. The curve will not necessarily be symmetric. A very flat and long tail is indicative of smaller downside risk. A steeper curve to the right indicates stronger upside. Sometimes, a business decision will be made to take an option with where the expected value is less, but the risks are significantly less also.

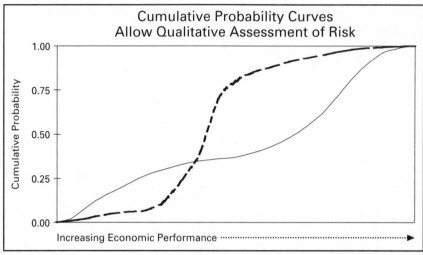

figure 3.9

Mitigating Risk

Use of risk data does not end after a go/no-go decision has been made for the project. Sensitivity and distributed probability studies remain quite valuable in assisting project execution planing. The project execution plan should include a comprehensive risk management plan that identifies and addresses mitigation. The components of a risk management plan include description of the risk, probability of occurrence, relative impact to the project, and relevant mitigation strategies. This useful tool provides the project manager with a reference of issues to be concerned with during the project, and allows him/her and the rest of the project staff to properly anticipate challenges.

A simple way to mitigate political risks is to use negotiation strategies that align with the amount of time you intend to stay in a country and your desired international reputation. Organizations that make deals where the benefits are largely in their favor have a much higher probability of undesirable government interference in their activities. The image created by a company with excessively aggressive negotiation strategies may impact ability to continue making deals in that, or other, countries. The best solution for a business that intends to stay in place with sustained growth over the long term is to strive for relations that are mutually beneficial for all parties. Remember, if something seems too good to be true, is most likely is.

Finally, we must recall that it is very difficult to anticipate all moves a government may make. Governments react to the changing world around them. There is a plethora of influences to a government policy, both internal and external. Wars, famines, weather changes, and other issues sometimes rise quite unexpectedly – and internal policies are revised in reaction. Sometimes the changes occur external to the country, yet they impact internal policy. With recognition that all changes are difficult to anticipate, a very important risk mitigation technique is simple diversification. Minimize investment in countries or businesses that are unfamiliar. By spreading the portfolio across several economies, or several businesses, an unanticipated crippling change in one area can be more easily absorbed.

Summary

Risks, when approached systematically, can be assessed and valued. Xenophobic attitudes can be detrimental to accurate assessments; care must be taken to separate less than desirable realities from actual risks which may be mitigated. Careful and comprehensive risk assessment is paramount to a successful project evaluation. A good assessment does not eliminate risks, but merely provides the developer a fair chance to identify areas of greatest risk, and, thus, enables an ability to develop mitigation plans.

Notes

[1] PT Data Consultants, "Electricity in Indonesia Entering the Privatization Era," September 1995.
[2] "Economic Trends Report – Indonesia," US Embassy/Jakarta, April 1997.
[3] PT Data Consultants, "Electricity in Indonesia Entering the Privatization Era," September 1995.
[4] Dr Purnomo Yusgiantoro, "Alternative Energy Resources in Indonesia," Advisor to the Minister of Mines and Energy, Indonesia, Presentation to First Indonesian Energy Outlook Conference, Houston, 1994.
[5] Don O'Shei, Oral Comments, "Geothermal Power in Asia '97 conference, Bali, Indonesia, February 1997.
[6] Ibid.
[7] Upstream Sector Employment Statistics, American Petroleum Institute, July 1997.

II
Lessons in the Management of International Political Risk from the Natural Resource and Private Infrastructure Sectors

Theodore H. Moran

Overview

Foreign investment in natural resource and infrastructure projects has long been among the most sensitive of all international corporate activities.

Mining and petroleum operations involve ownership or control of the "national patrimony." They deplete exhaustible resources. They invariably involve issues relating to "subsoil" rights. At the same time successful mining and petroleum projects can transform the tax base, bolster the balance of payments, raise the standard of living in the host economy like almost no other external investment.

Large infrastructure projects can create mega-economic complexes within host economies, tie regions together, transport materials and populations, raise the level of communication and interaction from levels associated with a previous century to levels associated with the next within a short period of time. The cost and degree of access to infrastructure projects may touch the lives of a host country's population with more widespread impact (and more popularity or unpopularity) than virtually any other kind of economic activity.

Beyond the issue of "sensitivity," natural resource and private infrastructure projects are more vulnerable to the dynamics of the "obsolescing bargain" than other kinds of foreign investor operations. As indicated in the previous Section of this volume, many manufacturing and agribusiness investors can rely on control over rapidly changing technology, and/or control over product differentiation and brand-name marketing, to mute unwelcome demands on the part of host country governments. Mining, petroleum, pipeline, power, transportation, in contrast, may find themselves with more limited options to defend themselves from diverse manifestations of economic nationalism in host jurisdictions, even when such economic nationalism stops well short of expropriation or confiscation.

As a result, foreign investors in natural resource and private infrastructure projects have been experimenting with methods of reducing their exposure to the "obsolescing bargain," and deterring its occurrence. As the five authors in this

Section point out, project finance has come to play a central role both in lowering exposure to the effects of changes in the terms of investment agreements and diminishing the likelihood that such changes will take place.

Project Finance and Political Risk

The term "project finance" can refer to a wide range of financial arrangements, but these arrangements have one thing in common: lenders look to the cash flow and earnings of the economic entity being financed as the source of funds from which a loan is to be repaid, and to the assets of that economic entity as collateral for the loan, not to the earnings or the assets of the parent investor. This allows the parent investor to avoid providing lenders with "recourse" (that is, access) to its own earnings or assets in case problems develop with the economic entity in question.

The use of project finance in natural resource and private infrastructure development has offered parent investors an opportunity to spread, share, and some offset political risk onto the lenders involved. Project finance syndications frequently incorporate a sizable number of participants, each of whom is exposed to loss if the project falters. The cost of project financing reflects the non-recourse nature of the lending. The length of time to arrange the syndication reflects the amount of coordination required.

But project finance has offered parent investors an additional dimension of protection as well, namely, the opportunity to structure the lending relationships in a way that may serve to deter harmful behavior on the part of host country authorities, through the involvement of what Robert Shanks has called "prominent victims" as financial participants.

This deterrence feature – whereby changes in the terms and conditions of operating a particular project will damage the interest of powerful actors who might then bring to bear their influence upon those who are responsible for those changes – has become one of the principal strategic objectives of parent investors and senior lenders in putting together the international project finance structure.

A pioneering example of the deterrent concept was launched by Broken Hill Proprietary of Australia to finance the $1.1 billion Escondida copper mine, which began producing in Chile in 1991.[1] Three-quarters of the output was committed with 12-year sales contracts to smelters in Japan, Germany, and Finland, giving them a large self-interest in a reliable flow of exports. At the same time, the $680 million loan syndication included development financing from the Export-Import Bank of Japan ($350 million), the Kreditanstant fur Wiederaufbau of Germany ($140 million), and the Kansallis-Osake-Pankki of Finland ($47 million) for the twelve-year duration.

The financing was executed on a non-recourse basis, with the Chilean subsidiary, Minera Escondida Limitada, as borrower of record, not the equity holders (BHP 57.5 percent, Rio Tinto-Zinc 30 percent, and a Japanese consortium headed by Mitsubishi 10 percent[2]). The Industrial Bank of Japan was appointed as trustee for the lenders, collecting proceeds from all sales in an account held outside of Chile. Any cause for interruption in production, in the estimation of Broken Hill, "would have the Export-Import Bank of Japan banging on the door of the Chilean government."

As the use of project finance to deter adverse actions on the part of host authorities has evolved, there has been a growing role for public and quasi-public institutions, including the multilateral agencies of the World Bank Group.

Project Finance, Political Risk, and the "Umbrella" of Multilateral Lending Institutions

The World Bank (IBRD) has developed two kinds of guarantees that may be of help in mitigating the political risk of investors.[3] The first consists of "partial risk guarantees" protecting repayment of loans against nonperformance of sovereign contractual obligations or against events defined under force majeure considerations. The second consists of "partial credit guarantees" covering a portion of the payments due under the loans (e.g. later maturities). The guarantees are made to lenders to projects. The direct protection to investors comes from specifying the circumstances in which the investor can withhold payments from a project, triggering (or threatening to trigger) a default. As noted below, there are indirect protections as well.

Partial risk guarantees cover risks arising from the failure of host governments to fulfill obligations spelled out in agreements with the project entity. These can include the performance of parastatal companies, the provision of inputs at given prices, the ability to sell output at given prices, and force majeure events such as changes in regulatory behavior and tax treatment.

In the Hub River Power Project, launched in Pakistan in 1994, for example, the financial package totaled approximately $1.8 billion, with 80 percent debt and 20 percent private equity. The loan portion included approximately $680 million in syndicated commercial bank debt, of which $320 million was insured by export credit agencies, and the remaining $360 million guaranteed by the World Bank and the Export-Import Bank of Japan. The project's revenues were secured through a long-term sales contract with Pakistan's national utility.

The World Bank guarantee can be called if Pakistan were to default on various undertakings made to the project company, such as performance of government-owned entities (payment obligations of the utility, fuel supply obligations, or Central Bank obligations to provide foreign exchange) or force majeure events (changes in law or political events in Pakistan). The government of Pakistan simultaneously promised, under an indemnity agreement with the World Bank, to reimburse the latter for any amounts disbursed to the lenders under the World Bank's guarantee.

Partial credit guarantees cover all events of non-payment for a designated part of the financing. This type of World Bank guarantee encourages the transformation of shorter-term to longer-term financing by covering the later maturities. It simultaneously provides comfort to investors and lenders concerned about the impact of the obsolescing bargain on the "out years" of an investment agreement.

In the Leyte-Luzon geothermal power project in the Philippines (1994), the World Bank assisted the $1.3 billion financing with a direct loan of $227 million. At the same time the World Bank provided backing for a $100 million bond issue on the part of the National Power Corporation by offering the bondholders an option to "put" the bonds (sell at par to the World Bank) at their maturity for the principal then due in year fifteen.

The fifteen-year maturity for the Leyte-Luzon power complex was a significant extension over the ten-year term previously available to Philippine borrowers. The guarantee of principal repayment enabled the bonds to be sold in the US institutional investor market (the so-called "Rule 144a" market), introducing the Philippines to a new investor base. The Republic of the Philippines provided an indemnity to the World Bank for providing the put option to the bondholders.

The "umbrella" of protection that results from the World Bank guarantee program is complex and subtle. First, to the extent that the World Bank is required to pay a lender for reasons triggered by violation of the undertakings made by the host government, the country will be required to reimburse the Bank as part of its indemnity agreement, creating a financial incentive for the country to avoid such violations. Second, since the World Bank has an interest in ensuring that sound business/economic practices are reflected in the initial host government commitments and in subsequent host government behavior, it has reason to exercise leverage to prevent claims from being filed and funds expended. Compensation and deterrence become blended together.

This leverage is not inconsiderable. Every loan agreement signed by the IBRD (and by the IDA, of International Development Association, the World Bank Group's lending arm for the least developed countries) permits the World Bank to suspend and eventually to terminate disbursements under the loan if the country breaches its undertakings to the Bank, and, under cross-default provisions, to suspend disbursements under all loans made to or guaranteed by the country.

"For most developing countries, the World Bank provides a significant portion of the country's development financing. In this context, the possible suspension of World Bank financing under all loans through the operation of cross-default provisions provides to the Bank substantial leverage to ensure that the country complies with its contractual undertakings to the Bank under a particular loan."[4] Such leverage extends to the delay or termination of new loans for future projects, and to the triggering of similar reactions on the part of sister donors.

The InterAmerican Development Bank and the Asian Development Bank have similar guarantee programs of smaller dimensions in early stages. As Linda Powers, Senior Vice President of Enron International argues later in this chapter, some of their initiatives – in particular, the InterAmerican Development Bank's partial risk guarantee program that does not require a host government counter-guarantee – are particularly useful to contemporary investors.

The International Financial Corporation (IFC) and the "Umbrella" of Protection Against Political Risk

The International Financial Corporation (IFC), as the organization within the World Bank Group that provides direct support to the private sector, has also played a growing role in constructing an "umbrella" of protection against political risk. This role has an equity as well as a lending component.

As part of the lending program IFC can provide funds from its own resources (referred to as "A-loans"). Of much larger size are loan syndications (referred to as "B-loans") in which the IFC mobilizes third-party funds for projects in the developing countries and economies-in-transition. In the latter the IFC both shares the risks of projects with the co-financing partners and remains lender-of-record. This helps projects receive longer maturities and less expensive terms than would otherwise be the case.

As an equity investor, the IFC is a unique institution within the World Bank Group. Its Articles prevent it from assuming responsibility for management, but it is naturally exposed to the commercial and political vicissitudes of any project in which it participates.

Unlike the IBRD (and the IDA), the IFC does not receive repayment guarantees from host countries for its projects. Host country governments do, however, commit themselves to various sound business practices when they become members of the International Financial Corporation. The IFC shares most of the same members, and the same Board of Directors, as the IBRD, IDA, and MIGA, ensuring that the latter three institutions would note any distressing conditions that IFC projects might be experiencing as they went about their business.

Limitations to the Expanded Use of Multilateral Guarantee Programs

Robert B. Shanks, Partner, Morrison & Foerster, provides a carefully nuanced appraisal of the growing utilization of multilateral bank guarantees to launch private infrastructure projects in the developing countries and the economies-in-transition.

The arrival of private developers in power generation and transmission, telecommunications, road and rail transportation, airports, ports, water and sewerage treatment facilities provides a welcome change from government-owned and financed infrastructure facilities, Shanks points out, but governments remain significantly involved as regulators of rates and as upstream sellers of inputs and downstream buyers of outputs.

Since infrastructure rates have customarily been heavily subsidized in the past, moving to a cost-based system with a rate of return needed to privatize the industry cannot avoid being highly sensitive politically. Converting local currency earnings into hard currency to service loans and pay dividends to international investors constitutes a special problem. As a consequence it is especially important that tariff adjustment formulas, accessibility to foreign exchange, and political force majeure events be clearly spelled out in the investment agreements.

The basic economics of all infrastructure projects must be sound, and local partners can use their experience and knowledge to bring significant cost advantages and help ensure completion and successful operation of a project. But reliance on well-connected local participants, as indicated earlier, can be a "two-edged sword," in Shank's estimation. It can lead to charges of favoritism and corruption, and produce a backlash against the investor.

Innovators and first movers, Shanks points out, occupy an especially awkward position. Rating agencies and international financial institutions are likely to be wary, according to Shanks, of terms that are "too out of line" with similar projects in other countries, especially when the deal resulted from particularistic negotiations rather than international competitive bidding. This puts high risk/high return "pioneer" projects in somewhat of a bind: the investors expect to receive high compensation for sailing in uncharted waters, but are prone to find themselves under intense pressure to renegotiate the more favorable aspects of their investment agreements at some time in the future.

To provide stability in this setting, explicit waivers of sovereign immunity are needed for contracts to be enforceable against public entities. Political force majeure clauses can help ensure the government's obligations in the face of events that may be controlled or at least significantly influenced by the government's own actions. Further protection may come with a host government buy-out obligation, triggered by force majeure events, sustained payment default, or other basic contract breaches.

In general, argues Shanks, the involvement of multilateral lenders to deter arbitrary host government actions justifies the potential delay and complications of dealing with such institutions. Their involvement has been important in bringing host authorities to the bargaining table to resolve disputes with project sponsors. Further protection may come from including major local financial institutions in a project syndication, with cross default provisions covering international and local loans.

But there are limitations to the ever-expanding use of sovereign guarantees, performance undertakings, and implementation agreements to protect investors against political risk, asserts Shanks. These result in a rapid build-up of contingent liabilities borne by the host government, and have adverse consequences for the country's creditworthiness. This is an issue that will be taken up at the end of this section.

Some carefully constructed projects in the Philippines, argues Shanks, may offer a useful new model to deal with this problem of accumulated liabilities, providing partial guarantees to replace the "all or nothing" sovereign guarantee approach. The public guarantee for foreign exchange availability and transfer, in these examples, falls away as the infrastructure entity achieves an investment grade credit rating. In the same vein, the adoption of clear formulas for tariff adjustments, and the development of reliable dispute resolution mechanisms (with mediation by a single expert or professional body preferred to full-blown arbitration) can help remove the burden of sovereign guarantees from the shoulders of host authorities.

Risk/Return Management in Infrastructure Projects in Emerging Markets

Timothy J. Faber, Managing Director for the Americas of GE Capital, introduces the term "risk/return management" as a corollary to the concept of the "obsolescing bargain." In contrast to industries such as biotechnology or computer software where publics accept the ability of innovators in the industry to reap a generous reward for products that benefit society, pioneers in infrastructure industries face public expectations that governments have a responsibility to make sure that the returns to investors remain within some socially acceptable bounds.

This management of returns "at the back end," after the project is successful and is earning "what in hindsight looks like a very healthy economic rent," is widespread in emerging markets. But, argues Faber, it is not absent in developed country markets as well – even where there are solid contractual procedures and legal institutions in place – as witnessed in New York state's renegotiation of power contracts with Niagara Mohawk.

There are several signs of progress, according to Faber, in helping investors to deal with host government tendencies to want to manage returns "after the fact." One is the expansion of the private political risk insurance industry, with longer maturities and more specialized risk coverage. Today it is possible to insure against an event as specific as losing a license, Faber points out. Another is the willingness of multilateral lending agencies to provide guarantees for projects that do not have export capabilities. A third is the consideration of the World Bank Group and some regional multilateral financial institutions about possibly offering guarantees for the obligations of sub-sovereign entities.

But, warns Faber, it is important to remember that official agencies – export credit agencies and multilateral lending agencies – have interests and motivations that are distinct from the private interests of investors. Their charters require them to support developmental goals, or export goals, while safeguarding the capital of the shareholders and taxpayers whom they represent. Investors and developers need to look closely, Faber concludes, at the extent to which the objectives of the private and the public parties are, and will remain, consistent over the life of any given project.

Enhanced Credit-Rating from Securitization of Export Receivables and Rights to Future Financial Flows

There are promising new benefits for investors, lenders, and host governments from securing financing for projects in ways that minimize the involvement of public authorities in the host country altogether, according to Patrice M. Jordan, Managing Director, Structured Finance, at Standard & Poor's. She provides a detailed analysis of how to rate debt issues secured by offshore receivables.

The basic vehicle is to set up a special purpose trust or other account offshore onto which are conferred the rights and into which are deposited the proceeds from the exports of a particular project. The example of Medimsa, Mexico's largest mining company, suggests Jordan, provides an illustration of the model.

As backing for a $525 million bond issue, Medimsa promised the receivables from export of copper and gold to the note holders, via a trust set up offshore. The note holders have first call on the export proceeds, but the financing is structured so that their claims constitute no more than a relatively small proportion of the total earnings from the project, leaving a substantial amount of "excess cash flow" to return to the issuer and protect the issuer even if prices in world metals markets decline.

To be sure, there are still political risks involved, including continuity of production, continuity of exports, and potential challenges to the claim of the offshore entity to the export receipts. But the interesting outcome of this arrangement, from the point of view of a risk rating service such as Standard & Poor's, is that the Medimsa bonds received a BBB grade, higher than the foreign currency sovereign rating assigned to the government of Mexico itself.

The potential for exploring the securitization of hard currency receipts from other kinds of transactions, according to Jordan, is quite large, including credit card vouchers, international telephone payments, even expatriate remittances, with the number of examples from Turkey, the Philippines, Pakistan, India, and Russia mounting rapidly.

The Pros and Cons of Choosing Project Finance Over Equity

The eagerness of new regions to invite investment by the international oil companies has not at all reduced the need to be concerned about political risk, according to Andrea MacDonald, Treasurer of Exxon Exploration Company.

Prior to 1990, Exxon estimated that private companies had access to roughly 35 percent of the world's undiscovered potential petroleum deposits. In 1997, private industry had access to approximately 80 percent of the world's undiscovered potential. Given the low levels of economic development and the low exposure to contemporary business practices in many of these areas, Exxon has made a point of offering assistance in drafting commercial legislation, frequently at the request of the host governments, even before the parent company has begun bidding on specific projects. The residual uncertainties of adoption, interpretation, and enforcement of such legislation are enormous, but so are the opportunities.

Consistent with William Irwin's finding in the first Section that project finance is likely to add 20 percent to the costs of an investment, Exxon finds that providing the capital itself is "by far" the cheapest way to finance a project (although this observation may not hold, MacDonald points out, for all oil companies). Self-financing also speeds the investment process by four to six years in comparison to project financing. But Exxon nonetheless occasionally adopts a project finance structure for three (or perhaps four) reasons.

The first rationale confirms the deterrent theory advanced earlier: the involvement of multilateral development agencies can lower overall project risk because the host countries "may be less likely to back away from agreements with international institutions upon whose continuing support they rely." For Exxon this is the principal appeal of seeking to involve the World Bank in a prospective project in Chad.

Second, the involvement of project lenders may be useful in convincing the host country of the importance of allowing the retention of hard currency offshore. International petroleum companies often have to accept production sharing contracts, where the investor receives "cost oil" to cover expenses, with what remains becoming "profit oil" to be split between the investor and host authorities. A vital consideration therefore is how to convert and retain the cost oil as hard currency offshore. When thirty banks deliver the same message to a particular would-be host country who does not allow the free remittance of foreign exchange, suggests MacDonald, this helps the investor to "be heard" at the highest levels.

Third, project finance can be useful in aligning the stakes of various partners, particularly for projects that require the incorporation of "weak partners" (public or private) who may not be able to fund their share of project expenditures. Rather than having some partners commit their own capital and other partners not, project finance becomes the common way to raise the required investment funds. The construction of the project finance package produces common documentation and a common timing sequence for all participants.

There may be a fourth rationale for using project financing as well, to reduce the parent corporation's exposure by greater leveraging of capital. But, argues MacDonald, for most downside risks, the reduction of the parent company's exposure is really quite limited since the sponsor always retains the riskiest portion of the cash flow in each operation where the company has a stake. Only in the rare event of a total disaster are the project lenders there to share the pain.

At the end of the day the investor has to consider the added cost of project finance, the concentrated risk of the investor's portion (since what is left after all the leveraging is always riskier than the original total), and the extra delay in bringing the project on-line, and ask whether the vulnerability that may be reduced by the project finance structure is worth the cost.

Moreover, there is the problem of "creeping recourse" for sponsors. Project lenders not only have a prior claim on cash flows from a project, they also look to other forms of corporate support on the part of sponsors, from completion guarantees and insulation from risks during the construction period, to take-or-pay commitments and throughput obligations, to cash flow cushions and generous coverage levels. In addition there are always contractual grey areas in so-called "non-recourse" arrangements. And, undergirding every form of operation, there is the parent company's compulsion to see the project continue rather than actually abandoning it.

Finally, the difficulty of separating political risk from other kinds of risks can either lead the investor to have too narrow guarantees (or too little political risk insurance coverage) or drive the investor to seek too broad guarantees (or to purchase broader political risk insurance coverage) than the parent corporation really wants. Political risk guarantees and insurance coverage rely on "but, for" clauses, MacDonald points out – "but for this political event," there would not be a problem. Suppose somebody comes along and throws a bomb at the train that hauls coal from Exxon's mines to Berinkea, suggests MacDonald: if the bomb thrower claims he was motivated by political concerns, the investor may be covered. If he claims he was motivated by environmental concerns, or by labor grievances, the investor may not. The investor may therefore have to choose between having a given set of operations insufficiently covered, or having to cover those operations for every eventuality, from commercial through political.

The Cutting Edge of New "Deal Structures"

The dilemmas that confront infrastructure projects, according to Linda F. Powers, Senior Vice President of Enron International, are in many ways similar to those confronting the natural resource sector but may be even more severe. The key to being safe and secure is having a project that is economically sound and broadly perceived as fair: "all the fancy structuring in the world will not save an operation that is fundamentally considered to be a bad deal." But what appeared as an appropriate level of prices or an appropriate level of returns at the front end when a project is being put together ceases to look so appropriate later on in the life of the investment.

The change in the perception of what is appropriate has an increasing cross-border dimension, according to Powers. A relatively few years ago, for example, power plants charged six cents per kilowatt hour; today the rate is under three cents per kilowatt hour. This squeezing of rates, and consequently of margins, does not just apply to mature investment sites, like the Philippines, that have done a number of private international power projects. It also spreads rapidly to comparatively untried locales, like Bangladesh, that are just launching their first international private power projects.

Another change in the marketplace is the emergence of "elephant projects" of more than a billion dollars apiece, often linked together in production, pipeline, and off-take arrangements such that no one elephant is economic without all the others working smoothly at the same time.

To further add complexity is the increasing number of multi-country projects, such as Enron's cluster of one thousand megawatt power plants to be built in Argentina for electricity to be sold in Brazil. The potential for such multi-country operations is attractive. Integrated regional power plants in Central America, for example, make a lot of economic sense, but raise difficult issues of overlapping political risk.

The forms such political risks take are becoming increasingly subtle. The classic case of expropriation – in which host authorities openly declare that they are nationalizing a facility – is, according to Powers, of less concern to project sponsors today. But not because the risk has disappeared. Quite the contrary. More sophisticated host countries are more likely to devise ways to blame the investor, cancel permits or withhold approvals, that place the foreign investor under intense pressure. Instead of losing the project permanently and totally via expropriation, such actions can easily result in a rather lengthy stoppage that (given the amount of fixed capital that is idled) causes sizable losses. Rather than being motivated by a desire to take over the project, the host country may simply be trying to gain leverage to force the renegotiation of investment agreement. Powers labels this politically motivated "business interruption."

In the face of these challenges, international investors find that many traditional methods of dealing with risk are actually disappearing. National governments are declining to offer guarantees for state and local infrastructure projects or for parastatal agencies. There is growing reluctance to allow automatic "pass-throughs" of unanticipated changes in the cost of foreign exchange, for example. Contract frustration coverage does not typically address the problem of politically-motivated "business interruption"; it is more geared, according to Powers, to the extreme case of permanent and total loss of the project.

To cope with these new challenges, project sponsors have undertaken three kinds of initiatives.

The first is to develop new deal structures, such as the InterAmerican Development Bank's Salitre municipal water project in Colombia. In this arrangement the municipality was required to buy-out the foreign investor if any of a specified list of force majeure events occurred. The IDB then provided a partial risk guarantee to make the payment itself if the buy-out were triggered and the municipality let more than ten days pass without making good on its obligation. A novel element was that the IDB did not require a counter-guarantee from the host country to back this partial risk guarantee; instead, it received a host country commitment not to contest IDB efforts to undertake salvage up to the amount needed to repay all the noteholders.

Second, there is a continuing search for risk protection outside of the deal structure via the involvement of export credit agencies, multilateral finance agencies, and public and private insurance agencies. Of particular note, according to Powers, is MIGA's cooperative underwriting program (CUP). In the CUP initiative, MIGA is insurer of record for its own account and for the coverage of the other insurers, including captive insurance entities associated with the project sponsor itself. In case of a claim, MIGA pursues salvage on behalf of all parties, and shares the recovered proceeds pro rata. As a result "MIGA can never be whole without the other parties – project sponsor and/or other insurers – being whole." MIGA's CUP program is examined further in the concluding section of this volume.

The third initiative is to continue the process of bringing new participants into the market for providing political risk coverage. Among these participants, it may be possible to add a new class of influential players with an interest in the stability of the project, in particular onshore capital market parties in the host countries where the projects are located.

The fourth initiative consists of experiments with introducing more flexibility as well as more liquidity into political risk coverage. The goal is to allow investors to move in and out of coverage positions as their evaluation of the need for protection evolves over the life cycle of a long project. Current political risk instruments, in Powers's estimation, do not permit such flexibility. Instead, they lock an investor into a fairly rigid structure for perhaps 15 years or so.

In pursuit of increased flexibility, Enron has been considering the use of credit derivatives not just for inconvertibility risk, but also for contract frustration and default risk. There is experimentation with default swaps, total return swaps, and credit link notes.

Another method of adding new players and increased flexibility is the CatEx system, which allows buyers and sellers to trade $1 million "bite size" chunks of exposure to hurricane and earthquake risk. In 1997 Enron initiated trade in political risk exposure on the system. Ultimately Enron might launch a political risk trading book, much like the contemporary gas and electricity trading books, making a two-way market in country and political risk.

These considerations by Linda Powers lead naturally to more intensive examination of the role of political risk insurance – private, national, and multilateral political risk insurance – as a tool of international investor strategy, which is the subject of the concluding section of this volume.

But first, the materials introduced here from the natural resource and private infrastructure sectors help address three of the most controversial questions about the future of international political risk management: first, to what extent can the growing availability of private sector financing simply replace the need for public sector participation in natural resource and private infrastructure development? Second, could there be ways to mitigate the risk of major changes in investment agreements by building in provisions for renegotiation at the beginning of the contract? Third, might host authorities in the developing countries and economies-in-transition actually be taking on too many commitments and obligations in the process of providing stability for external investors in the natural resource and private infrastructure sectors?

Questions and Concerns for the Future

First, to what extent can (and should) the expansion of private sector financing replace any need for public sector financing in petroleum, mining, pipeline, and other infrastructure projects? Or, is there an enduring role for public as well as private sector involvement in helping to provide stability for foreign direct investors – in particular, those most vulnerable to the dynamics of the obsolescing bargain, such as natural resource and private infrastructure investors?

A fundamental rule of public policy analysis is that public sector institutions should not intervene in markets where private sector actors are able to function on their own effectively and competitively. Public sector institutions are unlikely, as a rule, to be able to participate as efficiently as their private sector counterparts. Their intervention is liable to lead to a misallocation of resources. At best, their actions are redundant and therefore unneeded.

Only if there is some kind of market failure that prevents private actors from functioning effectively and competitively is there a legitimate role for public sector intervention.

With the vast growth of foreign direct investment and related private corporate borrowing documented in the Introduction to this volume, one might well question why national or multilateral financial institutions are needed to support the endeavors of the private sector. (A similar question will arise in the next Section, with regard to national and multilateral political risk insurers, as a complement to private political risk insurers.)

The analysis of the "obsolescing bargain" introduced in Section I, and the analysis of the participation of multilateral lending institutions in natural resource and private infrastructure projects introduced here in Section II, help provide an answer.

Foreign direct investors in natural resource and private infrastructure projects are typically required to make large lump-sum investments under conditions of uncertainty that require a sizable risk-premium over an extended period of time to justify the initial investment. Host government authorities prefer not to continue to pay the risk-premium indefinitely, long after the early uncertainties about the commercial prospects of the investment have dissipated. In particular, host government authorities who are successors to those who signed the original investment agreements are likely to want to renegotiate the contracts.

There is thus a political as well as an economic dynamic that undermines the ability of those who signed the original investment agreements to make credible commitments. This produces a manifestation of what the economics literature refers to as "imperfect contracts." It represents an inability of host government country authorities, no matter how initially sincere, to make reliable promises that extend more than a short way into the future, especially if those authorities are replaced by others.

Public policy analysts – from game theorists to nuclear arms negotiators – have long recognized that global welfare would be enhanced by developing "external" mechanisms to enhance the credibility of the commitments of actors who may simply not be able to ensure that their promises are otherwise honored.

The fundamental role of national and multilateral financial institutions (and, as examined in the next section, the fundamental role of national and multilateral insurance/guarantee institutions) is precisely to help reinforce the credibility of commitments embodied in international investment agreements. While their presence may involve the commitment of some capital (or the provision of some insurance), it is their participation *per se* that is important, their stake in guarding against fundamental transformations or abrogations, their influence as "prominent victims" if host authorities behave precipitously. In this sense what they provide cannot be substituted for by private sector actors; the role they play will be left empty by merely "letting markets work on their own."

Second, to what extent might the pressures for the "obsolescing bargain" be relieved by building adjustment mechanisms into the initial investment agreement?

As indicated above, on the one hand, foreign direct investors do need to be offered a high premium for particularly risky ventures or they (and their financial backers) will simply walk away from such ventures, helping neither themselves nor the would-be host countries.

On the other hand, host countries have a legitimate basis to expect that they will not have to continue to pay the initial risk premium forever (or, as in traditional concession agreements, for periods of thirty to fifty years), long after the early uncertainties have dissipated.

Moreover, there is also an objective conflict between the expectation of foreign investors that "successes" will pay for "failures" (i.e., that "gushers" will pay for "dry holes"), and the expectation of host countries that their own favorable projects and favorable policies should not be used to compensate foreigners for public and private mismanagement elsewhere.

In this setting, one option might be to plan for orderly change in the terms of an investment agreement. "Even when governments face great pressure to make changes in the arrangements, they may delay action if the contract calls for the change to occur automatically in a reasonably short period of time," argued Louis

Wells in the preceding Section. "On the other hand, if the agreement fails to provide for change, or postpones change for too long, the government may act immediately."

Is there some way to include the possibility of subsequent renegotiation into investment agreements without simply inhibiting the approval of the investment at the beginning?

One option, recommended by the OECD's "Expert Group" on investment policy for the Commonwealth of Independent States (CIS), is to set the horizon of stability for investment agreements at ten years. This should be adequate to compensate foreign firms for their initial risk since the discounted present value of changes beyond ten years is likely to be small.

But what standard might be set for the magnitude of subsequent renegotiations?

A standard that might be appealing to most parties is "national treatment" – that is, tax and input or output prices no different from those available to private sector actors in the economy at large. As Robert Shanks and Linda Powers point out in the this Section, investment projects that require special "better" treatment than other players in the local economy in order to be viable over the long term should be viewed with considerable skepticism by the international investment and financial communities. The World Bank and other multilateral lending institutions are unlikely to declare a country in default whose government makes foreign companies pay the same tax rates as national companies, once a reasonable period of "pioneer status" has expired.

Third, what is the optimum level of commitments that host governments should be expected to shoulder?　Are host authorities in the developing countries and economies-in-transition possibly being asked to shoulder too many obligations in helping to launch natural resource and private infrastructure projects?

Robert Shanks points out that while there may be an appeal to having host authorities standing behind the obligations of state-owned contracting parties in private infrastructure projects, there is a cumulative negative impact from having the government become potentially liable not only for a missed payment, but for all future payments, default interest, even the return to the investor. Neither host country interests, nor the global interest, is best served, he argues, by having host authorities adding contingent liabilities to their books indefinitely.

Echoing this concern in the next Section, Malcolm Stephens, Secretary-General of the Berne Union, observes that, while on the one hand developing countries and economies-in-transition are being told to privatize and deregulate their markets, on the other hand they are being required to issue counter-guarantees to the World Bank and to other financial institutions to cover the contractual requirements involved in new infrastructure and natural resource investments.

In short, host governments in the developing countries and economies-in-transition are being driven in contradictory directions, and ultimately there have to be limits on the extent to which they should be expected to use sovereign guarantees, performance undertakings, and implementation agreements to make up for predictable legal and regulatory systems in their own countries.

Notes

[1] This structure is described in more detail in Tilton, op. cit.

[2] The BHP strategy also incorporated the International Finance Corporation as an equity holder, with a 2.5 percent stake in Minera Escondida. The role of the IFC is analyzed *infra*.

[3] Philippe Benoit, *Project Finance at the World Bank: An Overview of Policies and Instruments* (Washington, DC: The World Bank, Technical Paper number 312, 1996).

[4] Ibid, pp. 62–62.

4

Lessons in the Management of Political Risk: Infrastructure Projects (A Legal Perspective)

*Robert B. Shanks**

Introduction

This paper addresses political risk management techniques concerning private infrastructure projects. Its purpose is to provoke discussion among very experienced practitioners. It is therefore drafted to be more provocative than comprehensive, inviting discussion around the general themes raised below.

Private Infrastructure: A Special Type of Investment

Significant private investment in developing country infrastructure projects is still a very recent phenomenon. The deregulatory movement in the United States during the 1970s and the wave of privatizations in Europe during the 1980s were the precursors of the efforts during the 1990s by many emerging market countries to meet their growing infrastructure development needs in power, telecommunications, transportation, and, more recently, water, by opening their doors to private developers and investors. The 1990s so far have witnessed a huge flow of private capital into such projects developed under build-own-transfer (BOT), build-own-operate (BOO) and various other concession schemes. Private development and financing of infrastructure projects in developing countries has grown from a small base a decade ago to an industry averaging about $60 billion a year at present.[1]

The Philippines BOT program, one of the most successful to date, provides a good example of this phenomenon. In the late 1980s and early 1990s, the

*Robert B. Shanks is a Partner, Morrison & Foerster LLP, Hong Kong; former Vice President and General Counsel, Overseas Private Investment Corporation (OPIC).

Philippines was suffering a severe shortage in power generation. Extended brownouts were common and lack of reliable power was perceived as a severe constraint on the country's development potential. The BOT program initiated following the election of President Ramos invited independent power producers (IPPs) to develop, finance and operate generating facilities, selling power under long-term, fixed price energy conversion agreements with NPC, the national utility. Because NPC was not creditworthy in its own right, the Government of the Philippines provided IPPs with Performance Undertakings, or guarantees, fully backing NPC's power purchase, fuel supply, and other contractual obligations. In the roughly five years since this program has been in existence, the Philippines has substantially increased its electrical generating capacity and eliminated its power shortage. In the past few years, the Government has extended the BOT program to stimulate development of toll roads, light rail projects, airport and port facilities, and water projects. Some of the experience gained and lessons learned from this program – particularly with respect to the government's role and policy respecting guarantees – will be discussed in more detail below.

Private infrastructure projects are unique among developing country investments in part because of their relatively brief history. In practically all developing nations, power generation and transmission, telecommunications, road and rail transportation, airports, ports, water and sewerage treatment facilities have all been developed, financed, owned, and managed, usually badly, by governments. Even where private developers and financiers have been invited in, governments remain very significantly involved as regulators and owners of utilities and other upstream and downstream facilities. Thus host governments remain important project participants and a part of the risk equation for infrastructure projects to a much greater extent than with respect to more traditional private sector investments.

Moreover, by their very nature, infrastructure projects provide critical services – power, telecommunications, roads, water – used by the general public. The public is therefore very sensitive to the level, quality and price of the services provided. Where, as usual, such services have been heavily subsidized in the past, moving to a cost-based system with a reasonable rate of return necessary to privatize the service can be expected to be politically sensitive in ways, for example, that the prices charged for exported manufactured goods or commodities, or hotel rooms for visiting business people, are not.[2] Infrastructure projects, therefore, are by their very nature more politically sensitive and more subject to political pressures than most other types of developing country investments. Such projects exist in sectors that, until recently, have been almost entirely government dominated, and they necessarily retain a "public" character to some degree. Moreover, few developing countries have well established legal systems or transparent regulatory systems for sectors so long dominated by government. It is therefore easy to appreciate that government interference in private infrastructure projects remains a major concern of infrastructure investors, lenders and their lawyers.

The Importance of Well-Structured Projects

Many investments can be structured to make political interference difficult or unattractive. For example, export-oriented manufacturing projects can be structured with a long-term exclusive distribution agreement with a separate company outside the host country and controlled by the foreign investor. Trade names and intellectual property rights can be owned offshore. Exclusive contracts can be entered into to control essential project inputs. Frequently hard currency export earnings can be captured offshore and remitted only to the extent necessary to meet in-country expenses. Unfortunately, however, many of these structural devices are not available for infrastructure projects, which typically do not export and earn most, if not all, of their revenues in local currency, which must be converted and remitted to service hard currency loans.[3] Infrastructure projects tend to be vulnerable to the full range of political risks.

These risks can be mitigated to some extent by assuring that the government, to the extent that it is at least a tacit participant in the project's risk structure, is on record as accepting the fact that project revenues must be adequate to meet debt service and fixed operating costs. Tariff adjustment formulas should be contractually linked to achieve this goal throughout the life of the project. The investor's right to receive the tariff and any applicable adjustments during the life of the project should be explicitly documented and not subject to discretionary government action. Ideally, tariffs should be indexed to the loan currency, and the investor's right to convert should be clearly documented.[4] If the tariff is subject to an adjustment formula, this should be carefully set forth in the concession agreement or other basic agreement. Finally, the risk of political force majeure events should be expressly allocated to the government or state-owned entities contracting with the foreign investor. It is especially important that the contractual documents establish without ambiguity that the obligations of state-owned entities to the investor will continue without regard to actions by the host government or other political events outside the investor's control.

As the rating agencies frequently remind us, artful legal and financial structuring can only go so far. Projects that are economically unsound will remain vulnerable to adverse government action no matter how skillfully project documents are drafted. Conversely, projects that are economically sound, and that contain financial incentives for all participants to perform their obligations, tend to be far less "accident-prone" than projects that are not. This applies to host governments as project participants as well as private parties. A well-structured project contains carefully designed economic incentives and disincentives – carrots and sticks – to encourage all parties to perform their respective obligations. No amount of legal and financial structuring can eliminate political risks from a project that is perceived as unfair, or in which slight changes in the legal and regulatory environment are likely to produce incentives for the parties to breach their agreements.[5] Rating agencies and commercial banks are thus justifiably wary of projects in which investors have struck "too good a deal" with host governments, or have tariffs that are out of line with similar projects in other countries, particularly where the deal resulted from negotiated transactions, rather than international competitive bidding.

As the current re-evaluation of IPP projects in Pakistan demonstrates, such projects are vulnerable to charges by political opponents that they are the result of political favoritism or corrupt dealings.[6] This risk is particularly acute for high risk/high return "pioneer" projects, where developers participating in the early stages of a country's private infrastructure development program understandably demand a higher rate of return than later stage projects in order to compensate for the increased risks of being the first investors in uncharted waters. While higher rates of return are justified for early stage projects, they tend to become vulnerable to attack once the perceived risks have lessened and the field has become more competitive. As technology improves and additional investors enter a sector squeezing margins, costs tend to come down. At this stage, pioneers may find themselves under intense pressure to renegotiate their tariff levels. It is therefore unwise for early stage developers to plan projects on the assumption that they will be able to command higher "pioneer" tariffs throughout the life of the project. Moreover, a project whose economic rationality is premised on a particular government program or incentive is extremely vulnerable to a decision by a subsequent government administration to modify the program or eliminate the incentive. The ability to insulate a project from the effects of such government decisions through guarantees and political risk insurance is very limited.

Assembling a Sound Project Financing Package

Assuming that a project makes good economic sense on a stand-alone basis, careful legal and financial structuring can help insure that it will achieve physical and operational completion and thereafter operate with a minimum level of complications. The list of tools available to construct an appropriate contractual package for project financing is well known and will not be discussed in detail here, except for those issues that are of particular relevance to infrastructure projects.[7]

Most privately financed infrastructure projects are financed on a limited recourse basis pursuant to BOO, BOT, or other concession arrangements. This structure limits the risk of project sponsors by limiting the security for debt repayment to the income stream and assets of the project. In order to accomplish a successful project financing, the project must generate an income stream that can be isolated and dedicated to debt repayment and that is sufficient to service debt and cover the fixed costs of operating the facility. All project risks must be allocated among experienced, creditworthy parties. Some of the typical tools of project financings include fixed-price turnkey construction contracts with performance obligations and/or liquidated damage clauses; carefully drafted completion tests; firm, fixed-price offtake contracts or other assurances that project revenues will be adequate to cover fixed operating costs and debt service.

In short, successful project financing depends upon the ability of the project participants to allocate all project risks among creditworthy parties in the best position to mitigate them pursuant to contracts that can be enforced with a high degree of certainty. This poses a problem in developing countries that lack well-tested commercial legal and regulatory systems with track records of enforcing complex commercial arrangements. Of particular relevance to infrastructure projects are those elements of the contractual package that address the unique role of the host government in infrastructure projects, including those provisions dealing with (1) government guarantees or performance undertakings, (2) provisions for adjustments in tariffs or other key terms during the life of the project, (3) dispute resolution/arbitration, (4) waiver of sovereign immunity, (5) political force majeure, (6) buy-out, or other remedies for fundamental government breach or sustained political force majeure events, and (7) careful attention to obtaining all required approvals. A few words about each of these is in order.

Government Guarantees/Performance Undertakings

As discussed above, optimal conditions for project finance – predictable legal and regulatory systems and creditworthy contracting parties – do not yet exist in many developing countries that nevertheless are in desperate need of private investment in infrastructure projects. In such situations, government implementation agreements, sovereign guarantees, performance undertakings, or support letters have been the mechanisms of choice to bridge legal and regulatory gaps and back the performance obligations of government utilities and other state-owned entities.

This practice of papering over holes in the project risk allocation structure with government guarantees or assurances has been necessary to get high priority projects off the ground without having to wait for needed legal and regulatory reforms, but it is unsustainable as a means of making infrastructure projects financeable in the long term.[8] While government guarantees of infrastructure project obligations can serve a legitimate transitional objective by providing needed assurances to commercial investors as governments move toward truly private infrastructure development, developing country governments are not in a position indefinitely to continue adding contingent liabilities to their books for all of their infrastructure needs. To do so would negate many of the advantages of private infrastructure development, would be inconsistent with the privatization objectives of responsible developing countries, would degrade the governments' own creditworthiness and, if unchecked, could ultimately lead to a replay of the 1980s debt crisis. Fortunately, some governments – notably the Philippines – are slowly shifting away from a model that would result in their accumulating unsustainable levels of contingent liabilities for project-related guarantees. Ultimately, of course, the answer to the dilemma developing countries are facing is to develop their legal and regulatory systems, and to privatize state-owned utilities, so that government performance undertakings or guarantees are no longer necessary.

The Current Reliance on Government Guarantees

Typically project financings involving state-owned utilities and other parties require some form of sovereign undertaking or guarantee to back power purchase and other contractual obligations. The government simply stands behind the obligations of state-owned contracting parties to provide an additional level of assurance that their obligations will be met. The system, therefore, is effectively one of broad payment obligations layered one of top of another. If the state utility or other party fails to pay for any reason, the government must. The government's obligations may then be insured through OPIC, MIGA or another public agency if the government's sovereign credit rating is not adequate to provide lenders with sufficient comfort. Usually no attempt is made to allocate specific political or commercial risks according to the government's ability to manage or control them. The risks covered by the government's guarantee usually include not only sovereign risks, such as expropriation and political force majeure events (many of which are within the government's control), but also foreign exchange availability (only partly within the government's control) and quasi-commercial risks associated with the demand for the infrastructure service and the state party's contractual performance (which may not be entirely within the government's control).

Under cross-defaults, acceleration provisions, and other lenders' remedies customary in project finance documents, including buyout clauses, such guarantees may render the government potentially liable not only for a single missed payment, but for all future payments, default interest, and even an investor's anticipated return on its investment. If the payment default results not from considerations specific to the project, but from a foreign exchange crisis, severe recession, or other major economic dislocation affecting multiple government-supported projects, the result could be multiple claims on the government treasury in devastating amounts. Lenders and rating agencies of course recognize the cumulative impact of guarantees on a country's creditworthiness and, over time, will discount their value for countries that rely upon them too much. Over-reliance on government guarantees can also complicate the process of privatization by making it more difficult for a government to sever its relationship with an entity that will continue to enjoy the government's financial backing, without corresponding government control, based on previously negotiated deals.

Some developing country governments have reacted to this concern by deciding not to provide any guarantees, to provide them for only a few high-priority projects, or to limit the types, scope, and duration of guarantees. Refusing to issue guarantees altogether, however, makes project finance extremely difficult, if not impossible, in some developing countries. The most obvious example is China – where the government has been determined not to issue sovereign guarantees to infrastructure projects and, consequently, few projects have gone forward. India has decided to issue counter-guarantees to back financially weak state electricity boards only for a handful of so-called "fast track" projects. Developing credit support for other non-fast track projects is a challenging task.

Unbundled Guarantees: The New Philippine Model

The Philippines has had great success in recent years in attracting private investment in their power sector, based on the government's willingness to provide guarantees backing the obligations of the National Power Company (NPC). As the government's contingent liabilities have multiplied, however, and as it has begun to extend the BOT model outside the power sector to toll roads, light rail, port and airport facilities, and water projects, it has begun to move away from this "all or nothing" sovereign guarantee approach, to "unbundle" its guarantees and to provide partial guarantees keyed to the specific financing needs of individual projects. The government's objectives are to minimize and better manage its contingent liability exposure to project risks, to create more flexible guarantee instruments that can be better adapted to the needs of specific projects, and to adjust to the "moving target" of the government's ongoing privatization and deregulatory efforts in power and other infrastructure sectors.

The new Philippine guarantee instrument is divided into three components: (1) a guarantee of the investor's fundamental rights, including assurances against expropriation, government action arbitrarily changing the "rules of the game" under which the concession or BOT contract is granted and upon which its economics are based, and certain political force majeure events; (2) a guarantee of foreign exchange availability and transfer; and (3) a guarantee of project agreements, backing the specific payment or other contractual obligations of state-owned utilities or other parties.

The Philippine government is also seeking effectively to limit its guarantees to the projects' senior debt, including construction and initial term financings. In power projects, this limited guarantee may take the form of a guarantee of capacity payments as a proxy for the project's debt service and fixed operating costs.

The guaranty of fundamental rights will always be given, as the sovereign risks guaranteed are within the government's control, and the guarantee covers rights that the government has already agreed to extend through laws protecting foreign investment. By separating the latter two guarantees, however, the government gains greater flexibility to tailor its guarantee package to the requirements of particular projects. Some projects, such as those that can be financed in local currency, do not require foreign exchange guarantees. A toll road being financed locally is going forward on this basis. Projects that require off-shore financing for major imported equipment, like power projects, require a foreign exchange guarantee primarily because the sovereign debt rating of the Philippines is not yet investment grade. By separating out the foreign exchange guarantee, this guarantee can be structured to fall away, or increase in price, once certain credit benchmarks have been achieved. The Batangas gas-fired power project was recently awarded based on a foreign exchange guaranty that will increase in price if and when the Philippines maintains an investment grade sovereign credit rating for three consecutive years.

Similarly, the guaranty of project agreements is presently required where state-owned enterprises, such as NPC, lack a sufficient credit rating to borrow based on their own balance sheets. Separating this guarantee allows it to be structured to fall away once the state-owned enterprise has been privatized and has achieved and maintained an investment grade credit rating. The Batangas project contains such a "fall-away" feature for the government's guaranty of NPC's obligations. Notably, Meralco, NPC's more creditworthy privatized sister utility, is already able to obtain financing without benefit of government support.

The "unbundled" guarantees also can more easily be structured to cover capacity payments or other obligations short of the "everything and the kitchen sink" form of guarantee under the old Philippine government performance undertakings backing all of a state-owned party's obligations. Moreover, by separating the guarantees, they can be market tested in bidding packages by informing the bidders in bidding instructions that excessive requests for government guarantees will be scored against bidders requesting them, thus using competitive pressures to bid down and thus to minimize calls on the government's scarce guarantee resources.

This approach is now being used in the Philippines in power and other infrastructure projects. The general idea has met with acceptance by both bidders and financial institutions. As more governments become successful in attracting significant levels of private investment into their power and other infrastructure sectors, pressures to move away from "all or nothing" guarantees of state-owned entities' obligations can be expected to grow, and more governments will begin to explore methods of better managing their scarce guarantee resources.

Adjustments to Tariffs and Other Key Terms

Infrastructure projects tend to be long term and frequently are being developed and financed in a changing legal and regulatory environment. Few countries have independent regulatory bodies upon which developers and lenders would be willing to stake their future ability to recover their investments in a project. Provisions for adjustments to tariffs and other key terms of the concession arrangement are often a critical element of the documentation package, at least outside the energy sector, where long-term offtake contracts have been the preferred mechanism.

For example, most countries' telephone systems have used international telephone revenues to subsidize domestic rates. International rates are coming down due to market forces; domestic rates therefore need to increase dramatically in many countries in order to cover the cost of providing basic domestic telephone service. The formula for tariff rebalancing as between international and domestic telephone service is therefore a critical item for negotiation and documentation in many telecommunications projects around the world. Tariff adjustment mechanisms may take the form of a mathematical formula keyed to inflation indicators or tied to performance targets, a guaranteed minimum rate of return, or a band within which a regulatory body may exercise its discretion. Whatsoever the particular mechanism, it is essential that the expectations of both the government and the private parties be clearly articulated and documented with respect to the trigger and timing for an adjustment and that the dispute resolution mechanism be carefully designed to deal with disputes involving the adjustment mechanism.

In the power sector, a number of countries, such as Thailand, Malaysia, and the Philippines, are considering following the lead of Argentina, the United Kingdom, and the United States by deregulating their power sectors and moving to a pool system in which power is purchased on a spot market without long-term power purchase contracts. This will obviously involve a fundamental change in the sector. How to assure that independent power producers developing projects under the current system will be adequately protected as the sector evolves will be a major concern for structuring international private power projects in the coming years.

Dispute Resolution/Arbitration

The politically sensitive nature of infrastructure projects, their relative vulnerability to government interference, and the participation of governments in them as regulators and frequently as owners of contracting parties, heightens the importance of a well-thought-out dispute resolution procedure. Developing countries typically lack independent judicial systems experienced in enforcing the kinds of complex contractual risk allocation provisions necessary for complex project financings. Moreover, investors should be concerned about the ability and willingness of local courts to enforce remedies on behalf of foreign investors and lenders against local parties, particularly government entities. It is therefore necessary to provide for resolution of disputes outside of the country's own judicial system. In most cases, arbitration outside of the country pursuant to UNCITRAL, ICC, ICSID, or other internationally accepted arbitration procedures will be the best option. Relatively few countries have entered into treaties to provide for reciprocal enforcement of judicial awards obtained in the courts of other countries. Enforcement of judicial awards obtained in New York or London will therefore be very difficult, if not impossible, in many developing countries. Most countries, however, are signatories to the New York Convention requiring enforcement of arbitral awards obtained abroad. In most cases, therefore, there are clear advantages to resolving disputes through international arbitration, rather than judicial procedures, because ultimately any decision will only be effective to the extent that it can be enforced in the courts of the host country.

Perhaps equally important, the dispute resolution procedure adopted should provide for a mediation procedure short of full-blown arbitration, which is likely to be expensive and slow. Many potential disputes are of a technical nature, or sufficiently specific so that the parties may be able to agree to be bound by the decision of a single expert or professional body acceptable to both. If the parties cannot agree to be bound by such a procedure, the clause can at least provide for a decision by an expert followed by a right of an appeal of the expert's decision to the full arbitral panel. Issues involving performance of equipment, construction, and tariff adjustment formulas are among those that are often appropriate for referral to an expert. Another effective method is to provide a period of perhaps 60 days during which a small committee of senior officials representing the government, the project, and lenders is convened to try to resolve the dispute prior to resort to arbitration.

Waiver of Sovereign Immunity

Waiver of sovereign immunity is of course essential for any contract agreement to be enforceable against a government or state-owned entity. It is therefore surprising that many agreements with state-owned parties do not contain explicit waivers and rely instead on implicit waivers from the "commercial" nature of the project.

Political Force Majeure

Because infrastructure projects typically involve contracting with governments or state-owned entities, contractual force majeure provisions should be drafted to reflect the fact that private and governmental parties are not similarly situated with respect to government or politically inspired force majeure events. Governments and state-owned parties should not be excused from performance of their contractual obligations by events which governments are able to control or influence.

The purpose of a force majeure clause is to relieve parties of the consequences of contractual non-performance due to events that are beyond their control. Governments and private parties are equally unable to control events such as earthquakes, storms and other "acts of God." However, force majeure clauses between private commercial parties also typically excuse performance due to "acts of governments," war, insurrection, and other events that may be entirely controlled, or at least significantly influenced, by governments. Project documents for infrastructure projects involving governments or state-owned enterprises should therefore contain a force majeure provision bifurcated to cover commercial and political force majeure events separately. The government's obligations, especially payment obligations, should not be excused during a political force majeure event.

Buy-Out Remedies

Ultimately, infrastructure projects are at the mercy of governments to abide by their fundamental contractual commitments and to refrain from arbitrarily changing the "rules of the game" – the fundamental elements upon which the economics of the project depend – during the life of the project. Because infrastructure projects cannot be economically repossessed and reused elsewhere, like an airplane leased to a national airline, most project structures provide for an investor's "put" of the project to the host government in the form of a government buy-out obligation that can be triggered by a sustained payment default, other uncured fundamental breach, or sustained political force majeure event. This provision may be made reciprocal, allowing the host government, as well as the investor, to precipitate a buyout. In practice, of course, a host government could always trigger a buyout by causing a default. There is some merit, however, to providing a government with a right to buy back a project according to a pre-negotiated price without precipitating a default that could impact on the government's future credit rating and attractiveness to other foreign investors in order to retire uneconomic projects and maintain legal and regulatory flexibility with respect to the sector.

While careful attention to these and other elements of project structure can help manage exposure to political risks, no contractual devices can do much more than seek to anticipate and avoid problems and provide procedural means for addressing them as they arise. No amount of contractual drafting can assure that a project that is perceived as unfair to or a burden on the host country will survive.

Government Approvals

Finally, a note on the importance of obtaining all required approvals for a project at the central government, provincial and local levels, is in order. This subject is far more complicated than it at first appears. In many countries, it can be very difficult, even impossible, to ascertain all of the approvals that may be required at various levels for a given project. Various approvals may be routinely overlooked or circumvented. In China, for example, the $30 million limit above which projects must obtain central government approval is frequently circumvented by arbitrarily dividing a project into components of less than $30 million, even though this practice violates the spirit, and probably the letter, of Chinese legal requirements. In other countries, local authorities and approval requirements may be ignored or overridden by central government authorities in the interest of moving projects forward without delays imposed by local parties. While these practices are not uncommon, it is important to recognize that every legal or regulatory approval not obtained has the potential to serve as a future pretext for a government's failure to honor its contractual obligations. Where a government is looking for a basis to avoid its obligations or renegotiate a deal, few arguments are as convenient as the failure of the project's sponsors to obtain all of the required legal and regulatory approvals.

The Advantages (and some potential disadvantages) of Local Equity Participation

Project companies formed to build, own, operate, and maintain infrastructure projects frequently contain one or more local participants as equity players. In some cases, local ownership is required under the law of the host country; in others, well-connected local players are added because they are perceived to add value to a bidding consortium, can assist in negotiations with the host government, or can help obtain necessary government approvals; in still others, a strong local player with experience in the country and local knowledge can bring significant cost advantages to the project as well as experience that will help insure completion and successful operation. Often some combination of these factors exists.

While strong local participants can provide important advantages for a project, reliance on "well-connected" local participants can be a two-edged sword. The more a project sponsor relies on the connections of a local partner to negotiate special arrangements with the host government outside of transparent bidding or other established selection procedures, the more vulnerable the project will be to charges of favoritism and corruption should the government's attitude toward the project, and its local participants, change. Today's well-connected insider can easily become tomorrow's embarrassment if the government administration changes. This possibility is particularly worth considering when doing business in certain developing countries without democratically elected governments where the relatives of the benevolent leader have a habit of turning up at the top of companies with lucrative participations in virtually every major project.

At the same time, experienced local companies with local knowledge can help keep a project on track and avoid unnecessary problems caused by the foreign investors' lack of experience in the business and legal environment. To the extent that the local partner's value added is based on experience and not just based on some familial relationship or other personal contacts, such a local partner may help the project avoid pitfalls and protect it from arbitrary government action directed at the foreign investor.

Multilateral, Export Credit, Bilateral Agency, and Commercial Bank Participation

Next to political risk insurance designed to cover certain specific risks associated with cross-border investments, discussed below, the broadest protection available against government interference in a project is probably obtained by involving in the project's financing structure one or more major multilateral lenders; export credit agencies (ECAs) or other binational lenders, such as the Overseas Private Investment Corporation (OPIC) or Japan's Overseas Economic Cooperation Fund (OECF); as well as major international commercial lenders. At least in theory, developing country governments are reluctant to default on obligations to major official lenders, upon whom they are dependent to finance high-priority projects and vital imports. The same theory extends to the major commercial lenders, who presumably will be reluctant to make new loans to projects in a country where their existing loans are in default due to government interference. The same argument could be made with respect to the likely reluctance of governments to cause defaults for projects financed in the international capital markets out of concern that their conduct will negatively affect their sovereign ratings and ability to tap the international capital markets for future financing needs.

The notion that the involvement of major multilateral and bilateral lenders in project financing packages acts to deter arbitrary government action is widely accepted, if perhaps difficult to prove objectively. The author is aware of cases in which the involvement of such institutions as project lenders has been an important factor in bringing governments to the bargaining table to resolve disputes with project sponsors. Whether they would have come to the table without such involvement, and what the results would have been is, of course, difficult to know. In at least one instance, however, in which a threatened expropriation is on-going, a host government has not carried out is threat to nationalize the project, at least in part because of its awareness of ongoing contacts between the sponsors and multilateral agencies. Even the original threat to nationalize the project was accompanied by assurances from the government that the nationalization would not adversely affect the interests of the major lenders to the project. This suggests that the prospect of withdrawal of access to major international credit lines was anticipated and taken seriously.

Because of the perceived umbrella effect of involving one or more major multilateral or bilateral institution as potential influential victims of government interference, such institutions are sometimes included in project lending structures despite the potential delay and complications of dealing with institutions that tend to be driven as much by policy as commercial considerations. The umbrella afforded by such institutions can be more or less explicit. Under the B-loan programs pioneered by the International Finance Corporation (IFC), for example, IFC remains the lender of record, theoretically extending some of the benefits of its preferred creditor status to the participating commercial banks. This arrangement is perceived by some national bank regulators as sufficiently secure to lower reserve requirements. Some deterrent effect may also be achieved by including major local financial institutions in the project's debt structure. Loans should be cross-defaulted, so that any default under a commercial loan agreement also triggers defaults under the official and local loans, thus putting additional pressure on the host government to avoid triggering an event of default.

Dealing with a number of different lenders, and with different classes of lenders, adds significant complexity to arranging debt packages and can raise difficult intercreditor issues among and between differently situated lenders. Efforts to deal efficiently with this situation have included evolution of common lending agreements as well as complicated intercreditor agreements. Significant issues have arisen – for example, the so-called "pledge of shares" issue involving the conflicting needs for a pledge of stock in the project company as collateral for senior lenders and for control of the same stock in order to pursue salvage rights of political risk insurers.[9] Participation of different classes and types of lenders, with different layers of debt, equity and quasi-equity participations, also adds considerable complexity to financing structures.

Political Risk Insurance

Political risk insurance has long been available from public sector agencies and is increasingly available from the private sector as well. Political risk insurance is available to cover certain major defined risks of foreign direct investments including expropriation, currency inconvertibility, and political violence. To the extent that such insurance protects investors and lenders from risks that they are unwilling to bear, it plays a critical role in leveraging private sector equity and debt for investments in developing countries. In recent years, the growing number of developing country infrastructure projects has provided a large and growing market for political risk insurance providers.

At the same time, it is important to note that political risk insurance is not perfectly tailored to infrastructure projects and provides only limited protection keyed to certain defined risks. This is not surprising in that, until recent years, infrastructure projects have not been a major focus of foreign direct investments in developing countries. Existing political risk insurers, for the most part, designed their policies with other types of investments in mind.

Outright expropriations are rare in this day and age. While expropriations of foreign investments were common in the 1960s and 1970s, host government interference with foreign investments tends to be much more subtle now. While political risk insurers typically cover "creeping" expropriation, as well as outright nationalization, distinctions between creeping expropriation and valid regulatory measures can be murky, inviting disputes under policies. Expropriation insurance does not cover general deterioration in the legal or regulatory environment, changes in attitude toward privatization or foreign investors, and most contractual breaches.

While currency inconvertibility and transfer risk coverage can provide very important protections for projects that depend, as most infrastructure projects do, on revenues earned in local currency,[10] this coverage does not protect investors from devaluations in local currency that diminish its value against hard currency in which project loans are denominated. Investors must therefore negotiate currency indexation arrangements with local governments and rely on hedging currency risks. While the sophistication of hedging devices has increased in recent years, investors in infrastructure projects frequently will be unable to hedge against the very long term risks facing some projects. The recent significant devaluations of almost all Southeast Asian currencies serves as a vivid reminder of the exposure of infrastructure projects to currency risks.

Perhaps the most significant risk category that remains largely uninsurable under today's political risk policies includes breach by a host government or a state-owned enterprise of the concession agreement or other project documents, or unilateral changes in key terms, such as tariff adjustment provisions, or other arbitrary changes in the basic "rules of the game" upon which the investment was premised.

As a purely legal matter, breach of a host government's or state-owned party's contractual obligations may or may not amount to an expropriation under political risk insurance policies, depending upon a number of factors, including whether the breach is accompanied by a denial of remedies, constitutes a violation of local or international law, or discriminates against the foreign investor. As a practical matter, however, arbitrating these issues under a political insurance policy will always be a long and costly exercise.

Some effort has been made by MIGA and OPIC to provide insurance tailored to this risk. To date, however, contract repudiation coverage has been tied to arbitration clauses contained in underlying project documents. While this form of coverage is certainly helpful, it usually requires investors to exhaust cumbersome contractual and administrative remedies and seek to obtain an arbitral award against the host government or state-owned enterprise. The coverage is triggered by a refusal to honor the agreement to arbitrate or pay an arbitral award. This effort to exhaust contractual remedies could easily require a year or two, or longer, during which time a project "meltdown" very likely will have occurred.

This is perhaps the risk for which improved insurance coverage is most needed. If, for underwriting reasons, it is necessary to tie coverage to an arbitral award or a refusal to arbitrate, then perhaps a streamlined arbitration procedure could be devised for resolution of contractual disputes with host governments concerning infrastructure projects. ICSID, UNCITRAL, and the ICC would be among the logical vehicles for such a streamlined procedure.

Conclusion

Private infrastructure projects are highly vulnerable to political risks because of the relatively brief experience with such projects, their "public" character resulting from the history of government involvement in infrastructure sectors, and the public sensitivity to changes in the cost and level of service associated with privatization and elimination of government subsidies. The ability to structure around political risks is very limited because of the captive nature of such projects in the host country and their relative lack of interdependence with upstream or downstream projects located outside the host country. Certain contractual mechanisms can help, as can inclusion of local participants with experience and local knowledge. The greatest potential for minimizing and managing political risks, however, probably lies in structuring the financing package to include influential multilateral, bilateral and commercial institutions upon whom the host government must depend for access to capital for its future needs, and political risk insurance, which covers certain defined risks (expropriation, inconvertibility, and political violence) extremely well and others (contract repudiation by state-owned entities) less well.

None of these devices alone can fully insulate private infrastructure projects from exposure to political risks. A well-structured project requires careful attention to all.

Notes

[1] See Jae So and Ben Shin, "The Private Infrastructure Industry: A Global Market of $60 Billion a Year," in *Public Policy for the Private Sector: Infrastructure* (Special Edition), The World Bank (June 1996).

[2] The increased prices charged for some infrastructure services, e.g., water tariffs, are likely to be more sensitive than others, e.g. airport departure taxes or landing fees, based on the degree of exposure of different economic levels of the general public to the increase, as well as the extent of past subsidies.

[3] Certain projects, such as telecoms or airport projects, may enjoy offshore hard currency revenues through international settlements, landing fees, or other hard currency charges. Some governments including, until recently, the Philippines, have also permitted capacity payments for power projects to be denominated in dollars or other hard currency. Government policies regarding offshore accounts and hard currency payments are subject to change, however.

[4] It is very doubtful that a contractual conversion right can ever prevent a host government from rationing scarce foreign exchange reserves or otherwise restricting conversion during a foreign exchange crisis, but an effort nevertheless should be made to establish a legal priority of access to foreign exchange for the project.

[5] See, e.g., "Project Finance Debt 1995: Standard & Poor's Credit Perspective in Global Project Finance," Standard & Poor's (October 1995), p. 6.

[6] See, e.g., "Foreign Power Firms Fear Widening Probe in Pakistan," *The Asian Wall Street Journal* (June 4, 1997), p. 3.

[7] A project risk "template" with suggested risk mitigation tools is included as an Appendix to this paper.

[8] See Felton MacJohnston, Ashoka Mody and Robert B. Shanks, "House of Cards," *Project & Trade Finance*, vol. 154 (February 1996), pp. 40–42.

[9] See H. Glaser and F. MacJohnston, "Collision Course," *Project & Trade Finance* (March 1995), p. 46.

[10] Inconvertibility coverage can be important even where a project is paid in hard currency or permitted to maintain an offshore hard currency account, as these privileges are subject to changes in law or government policy.

Appendix

Risk During the Construction Phase

I
Abandonment

Issues	Mitigating Factors
Failure to obtain regulatory approval from each relevant governmental authority	• Equity contribution
Financial failure or technical incompetence of the contractor	• Completion guarantee from Sponsor
Financial failure of the sponsor	• Sponsor's creditworthiness, management, and dedication to the project
Uninsured casualty losses and other force majeure events	• Liquidated damages
Dramatic shifts in market conditions for the contractor	• Contractor's creditworthiness, reputation, and experience with similar projects
	• Insurance against casualty losses and conservative definition of force majeure events
	• Use of long-term sales and supply contracts

II
Completion Delay

Issues	Mitigating Factors
Delay in equipment delivery	• Liquidated damages provision from contractor
Inaccurate time estimate	• Independent Engineer to opine on construction schedule and contractor's capabilities
Incompetent contractor	• Analysis of import and export laws of the host country
Financial failure of sponsor and/or contractor	
Casualty losses and other force majeure events	

III
Cost Overrun

Issues	Mitigating Factors
Incomplete cost estimate	• Use Independent Engineer to verify all cost estimates
Inaccurate cost estimate	• Use turnkey contracts
Misappropriation of funds	• Require sponsors to be liable for cost overruns
Regulatory/environmental changes	• Require progress reports
	• Routine engineering monitoring by Independent Engineer
	• Link loan disbursements to progress reports and engineering reports
	• Authorize Independent Engineer to terminate payment if contractor fails to perform

IV
Performance Risk at Commission

Issues	Mitigating Factors
Defects in design	• Liquidated damages for defects in design
Defects in equipment	• Manufacturer's warranty for defects in equipment
Inexperienced staff	• Require performance testing
Inferior inputs	• Use of inputs compatible with equipment and plant design
New or obsolete technology	• Contractor's reputation and experience
	• Use proven technology or new technology with wide industry range
	• Careful review of technology's performance in other projects

V
Reduced Output of Operating Rate

Issues	Mitigating Factors
Facility design and/or construction	• Stringent performance test during the testing phase, which if passed according to the Independent Engineer, gives a very low likelihood of reduced output under actual operating conditions
Inexperienced or inept operator	• Monitoring of the design and construction phase by the Independent Engineer
Inappropriate technology or new application of old technology	• Equipment (supplier) warranties
Reduced yield, particularly from loss of tax credits, depreciation changes, or increased rates	• Post-completion warranty and/or liquidated damages from the contractor
	• Use experienced operator with positive track record
	• Meaningful liquidated damage/bonus-clause in operations and maintenance contract
	• Subordination of O&M fees to debt service if inexperienced operator used as incentive for good performance
	• Project feasibility study reviewed by Independent Engineer
	• Stringent performance tests with liquidated damages
	• Tax law change indemnification transferring risk from debt to Project Sponsors

VI
Unexpected Major Capital Expenditures

Issues	Mitigating Factors
Construction with inappropriate or inferior materials	• Standby equity or other sponsor support
Acts of God	• Do not finance new technology risk
Changes-in-law	• Independent Engineer's opinion on appropriateness of materials selection
	• Boiler and Machinery Insurance
	• Force Majeure Insurance
	• Capital Expenditure Reserve Fund

VII
O&M Expenses Exceed Budget & Impair Debt Service

Issues	Mitigating Factors
Higher than expected operating expenses	• O&M Reserve Fund
O&M Contractor does not control costs	• O&M contract clauses which provide "ceilings" for O&M expenses
Unexpected repairs	• Avoid "pass through" or "cost plus" contracts
	• O&M contract clause which subordinates O&M expenses above budget to debt service
	• Revenues linked to increases in O&M costs
	• Verify that O&M contractor has good long-term contracts with their suppliers at competitive rates

Risk During the Operating Phase

I
Availability, Cost, Distribution, and Quality

Issues	Mitigating Factors
Resource is scarce and prone to shortages	• Project ownership of resource
Resource price variance does not correlate with revenues	• Use of long-term supply contracts
The means of delivering the resource fails	• Identification of contingent supply sources, secured by contracts if possible
Resource is subject to variances in certain characteristics which can affect project performance	• Maintenance of inventories of the resource at the project site
	• Strong credit quality of suppliers
	• Suppliers should have a strong performance record
	• Project location is sufficiently close to supply sources to facilitate access to normal distribution channels
	• Transportation agent (i.e. shipper) should be of strong credit quality and enjoy a strong reputation for performance
	• Contractual guarantee ensuring (i) specifications are met and (ii) supply cost changes will result in an adjustment to revenues
	• Extensive market studies indicating high predictability of resource prices

II
Environmental Compliance

Issues	Mitigating Factors
Environmental compliance can be affected by resource variance and/or legislative changes	• Sampling, for project-owned resource, recourse to suppliers and/or equity for the additional costs required to attain environmental compliance • Review of statutory and regulatory environmental requirements of the host country and the financial institutions that finance the project (e.g., the World Bank environmental standards)

III
Reduced Demand/Collapse in Prices for Project Output

Issues	Mitigating Factors
Unrealistic economic/market assumptions	• Rely on independent market survey
Oversupply of product in market	• Sensitivity analysis reducing prices, volumes and utilization (should have adequate coverage even in worst case scenario)
Output cannot be sold profitably	• Assess project's relative cost position (in addition to revenue stream) under the theory that a project with a position as low-cost producer can retain competitive advantage even when market is depressed
Technological obsolescence	• Assess likelihood of regulatory or other governmental changes • Utilize proven technology or widely accepted new technology • Tie contractual prices to prices in supply contracts, raw materials costs

Output Market Risk

I
Breach or Renegotiation of Contract

Issues	Mitigating Factors
A. Type of Contract	
Purchaser finds it uneconomic to continue buying under contract	• Full sponsor guarantee to take output (unlikely)
Contract becomes uneconomic due to supply side	• Take-or-pay (hell-or-high-water) contract
Contract expires before loan is paid off	• Take-and-pay (take-if-tendered) contract
Purchaser has no obligation to take specified quantities	• Contract ties to payment in full under financing agreement
B. Parties	
Purchaser is experiencing financial difficulties	• Purchaser's credit quality
Purchaser no longer has use for output	• Purchaser's management quality
Purchaser has multiple contracts for same or similar project	• Satisfaction that purchaser's need for output is clear and ongoing
	• Assessment of purchaser's interest in project (ideally buyer is project sponsor with equity interest)
	• Awareness of existing contracts for output similar to the project's output

5
Progress in Privatizing Infrastructure in Emerging Markets

Timothy J. Faber[*]

Today in infrastructure finance, there is a general recognition that privatization – whether through Build Own Operate (BOO), Build Operate Transfer (BOT), Independent Power Producer (IPP), or some other structure – is necessary to attract capital required for the huge infrastructure needs of these countries. That said, the required regulatory frameworks are still in early stages of development. Risk profiles, investor appetites, government programs are all changing rapidly.

And, as investors, we see returns shrinking as more players come into the market, more capital chases projects, and a more demanding "consumer" of infrastructure emerges, i.e., the governments and consumers in the local markets. It may be a generalization, but in some ways the balance of power is shifting from the investor/developer to the consumer governments, and with that balance of power shifting, the question arises as to whether we are adapting our methods of mitigating political risk appropriately and quickly enough.

The first area I would like to highlight is, for lack of a better name, "risk/return management." It is probably a corollary to the concept of the "obsolescing bargain" or, as Robert Shanks termed it, "pioneer project risk." In many emerging markets, governments try to manage the return received on infrastructure projects.

If you look at other types of industries such as software, biotechnology, and delivery services, the idea of a premium return for getting into the industry early is widely accepted. Nobody questions the person who gets rich developing a software package that changes the world or comes up with the concept of Federal Express, a delivery service that helps the rest of the business world operate more efficiently. However, because of the nature of infrastructure as what some would call a public good or at least a good that is highly visible, it is much more difficult to allow investors to achieve what in hindsight looks like a very healthy economic rent.

[*]Timothy J. Faber is Managing Director for the Americas, GE Capital.

We have seen in markets like India, Pakistan, and even Thailand, efforts to manage returns after the fact, and, in markets like China and Turkey, efforts to manage returns as projects are being negotiated. Where governments try to manage returns on the front end, we tend to end up with bottlenecks as project development moves slowly. Where the management of returns takes place at the back end, the process starts raising questions in investors' minds. This is not a risk that can always be mitigated by solid documentation and a strong legal system – witness the systematic renegotiation of power contracts in New York state with Niagara Mohawk. And, because of the need to entice investors into early-stage development programs via initially generous terms, it is a risk that will continue to confront infrastructure investors in the emerging markets.

Next I would like to focus on the role of government support, a subject that is also apropos of the discussion earlier on local partners. When a key participant in the project is the government, this can often appear to align the government's interests with the investor's interests in the project. What people often lose sight of, however, is that the investor has a very specific commercial interest in the project, while the government has a much broader set of interests that change over time in a very dynamic environment. A local partner, whether it's the government or a local investor, whose interests today may be aligned with the investor's, and who may be helping the investors manage political risks, tomorrow may have other more pressing interests. Now the investor has a liability rather than an asset in the local partner.

At the same time, with increasing frequency, local government bodies are participating and putting up their local assets for privatization or allowing projects to be sponsored in their jurisdiction. Instead of relying on the central government to fulfil the obligations associated with the project, the investors must rely on a local government entity. The official political risk insurance world is not set up to deal with local government obligations. There are some encouraging signs coming from the World Bank Group and some of the regional multilaterals, and we look forward to development in this area.

My third concern relates to the way investors and developers approach official agencies to participate in projects. The inclusion of Export Credit Agencies and multilateral lending agencies in infrastructure project financings is a widely accepted mechanism for the mitigation of political risk. The view is that having them in the project offers a certain umbrella of protection, and there is a lot of merit in that argument.

What people may lose sight of in so structuring a project is that those official bodies also have valid motivations other than commercial interests of the private investor. By their charter, these institutions must support exports or support development while safeguarding the capital of their shareholders and taxpayers. People often complain about the difficulty in dealing with these institutions, but the complaints leave out the fact that the institutions are following their charter. Investors and developers need to look at whether the involvement of the institution is in fact appropriate in the particular case. In structuring a project, we should turn to these agencies only to the extent that their objectives are consistent with the objectives of the project.

There are several encouraging developments:

First is the expansion of the private insurance market. In the last 12 to 18 months, there have been a number of new entrants into the market. Traditionally there were two or three players who offered private insurance and the coverage was typically three years. The new players coming in have forced the market to look at longer coverage, in some cases going out to ten years.

Also, more specialized risk coverage is available today. Once can insure, for example, something as specific as the risk of losing a license. And there is more appetite in more markets. Competition among providers now has made it easier to get the appropriate coverage in more cases than in the past.

The new multilateral and bilateral initiatives are also encouraging. Export credit agencies are very involved in project finance. They have been helpful in a number of areas, and will continue to be important players in project finance in the emerging markets. The regional development banks are also moving into project finance so that even in infrastructure projects where there are not large export components, a multilateral umbrella is available for an investment. There is still development work to be done on the World Bank and IFC guarantee programs, but these programs have filled a very important need to date. Some of the things that the World Bank Group is looking at right now, such as the subsovereign guarantee, will also address some of the issues raised earlier.

Finally, there have been some very successful infrastructure privatizations. I would define success by determining whether enough capital has been attracted to get the resource that is needed to the consumers at an effective price. In a number of the telecommunications and power markets, the price of power or telephone services has come down and consumers are no longer experiencing shortages. Investors are reasonably satisfied with their experience in many of these markets as well. As the lessons learned in these markets filter out to other governments, we hope to see continued success.

6
Rating Debt Issues Secured by Offshore Receivables

Patrice M. Jordan[*]

Over the past several years, Standard & Poor's has rated a variety of offshore receivables financings. These are secured transactions that are structured to reduce the risks of cross-border debt issuance. Typically, these involve a company that exports a product, usually a commodity such as oil or copper. The exports generate offshore dollar-denominated receivables under contract with a foreign buyer or from sale through an established exchange such as the London Metal Exchange. The cash generated from the future receivables is captured offshore and is used to service the debt.

Offshore receivables transactions, known generically as future flows, have also been done with financial flows such as airline ticket receivables, net long-distance telephone payments, and expatriate remittances. This type of financing has generated capital markets funding for companies located in Brazil, Argentina, Mexico, China, Turkey, and Pakistan, and numerous other countries, with the list expanding each year.

Export receivables transactions, such as those involving oil, or another natural resource, are the most common type of capital markets future flows financing. In analyzing an offshore export receivables transaction, seven major factors must be considered:

- the company;
- the company's ability to produce;
- the company's ability to export;
- the nature of the product;
- the nature of the receivables and any purchase contract;
- the size and term of the debt issue; and
- the terms and legal structure of the debt issue.

[*] *Patrice M. Jordan is Managing Director, Structured Finance, Standard & Poor's.*

The Company

Assessing the underlying strength of the company producing the product is the first step, since it clearly has a bearing on the ability to produce. In this process, Standard & Poor's examines both the underlying business risk and financial risk of the company. This is the same procedure used in assigning any corporate credit rating. As a part of this corporate credit rating process, Standard & Poor's assesses the ability of the company to meet all its financial obligations, whether denominated in foreign or local currency, on a timely basis.

The Company's Ability to Produce

Standard & Poor's recognizes that a credit rating does not exactly quantify the probability of continued production, since the former only assesses the likelihood of timely payment of financial obligations. A company can be in default, or even in bankruptcy/receivership, and still continue to produce a given product. Therefore, the probability of continued production could be higher than the probability of timely payment connoted by a local currency credit rating.

The strength of a given company within its industry and its competitive position form a basis for estimating the likelihood of continued production. A company's position related to a specific product may be more pertinent than its overall business position, especially in the case of diversified firm.

The overall financial condition of a company is still relevant in this analysis. A company close to bankruptcy or in bankruptcy/receivership as a result of its financial condition, regardless of its underlying business strength, is more likely to be unable to meet production and delivery obligations than one with a strong financial profile. Standard & Poor's also reviews the local laws for bankruptcy/receivership to assess whether and to what degree these might affect a financially stressed company from meeting its obligations. For example, do the regulations allow for the abrogation of existing contracts? Can secured creditors execute quickly against assets assigned to them as security?

Companies considering issuing securitized receivables debt frequently are in countries with low credit ratings. Typically, operating conditions in such an environment are more difficult or volatile than those in a higher-rated country. Country considerations that could affect the ability to produce include the impact of sovereign risk on the local business environment, including changes in economic activity, the price and availability of credit, market volatility, competition, and labor relations. A second consideration is the potential for regulatory oversight and/or government intervention affecting pricing, production, distribution, and access to raw materials and other imputs as well as potential nationalization.

The Company's Ability to Export

The ability to produce must be followed by continued ability to export the commodity or finished product. The historical track record of the country, in terms both of controlling exports generally and controlling exports of a specific product or industry, is the starting point for this analysis. However, since governments, industries, and products change, the historical track record is just one factor to consider in determining the continued probability of export. Overall, what must be assessed is the existence of strong underlying economic and/or political incentives to allow the continued export of the product. Some factors that are considered include:

- **Factor 1. How important is the product to the country?** This can be either positive or negative, depending on the circumstances. If exports of the product are a large generator of foreign exchange, the country would have a strong incentive to permit continued exports. A product deemed to be strategically sensitive may be treated differently. Brazil, for example, is a net importer of oil, and has defined oil independence as a policy goal. The Brazilian government's view of oil exports would probably be very different from the view of Venezuela, which produces far in excess of its domestic needs and its oil exports represent approximately 90 percent of foreign exchange generation. Another example is gold, which can be used as a reserve asset to back up the country's foreign reserves or settle balance of payments deficits. As a result, some countries could view gold as strategically important. Thus, there is a higher likelihood of interference with gold exports.
- **Factor 2. Is the product a net export?** If the country produces more of the product than can be used domestically, the likelihood of continued exports is higher than that likelihood in a situation where the country is a net importer. The previous example of Brazilian and Venezuelan oil exports also applies here.
- **Factor 3. Does the industry or the company specifically represent an important source of employment to the country?** The exports of such an industry or company would most likely be viewed more favorably, since failure to allow the exports could involve increased unemployment.
- **Factor 4. What raw materials are used to make the product?** If the industry or company must import the raw materials to produce the product, it is possible that in a crisis these imports would be limited. On the other hand, if domestic raw materials are used, the relative value added and consequent ability to generate foreign exchange from export could be more important. In general, the greater the proportion of value added in the country, the greater the likelihood that exports would continue.
- **Factor 5. How large a proportion of export receivables must be used to meet external debt service?** This factor is addressed for the company, the industry, and the country. For example, if such a transaction or series of transactions represents an important percentage of a country's export receipts, there is a greater likelihood that the government might interfere with the exports or the cash flows generated by the exports to ensure repatriation of the receipts rather than

allow their use for offshore debt payment. At the company level, the greater the percentage of the receivables that will ultimately flow back into the country to meet raw material or labor costs, the greater the incentive to continued production and export under the terms of the transactions being securitized.

- **Factor 6. Are the export sales contracts arm's length?** A contract that is generated under standard market conditions and containing standard market terms, including pricing, is less likely to be modified by a government than one that represents a one-sided benefit to the foreign buyer. For example, a 20-year contract with an offshore affiliate company using transfer pricing to maximize remittances or avoid taxes or potential exchange controls has a greater risk of being modified or abrogated by the producer's government. The terms of the contract, particularly how easily one of the parties could renege on its obligations, also are critical. Any terms that reduce the uncertainties, whether in terms of price or volumes, make the transaction easier to analyze.

- **Factor 7. Could interference with exports affect future foreign investment in the country?** A unilateral modification or abrogation of an offshore third-party sales contract could jeopardize the amount of investment coming into that country. Depending on the importance these inflows have for economic development, the likelihood of reduced foreign investment as a result of government interference, and the degree of governmental concern for the nation's economic welfare, these risks to the country could represent an important deterrent to governmental intervention.

This list represents the major considerations that must be addressed in determining the likelihood of continued exports, although it is not comprehensive. Each situation must be addressed on a case-by-case basis, as each country, industry, and potentially, each company or export contract, will present a different mix of issues.

Nature of the Product

Apart from any potential governmental interference with the export of the product, demand for the product in the international market is an important factor to consider. Commodity products with deep international markets, such as copper traded on the London Metals Exchange, tend to be viewed more favorably for these transactions, since they enjoy the depth and liquidity of the international market to support sales under a specific export contract. Manufactured products tend to lack the liquidity inherent in commodity products, though there are exceptions. A manufactured product that may be more difficult to sell readily on the international market may still be viewed favorably if the exporter is an important source of the goods for the offshore buyer and other sources are not readily available. For example, MABE Export S.A. de C.V. in Mexico is the only significant supplier of gas ranges for General Electric Company to sell in the US market.

The Receivables and the Purchase Contract

Typically, these transactions are structured so that receivables are generated from a long-term sales contract for the purchase of the product by an offshore buyer. Alternatively, for certain commodities the sale may be made through a recognized market. If the transaction relies on a purchase contract, the underlying credit strength of the purchasers is assessed to determine its ability and willingness to honor its contractual commitments and generate the receivables.

Standard & Poor's also assesses the importance of this particular source of supply for the buyer. Standard & Poor's considers whether there are strong economic reasons for the buyer to honor the contractual arrangement. A tightly structured, long-term contract containing minimum purchase requirements with a strong offshore entity strengthens the transaction. However, it is possible to have loosely worded contracts, short-term renewable contracts, or no contracts at all. These transactions would rely on the liquidity of the product in the international markets.

Purchase contracts are reviewed. This analysis includes the sensitivity of the contracts to commodity price declines, production interruptions, volume fluctuations, and exposure to construction and/or technical risks. Standard & Poor's notes the ability to increase the volume of exports if the price should decline. If the product is a commodity and a fixed quantity of product is being purchased, the strength of debt service coverage during a down cycle is assessed. Standard & Poor's expects strong coverage ratios even in the down cycle. Standard & Poor's also reviews the likelihood of supply interruption. This helps to determine the size of any reserve fund that is set up for contingencies.

Ownership of the producer by the buyer, whether full or partial, can enhance secured debt issues where the offshore entity has a strong credit rating. To be viewed most positively, the ownership interest must be a controlling interest, must represent an important part of the offshore entity's global operations or source of product supply, and should be accompanied by a clear statement of support. In addition to statements made by the offshore entity, Standard & Poor's also looks for evidence of tangible support by the offshore parent in times of crisis. Such a relationship can increase the likelihood of continued cash generation to service the debt obligation.

Limitations on securitizing additional receivables are important. One of the positive factors in these transactions is the preferred position in which such bondholders are placed relative to other creditors and the offshore cash flow. Often holders of this securitized debt are effectively placed in a position superior to all other creditors of the issuer, even those notionally secured. However, if a significant portion of the future receivables can be used as security for future debt issues, these benefits are largely undone.

Size and Term of the Debt Issue

The size of the transaction relative to the seller's cash flow also is important. If the cash generated by a relatively large amount of receivables is diverted to pay the specific debt obligations, the seller could face a crisis if the export receipts, which are being used for the sole benefit of securitized debtholders, are unavailable, and the company needs their receipts for working capital purposes. This would be a difficult situation for a company to handle for any length of time, and might increase its incentive to divert production away from the securitized transaction to other purchasers. The likelihood of a default under the contract by the company would be higher. A smaller debt issue relative to the cash needs of the company would be easier to service and would not provide this type of diversionary incentive.

Likewise, Standard & Poor's prefers amortizing debt issues with a sinking fund. Bullet payments imply the need for refinancing and again subject the debt to company and country risks. An amortizing issue will have principal paid from the cash generated by the receivables on a regular basis and allows the amortization of the debt to benefit from the structure of the transaction. In addition, the shorter the term of the issue the easier it is to predict the severity of the risks involved and to rely on any mitigation factors.

Structure of the Issue

Many of the characteristics of traditional asset-backed securitization also are used to help mitigate potential disruptions in the generation of cash to service debt. One of these aspects is the establishment of an offshore bankruptcy-remote issuing vehicle and collection accounts in which all the cash flows are held. These structures are used to help distance the issue and the cash flows from the uncertainties within the home country, and facilitate control and security interests in the underlying receivables and cash flow. However, unlike typical structured transactions, most of these debt issues are also backed by a guarantee from the producing company. This guarantee gives additional recourse and protection to bondholders and added motivation for timely payment.

Standard & Poor's recognizes that in some very limited instances, the offshore bankruptcy-remote issuing vehicle may not be needed. In one transaction, YPF S.A., a major Argentine oil company, securitized receivables from the sale of oil to Empresa Nacional del Petroleo-Chile. In this structured export note transaction, which was rated 'BBB,' YPF was the borrower. Sales were made directly by YPF to ENAP without the benefit of an offshore special-purpose vehicle (SPV).

The solid underlying business position of YPF in Argentina, coupled with strong governmental incentives to assure continued production and the export of oil, allowed a debt structure without an SPV for this transactions.

A second characteristic of asset-backed securitization is secured export volumes that result in receipts from the purchase contracts or market sales that cover multiples of the issuer's debt service. This coverage helps to ensure timely cash flow if there are changes in contracts, productions, and/or international markets or prices, which could reduce overall cash flow availability. For example, an export contract calling for delivery of a fixed volume of goods at current market prices that just exactly meets the amount of debt service provides no protection if market prices decline. If the volume of exports under contract at current market prices covers several times annual debt service, there is substantial inherent protection against such price changes.

A third characteristic is the establishment of a debt service reserve fund. Generally this reserve, established at the outset of the transaction, is equal to at least one scheduled principal and interest payment. This amount can be greater depending upon the nature of the product, the contract, the underlying risk of the sovereign, and the frequency of payments. Such a reserve acts to cover temporary interruptions in product delivery and cash flow, whether from reduced prices, delayed receipts, or other occurrences.

A fourth characteristic consists of triggers in the transaction documents that require trapping of all cash flow at the issuer, that is, the SPV level, if certain adverse events occur. This helps to provide more cash to bondholders to assure timely payment and additional security when these adverse events occur, regardless of whether they are the result of action by the sovereign or events affecting the issuer/producer, product purchasers, or the market as a whole. For example, the imposition of export restrictions or currency controls that might serve to undermine the transaction, declaration of force majeure, radical changes in the market for the product, or similar occurrences might set off such triggers. The triggers also provide strong incentives to the ultimate producer either to prepay the issue or to quickly and satisfactorily resolve the events that caused the trigger mechanism to come into play.

The fifth asset-backed characteristic that helps mitigate potential disruptions in the generation of cash to service debt is legal assignment to the SPV issuer of all the sales and purchase contracts, and rights to all the relevant cash flows, rather than those attributable to just one or a narrow group of purchasers. This eliminates any incentive to either the producer or the sovereign to divert supply to purchasers outside of the security arrangement and ensures that the preferred status of the secured debtholders is preserved and timely payment met.

Popularity to Grow

The relative weight placed on each of the elements of the transaction varies depending on the nature of the particular transaction. The greater protection and strength of one element might offset some relative weaknesses elsewhere. Standard & Poor's rating of the debt issue ultimately reflects the inherent economic viability and strength of a particular transaction along with its legal structure. Together, these factors determine an issue's likelihood of timely payment.

A well-structured transaction offers benefits to both borrowers and lenders. One example is Grupo Mexico Export Master Trust No. 1, a $525 million secured export note issue backed by mineral export receivables done in March 1996. The seller of the future export receivables, and the recipient of the issue proceeds, is Mexico Desarrollo Industrial Minero S.A. de C.V., "Medimsa," Mexico's largest mining company. The future receivables sold to the issuer by Medimsa represent a relatively small proportion of the overall earnings of Medimsa, however. They provide a sizable cash flow cushion to investors in the event of falling metals prices in the global markets. The combination of the case flows and the structure of the transaction, whereby the payments on the receivables are made and kept outside of Mexico, resulted in the issue receiving a "BBB" rating from Standard & Poor's which is higher than Mexico's foreign currency sovereign rating of "BB."

Standard & Poor's expects that the popularity of export receivables and other types of future flow transactions will continue to grow around the world, and the nature of these transactions will continue to evolve. For these transactions to gain even greater acceptance with investors and issuers, they must be carefully structured to provide real economic incentive and proper legal certainty.

7

Challenges in the Financing of International Oil Operations

Andrea L. MacDonald[*]

First, let me set a framework around why the topic of political risk management is of interest to the oil industry today. None of us are strangers to the world of international commerce. More than half of Exxon's income is earned in our non-US businesses and our emphasis on international growth is expected to continue for the foreseeable future.

Due to dramatic changes that have marked the 1990s, international opportunities, particularly upstream, have expanded in geographic areas that are either new areas or those that have re-opened after being inaccessible to us for many years.

The map on page 124 shows the different areas of the world and their accessibility to international investment. We estimated that prior to 1990, international capital had access to roughly 35 percent of undiscovered oil and gas potential. With the areas shown with line shading opening up, we now estimate that private industry's access to the world's undiscovered oil and gas potential has more than doubled to approximately 80 percent. Moreover, there are also large volumes of discovered, but undeveloped, resources that have opened up in recent years.

The circled areas show key high potential areas for oil and gas development. Since these are the areas where resources are concentrated, these are the areas where companies are flocking. There are certainly commercial challenges associated with resources in many of these areas. The opportunities tend to be capital intensive and often include a greater level of technical risk. The number of oil and gas projects and the amount of capital investment being contemplated in such areas are increasing rapidly.

There is both an opportunity and challenge in these developments for the oil industry – for both the resources themselves and the enormous amount of capital required to develop them.

---

[*]Andrea L. MacDonald is Treasurer, Exxon Exploration Company.

These opportunities are potentially attractive for the industry, but they bring political risks or a size, significance and scope of a different magnitude than experienced in the last several decades.

In a number of cases, political risk stems from the low levels of economic development, lack of infrastructure, and governmental systems that are in early stages of democratization. Many of the countries in newly accessible areas are still in the process of developing the economic, legal, and fiscal regimes necessary to attract and support major private investment initiatives. They may also be struggling to define specific arrangements that both make sense to them and are acceptable to investors.

Political risk associated with large-scale projects in the developing world is a reality that must be thoughtfully assessed and carefully addressed in project planning. By this I am referring to political risk in its broadest sense, covering the full range of non-technical and non-market risks that these projects face.

Long before considering insurance or financing as a source of risk mitigation, companies look not only at the technical aspects, but the fiscal terms of a deal. I have been involved with several opportunities where issues like foreign exchange rights could have killed the project if not resolved.

Agreements have to work in the long term for upstream or mining projects to work given the long lead-time involved and the high front-end costs. In many cases we are also asked for input on laws which, in some cases, need to be drafted from scratch. Setting the framework for things like the right to export and the rights to retain hard currency offshore are important whether or not someone is considering using insurance or debt as a means of risk mitigation. However, clearly in the case of debt these are also something lenders would like to see.

Project Finance

There are a number of potential benefits to project finance.

- It can help to mitigate political risk. Involvement of multilateral agencies in developing parts of the world can lower overall project risk, as these countries may be less likely to back away from agreements with international institutions upon whose continuing support they rely. The involvement of such lenders can also help countries understand the importance of policies allowing for retention of foreign currency abroad and of designing appropriate fiscal regimes.
- It can also be useful in aligning the stakes of various partners. This is particularly true of projects that involve financially weaker partners, public or private, who may be unwilling or unable to fund their share of project expenditures. However, there are ways to handle situations where some of the participants require project financing, but others are unwilling to bear the cost of project finance.
- Project finance not only helps align stakes among partners; it can also reduce the total stake. For most downside risks, this stake reduction is of little value since the sponsors will always retain the riskiest portion of the project cash flow. However,

in the event of a total disaster, such as outright expropriation without compensation, the lenders are there to share some of the pain.

- Furthermore, limiting one's stake may expand the number of projects companies are willing to participate in.
- For some companies, very structured project financing can actually reduce costs and, in some cases, allow them to break through sovereign credit ratings. This had been seen in a number of financing transactions, most recently that of Ecopetrol in Colombia.

Securing project financing is not without challenges or cost.

- First, and probably the only quantifiable item, limited recourse finance usually involves a significant borrowing premium over the normal cost for a major oil company.
- Invariably, the lenders have a prior claim on project cash flows, which increases the riskiness of the net back flow to the borrower.
- In addition, the lender is likely to look toward other forms of sponsor support.

As the loan negotiation process unfolds sponsors may find themselves more deeply committed to support the project debt than originally anticipated. The "creeping recourse" could result from contractual gray areas or from simple economic compulsion to see the project continue. As the supplementary protection measures expand, the benefit of risk shedding is compromised.

The first clear area of sponsor support comes in the form of completion guarantees, shifting construction risk squarely back on the shoulders of the sponsors.

Lenders will also look for some degree of certainty on their portions of project inflows. This frequently involves take or pay, throughput or other fixed obligations from the sponsor; these obligations again effectively shift ownership risk back to the sponsors.

Another form of protection comes in the form of a cash flow cushion or high coverage levels. This helps to ensure repayment even in downside scenarios, lessening the chance of default in all but catastrophic situations.

- Finally, the introduction of various third parties at different stages in the development process inevitably leads to some loss of flexibility. Obviously, if lenders are looking solely to a project for repayments, they will need to satisfy themselves as to its commercial soundness and may offer their own opinions on how things should be done.

As you can tell by looking at any of Exxon's annual accounts, we most often borrow centrally. This has minimized borrowing costs by capitalizing on deep, efficient markets and drawing on the cash flow support of our global operations. However, despite our predilection for funding most projects from central sources, we believe project finance can make a constructive contribution to managing risk of projects in a number areas.

While the involvement of multilateral institutions and other lenders adds complexity, their presence can enhance host country commitment and mitigate political risk.

As we consider large projects with varying financing capabilities among participants, project finance can also help to align the "at risk" stakes among the partners.

However, project finance is not a panacea. We need to assess whether the added costs entailed are worth the various risk mitigation steps achieved.

Political Risk Insurance

There are very limited levels of insurance available from many agencies relative to the size of upstream investments. This, combined with the requirement to turn over the keys to a given project in order to collect on the expropriation coverage, raises questions about its applicability to multi-billion dollar investments.

Additionally, in many cases, it is very hard to separate political risk from commercial risk. Political risk insurance uses "but-for" clauses: but for the political event, there would not be a problem. The dilemma here is that if an investor wants to shed political risk, he may have to pay for coverage for events that are really part of his everyday business.

Suppose somebody comes along and sabotages a pipeline moving oil across a country. He may have done it for political reasons, but if he says he did it for environmental reasons, then political risk insurance will not reimburse the investor. So if you want to cover this kind of risk you have to insure yourself against practically all contingencies, including risks you might prefer to keep.

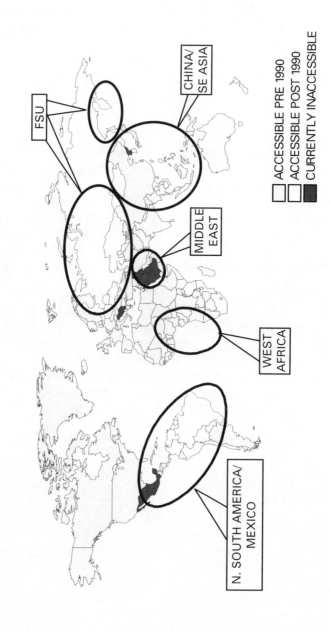

HIGH POTENTIAL - CHALLENGING AREAS

75% OF WORLD'S UNDISCOVERED AND DISCOVERED REMAINING RESOURCES

8
New Forms of Protection for International Infrastructure Investors

Linda F. Powers[*]

Infrastructure is a special category of industry. It has high visibility and high sensitivity. The services are critical and they have a public character. Given these factors, the key to being safe and secure as a project sponsor is having a project that is economically sound and fair. All the fancy structuring in the world will not save a project that is fundamentally a bad deal.

However, the main challenge for project sponsors – determining what constitutes an economically sound and fair deal – is very much a moving target. It is a moving target partly because of what has been called the "obsolescing bargain" – the idea that what looked like an appropriate level of return and pricing at the time the project was put together on the front end does not look so appropriate later on in the life of the project.

But there is more to the problem than this. In our marketplace in particular – energy infrastructure – what is considered an appropriate level of pricing and return on the front end is itself changing very substantially and very fast. To give a sense of this change, just a few years ago independent power plants in emerging markets were charging their customers (the utilities) six cents a kilowatt hour, and now the rate is down to under three cents a kilowatt hour. And that is true not only in countries like the Philippines that have done a number of independent power projects and have a track record, but also in countries like Bangladesh that are just doing their first independent power projects.

This rapid squeezing of project economics is having a huge impact, placing much greater emphasis on the issue of risk because there are no margins in the projects anymore to absorb problems or pay for a lot of protection. For example, in the past, project sponsors often purchased political risk insurance. Such insurance could cost anywhere from 2–4 percent of the covered amount per year, depending on the source of the insurance, the scope of coverage, and the duration and riskiness of the

---
[*]*Linda F. Powers is Senior Vice President, Global Finance, Enron International.*

undertaking. Now, with project economics so compressed, many projects can no longer support the cost of such insurance.

As a comparison, natural resource investments are highly sensitive too, but are not experiencing the rapid and severe compression of project economics that energy infrastructure is experiencing. Indeed, few businesses outside of high technology sectors face such a pace and degree of change in their fundamental economics.

Another important shift exacerbating the risks involved is the growing size of energy projects. There is an increasing number of "elephant" projects in the market, costing a billion dollars and more each. These are extra large and extra complex. The sheer magnitude of the risks can far outstrip the capacity of traditional risk protections, such as insurance, and may also dwarf the returns a project sponsor stands to earn. Sometimes, more than one "elephant" project has to fit together with other "elephants," and no one project is economic without the others (e.g., a large pipeline project and a large off-take project). In these cases, the risks become truly staggering.

Another significant trend is toward an increasing number of multi-country projects. In these, political risk is multiplied and compounded, as the projects must address multiple sets of country and political circumstances simultaneously. For example, the production activity (e.g., electric power generation, or gas field production) is often located in a different country than the consumption activity (e.g., off-take projects using the electricity or gas). This not only makes it more difficult to put the project together in the first place (permits and approvals are needed from each country's government, deal terms and structure must be negotiated with each government). It also makes the political risks more difficult throughout the life of the project, because the project is exposed throughout this time to risks of governmental interference, foreign exchange difficulties, elections and changes of government, and contract renegotiation, in multiple countries simultaneously. This compounds risk on top of risk.

Yet, from a business and engineering standpoint (in contrast to risk-profile considerations), multi-country regional projects increasingly make sense. For example, in the fall of 1997, Enron was awarded a project for a thousand megawatts of power plant capacity to be built in Argentina, with all of the electricity to be sold in Brazil. Another example involves an ongoing effort to develop an integrated regional power plant for six countries in Central America. A single large regional plant would be much more efficient and cost-effective than six separate small plants. The real difficulties are the country and political complexities.

In sum, energy infrastructure project sponsors are grappling with increasingly difficult market conditions: severe compression of project economics, and increasing project size and complexity. At the same time, project sponsors are facing a decreasing ability to use traditional structuring solutions to handle these risks. With regard to the security package, for example, project sponsors can no longer get federal government guarantees from most host countries. The security package is a set of provisions built into the structure of each deal, which provide a financial cushion (e.g., escrow of an extra six or twelve months worth of debt service) plus various forms of protection (e.g., guarantees) to deal with unexpected revenue shortfalls, cost overruns, or other difficulties that would otherwise jeopardize a project.

Until recently, one of the most important components of the security package has been a guarantee from the host country government promising that, if certain risks materialize, the host government will bear the economic loss or cost rather than the project. Such guarantees made very good sense, because most of the key risks projects faced would only be likely to materialize because of various acts or omissions of the host government. However, as the marketplace has tightened (as already described), many host countries have started refusing to give such guarantees anymore. With heightened competition among project sponsors, host governments no longer feel it is necessary, and they prefer to save their credit capacity for more public uses.

The same is true of pass-throughs. Pass-throughs are contractual provisions in project agreements that allocate specified risk exposures to a local party – usually the customer, who is usually a state or parastatal entity (e.g., state utility or state electricity board). These provisions protect project sponsors by transferring or "passing through" to the local party the risk exposure that the project sponsor would otherwise bear. The risks selected for such pass-throughs are ones that the local party is, at least in theory, better situated to prevent or handle than the project sponsor is. A leading example is foreign exchange risk. Project sponsors are generally unable to hedge emerging market currencies for a substantial forward period at any manageable cost. Sponsors are also unable to bear a further squeeze on project economics (beyond that already described) from bearing foreign exchange problems themselves. But now the marketplace is changing such that sponsors cannot deal with foreign exchange risks by using pass-throughs.

A further change in the marketplace that is accentuating the risks for project sponsors is the fact that there is decreasing opportunity to tailor projects and project structures to individual countries' circumstances. This is because nowadays projects are increasingly being awarded by competitive bids with deal terms that are set. A sponsor either enters a bid on those terms or does not. The reality is not quite that cut and dried, but there is less opportunity to tailor projects even on the first power plants in a country let alone on the fourth or fifth set of projects.

So, these are some of the main changes occurring in the marketplace for energy infrastructure projects. These changes are making risk profiles more complicated, squeezing project economics rendering insurance and other protections less affordable, and preventing project sponsors from using other structuring solutions (such as guarantees and pass-throughs) to mitigate the risks. The net result is that project sponsors are having to take on more and more risks themselves, and to devise new ways to cope with them.

Among the various risks, some are of greater concern to project sponsors than others – and this, too, is changing along with marketplace changes. For example, classical expropriation – in which a country actually *says* it is nationalizing a company or a project, is no longer a top concern of project sponsors. Why? Not because the risk has gone away, but because nowadays countries are much more sophisticated about their methods. They are more likely to find ways to blame the project sponsor, withhold or cancel key permits or approvals, and so forth, resulting in "contract frustration" rather than outright expropriation.

Contract frustration can be considered, in essence, simply a more subtle form of expropriation. The result is a permanent and total loss of the project, just as with a classical expropriation. The loss can even be worse than with an expropriation, because it can be difficult or impossible for a project sponsor to obtain compensation for a contract frustration loss. There is no clear body of international law establishing a right to compensation from the host country, as there is for expropriation. Insurance policies often cover only expropriation, not contract frustration. And even when an insurance policy does include coverage for contract frustration, proof is always difficult because these cases always turn upon murky factual issues about fault and causation.

Another increasingly common scenario of high concern to project sponsors is what I would call "political business interruption." In these cases, the sponsor does not end up losing the project permanently and totally... but *does* experience a project stoppage that is politically based. Perhaps the most frequent situation in which this occurs is when there has been a change of government, and the new regime wants to gain leverage to force a re-negotiation of the deal. This is becoming increasingly common – even in cases where an election has been won by the same political party that negotiated the existing deal – and is a very serious threat to project viability. The losses from a project stoppage can add up very quickly – especially for large infrastructure projects – and there is no traditional insurance instrument, or coverage category, which covers this type of business interruption.

With these considerations in mind, let me now turn to what we, as project sponsors, have learned out of all this. I would like to describe four lessons that we have learned and (unfortunately) continue to learn every day.

First Lesson:
Need for New Deal Structures

The first lesson is that, since traditional structuring solutions (e.g., pass-throughs, guarantees), are often no longer available, we must develop new mechanisms to provide the necessary financial cushion for revenue shortfalls or cost overruns, and for other sorts of risks. A lot of attention and effort are currently being focused on developing various kinds of escrow accounts and lien arrangements which would enable an infrastructure project to tap certain revenue flows to the project's customer (the state utility) or the host government. A project's right to tap those revenues would only be triggered if specified risks materialized – the same kinds of risks that previously served as triggers for pass-throughs and guarantee coverage (i.e., risks affected by host government acts or omissions). Such arrangements would have the same result as pass-through provisions and guarantees used to have: they would enable a project to access the financial resources of the state utility and/or host government to compensate for problems which those parties either caused or were better situated to bear.

The key obstacles to developing such arrangements have been the difficulty in identifying state utility and/or state government revenue streams and, most importantly, figuring out how to establish a legally enforceable and sufficiently senior lien position to give the projects meaningful protection. These are new and uncharted areas. Both the facts and the laws concerning the revenue streams (tax revenues, funds transfers from the central government, utility customer receivables, etc.), the state utility's or government's own rights to them, and the status of other existing pledges or claims upon them, tend to be very murky. The laws concerning a private third party's potential lien position (enforceability, seniority, etc.) are even more unclear and uncertain. Thus, project sponsors and their lenders have a lot more work to do in this area.

Another example of new deal structures under development involves the InterAmerican Development Bank's (IDB's) new partial risk guarantee program and the first project done under this program: the Salitre municipal water project in Bogota, Colombia. After a long period of study, the IDB has established a new program that provides IDB guarantees to cover selected risks in a project which are beyond the control of the project sponsors, are critical to the project's viability and, typically, involve some act or omission by the host government. Thus, the IDB guarantee can to provide the missing protection that project sponsors have become unable to obtain through host government guarantees or otherwise.

The IDB deserves great applause for its design and launch of this partial guarantee program. The guarantees are very efficient and surgical, custom tailored in each deal to cover only risks that are essential and that the project sponsors do not have other means to protect against. Most importantly, the IDB guarantees are flexible and realistic, in that they do not require any counter-guarantee from the host country government. This enables host countries to preserve their credit capacity for public sector uses, and recognizes that host governments have become unwilling (as discussed earlier) to use that capacity to provide any guarantees for private infrastructure projects (including indirect guarantees structured as counter-guarantees for another party's direct guarantee). In contrast, the World Bank's partial risk guarantee program *does* require a host country counter-guarantee for every one of its guarantees. This has greatly undercut the effectiveness and usage of the World Bank's program.

The recent Salitre project provides a good illustration. This was a $100 million water project at the municipal level in Bogota, Colombia, developed by Lyonnaise des Eaux. Although there was a strong project sponsor, there was no established track record of municipal creditworthiness, and there were significant risks to the project's revenue stream beyond the project sponsor's control (e.g., currency inconvertibility). Some protections were built into the project agreements: if any specified force majeure events materialized, the municipality would be required to buy out the project sponsor. However, in the absence of a municipal creditworthiness track record, these agreements on paper were not enough. Without some form of back-up, the project was not financeable.

The IDB provided a partial risk guarantee to Salitre which covered two risks: currency inconvertibility, and the failure of the municipality to make good on the buy-out obligation if the force majeure events occurred. If the municipality failed to make the buy-out payment within ten days of when it was due, the IDB would step in under its guarantee, make the buy-out payment to the project sponsor and lenders, and then pursue recovery itself. By covering just these two critical risks, the IDB enabled the project to go from being unfinanceable (and thus not doable) to getting an investment grade rating. (The financing for the project came from the issuance of $30 million of A notes and $70 million of B notes. The value of the IDB's partial guarantee enabled both the senior and junior notes to achieve investment grade ratings of A and BBB, respectively.) The investment grade rating not only made the financing obtainable but minimized its cost for the project and, and hence, for the country. All in all, a big success story for which the IDB deserves great credit.

These are the kinds of new deal structures that must constantly be developed and improved to keep pace with changing market conditions. We hope that other mechanisms, such as the escrow accounts and lien arrangements described earlier, can also become successful. However, structuring solutions such as these are only part of the answer.

Second Lesson:
Need for Protections Outside Deal Structures

We still need risk protections outside of the deal structure because structural provisions alone are not enough. One such external protection is the involvement of the right parties. The participation of the multilateral banks, export credit agencies, and investment finance agencies does have an important effect. We really do need their presence.

In order to be most effective, we need to have the multilateral and bilateral agencies' participation related to the risks that project sponsors are most concerned about today. Recently, MIGA has been playing an important leadership role in this regard by recognizing sponsors' heightened concern over contract frustration and initiating a review to determine whether expanded insurance coverages are needed for this risk. While MIGA's current coverages could be interpreted to cover contract frustration if those situations otherwise meet the definition of expropriation (by being a sufficiently total and permanent deprivation, etc.), the language is rather unclear and uncertain. We applaud MIGA for initiating its review, and hope that the Overseas Investment Corporation (OPIC) will likewise consider an expansion or clarification of coverage for contract frustration.

There also remains a need for each of the multilateral and bilateral agencies to take a look at the "political business interruption" risk I described earlier, and devise ways to cover that risk effectively. We hope that both MIGA and OPIC will recognize the growing frequency and seriousness of this type of project interruption risk, and play a leadership role in helping create solutions.

Traditional players, such as Lloyd's of London, are moving fairly slowly and incrementally. In the past, these private insurers would only cover confiscation/expropriation/nationalization (CEN). They are now willing to write modest amounts (in the tens of millions of dollars) of contract frustration coverage and some types of political violence coverage, for somewhat longer durations (e.g., seven years instead of one to three years). However, these coverages still fall far short of the public insurers' coverages, and of the coverages needed in large infrastructure projects.

A number of new private insurers have also begun to enter the political risk insurance arena. These new players are focusing on covering all three types of political risk which the public insurers have been covering (CEN, currency inconvertibility, and political violence), which is helpful. However, even these new players do not have nearly as much capacity for political risk insurance as the public insurers do, and are not able to provide nearly as long a duration as the public insurers do. So, the public insurers (e.g., MIGA, OPIC) remain essential for infrastructure projects.

In designing risk protections external to the deal structure, we all need to get more sophisticated and more surgical about the way risk allocations are done. To do so, we have to start by "unbundling the risks, because, as I indicated earlier, project sponsors simply cannot afford to pay other parties to bear any more risks than they really, really have to, as project economics get squeezed. This also gives agencies like MIGA and OPIC more mileage from their existing capacity, as their coverage becomes more surgical.

Here again, I would like to applaud MIGA for their new cooperative underwriting program (CUP). Both insurance companies and non-insurance companies (such as infrastructure project sponsors) are eligible to set up CUP arrangements. A non-insurance company need only set up a captive insurance company to participate in the CUP program. (A captive insurance company is an entity established by a non-insurance company to handle only the risks generated by that non-insurance company and its affiliates – in essence, a sort of in-house insurance company.)

MIGA's CUP arrangement is modeled upon the IFC's co-lending structure of A loans and B loans, in which the A loan is for the IFC's own account and the B loan is syndicated to other (private) banks. MIGA's CUP is a co-insurance arrangement, in which one tranche of the insurance exposure is for MIGA's own account and the other tranche of insurance exposure is borne by the "Cooperating Underwriter" (i.e., the private insurance company or the captive insurer set up by a non-insurance company).

The key elements of the MIGA CUP structure are that: 1) MIGA serves as the insurer of record for *both* tranches of insurance exposure (the one for its own account, and the one borne by the Cooperating Underwriter); 2) if a covered risk materializes, MIGA and the Cooperating Underwriter each pay their respective share of the claim to the insured party (typically, to the project company); 3) MIGA pursues recovery on behalf of *both* itself and the Cooperating Underwriter; and 4) any recovery obtained by MIGA is shared pro rata between MIGA and the Cooperating Underwriter. Thus, MIGA can never be made whole without the Cooperating Underwriter also being made whole. This is a very powerful structure because unless and until MIGA is made whole, the host country that caused the problem is in bad standing with the World Bank Group. That is a strong lever.

Another example of being more sophisticated and more surgical in managing political risks can be found in our work with private insurers to develop new types of insurance products. Enron has a special group in Houston that is working with private insurers to develop a number of new instruments, including a hybrid which is part risk-transfer and part risk-financing.

Traditional insurance – including traditional political risk insurance – consists of risk *transfer*: the specified risk exposure is taken off of the insured party and placed onto another party (the insurer). In the late 1980s, a different type of instrument was developed which involved only risk *financing* – not risk *transfer* – for situations in which a loss was virtually certain to occur (and thus could not be insured, in the traditional sense), but the party at risk wanted to spread out the impact of that expected loss. This instrument – called "finite insurance" – essentially involved installment payments of the expected loss amount into a reserve account over a set period of years (both before and after the loss event), thus spreading the impact but leaving the full amount of the impact on the original party.

The hybrid instrument that Enron is now working with private insurers to develop combines portions of both risk *transfer* and risk *financing*. For our purposes, we are mixing about one-third risk transfer and two-thirds risk financing, but the relative proportions can be varied in almost any mixture, depending upon the probability of occurrence and potential severity of the loss being covered, upon the insured party's tolerance for self-exposure, and upon the insurance company's appetite and pricing for the exposure involved.

With this hybrid instrument, a total coverage amount is specified, a portion of that exposure amount is borne by the insurance company (risk transfer) and a portion is funded by the insured party's own installment payments (risk financing). The insured party under this hybrid instrument makes payments into a reserve account which consists of premiums for the risk transfer portion and installment payments for the risk financing portion.

This structure has a number of interesting benefits. First, if the risk transfer portion is substantial enough, the entire combined payments become tax deductible. (On a stand-alone basis, traditional insurance premiums are deductible, but installment payments into a reserve account are not.) Second, the funds in the reserve account accrue interest, and if no loss event materializes, the funds attributable to the risk-financing portion, plus interest, are returned to the insured party at the end of the policy. Third, if a loss event does occur, the insured party achieves meaningful mitigation of the impact, as part of the loss is borne by the insurance company and the rest is spread out over time through the sponsor's installment payments. Fourth, the cost of this hybrid coverage can be much lower than traditional full risk transfer.

For what situations is this hybrid insurance appropriate? It is best deployed for situations involving a sophisticated project sponsor who can thoroughly analyze the risks, who can afford to bear a substantial portion of the risks, and who feels fairly confident that a big problem or loss event is not very like to occur – and, if such a major loss event does occur, the sponsor has some effective means of solving or handling it. In short, the hybrid instrument provides tailored (surgical) coverage for situations in which a sophisticated party feels *pretty* sure they will not encounter a big problem – and thus does not want to pay (or, with the squeeze in project economics, cannot afford to pay) very much for protection – but does not feel *so* sure about this that they can afford to go "bare" without any protection at all.

Thus, the second lesson Enron has learned about handling political risks is that we still need protections outside of the deal structure (as deal terms become increasingly rigid, and pass-throughs and other internal solutions become increasingly difficult to obtain), but that we also can and should push ourselves to make those external protections as surgical and economical as possible.

Third Lesson:
Need for New Sources of Political Risk Coverage

The third lesson we have learned about handling political risks is the importance of bringing new players into this arena as coverage providers. The new players are needed not only to add more capacity for existing types of coverages, but also to expand the types of coverage available and help develop new forms of protection. Fortunately, a substantial number of new players have been piling into the political risk arena since 1995. Their names are now familiar, including ACE, Exel, Sovereign, Chubb, CIGNA, Zurich Re, and AIG.

Perhaps the most important contribution of these new entrants has been to lead the way in pushing the edge of the envelope – lengthening the duration of coverages, widening the scope of risks covered, increasing the amounts of coverage available per project – beyond what traditional players had been willing to provide. Thanks to this new infusion of competition, even the traditional players have been dragged along and have expanded their own horizons.

With these considerations in mind, Enron is also working actively to try to help draw more new players into the political risk arena. Enron's special working group in Houston, which is developing the new hybrid insurance instruments I have already described, is also in discussion with a variety of new players about how they can become involved. One of the most important groups of potential entrants consists of onshore parties in the host countries where the infrastructure projects are located – local pension funds, financial institutions, and so on.

These parties offer two very important attractions. First, they have available financial capacity. As project sponsors, we have long tried to figure out how to tap that capacity for direct lending to infrastructure projects. The difficulty has been that the yield these parties needed to earn has been too high for the infrastructure projects to afford (especially as project economics get squeezed). However, if these parties take a more surgical role – bearing political risk exposure as a contingent liability – it may be possible to provide sufficient yield to them and still be affordable for the projects. Second, these parties offer important de facto political risk protection, beyond the actual coverage they may provide. A host government should be less likely to cause or allow problems for a project if doing so will hurt important local pension funds or financial institutions. And, if a host government does so anyway, the local parties should be in a stronger position to object and to help solve the problem.

In addition to local parties in the host countries, Enron is also seeking ways for non-insurance company capital market players to become involved in providing political risk protections. For example, we have been working with some investment banks to develop catastrophe bonds ("CAT bonds") modeled upon the CAT bonds created for hurricane and earthquake exposures, as well as certain types of derivatives (e.g., default swaps), for use in covering political risk exposure. Both of these will be discussed later.

So far, under current market conditions, we have not been able to make the numbers for these instruments price-competitive with insurance. However, the capital markets remain an important focus because market circumstances will change over time, because the capital markets' potential capacity is enormous (many, many times the size of the insurance markets), because the capital markets can handle risks of much longer duration than insurance markets have been willing to take, because the capital markets tend to be more readily receptive to new types of risks and structures than insurance markets have been, and because the capital markets offer liquidity that has not been available in the insurance markets. This leads to the fourth lesson.

Fourth Lesson: Need for Liquidity

The fourth, and final, lesson we have learned (so far) at Enron about handling political risk is that we really need to find ways to introduce liquidity into the protection mechanisms we use. In fact, this is part and parcel of being surgical about the protections we buy. Infrastructure projects typically take several years to put together, and have a project life of at least fifteen years – sometimes twenty years or more. During this time, a host country typically goes through quite a few election cycles, potentially a number of changes of government, potentially wide swings in economic conditions, and many other changes in circumstances – all of which can greatly affect the level of political risk faced by a project. In addition, the level of a project sponsor's economic stake in a project, and that project's importance in the sponsor's total portfolio of projects, can also vary greatly over the life of the project. Consequently, the amount of political risk protection it makes sense for a sponsor to buy, and the price it makes sense to pay for such protection, can also vary greatly over a project's life.

Traditional political risk protection mechanisms, however, do not allow a project sponsor to move in and out of coverage positions – i.e., do not provide liquidity. The traditional instruments are essentially rigid: they can only be put in place and left in place, or canceled *once*. Even some of the new instruments, such as the hybrid of risk transfer and risk financing that I described earlier, likewise lack flexibility. To overcome this rigidity, Enron is working on several avenues to introduce liquidity, including the use of credit derivatives (such as default swaps), use of the CATEX electronic trading forum for catastrophe risk exchanges, and development of our own political risk trading floor for two-way trading of country and political risk. Let me describe each of these very briefly.

Credit derivatives are financial instruments that isolate credit risk and package it into a tradable form. A default swap, for example, is functionally similar to an insurance contract, in that a protection-buyer (like an insured party) pays a set amount (like a premium) to a protection-provider (like an insurer) for the right to receive a lump sum (like an insurance claim) from the protection-provider if a specified default event (i.e., a covered risk) occurs before the swap expires (i.e., during the term of the coverage). The specified default event – or "default trigger" – can be something rather standardized, or can be highly customized, just as insurance policies can be standardized or customized.

Although there are plenty of naysayers who argue that credit derivatives are not suitable or useful for handling political risks, in fact such derivatives are already starting to take off. Already a very large volume of these instruments is being used to handle one of the key political risks – currency inconvertibility. That type of political risk lends itself to largely standardized derivative instruments. Although the duration of many of the inconvertibility swaps being done today is still only a few years, the volume of longer term swaps (up to ten years) is growing rapidly.

At Enron, we are also optimistic that credit derivatives can be developed to handle an even more difficult type of political risk – contract frustration or contract default. Such instruments may take the form of default swaps, total return swaps, credit-linked notes or other structures. As indicated earlier, contract frustration has become a top concern among project sponsors – ahead of expropriation risk, as such. The key challenge in using credit derivatives to cover contract default risks is that such derivatives must be customized (because contract terms, parties, and risks are different in each contractual arrangement), and this is proving to be a struggle.

The key difficulty causing this struggle is that the kinds of portfolio investors who would typically buy derivatives are not ones who are willing or able to get down and do the kind of project-by-project, or utility-by-utility, due diligence that traditional lenders and insurers would do. These portfolio investors are accustomed to looking at sovereign credits, and cannot afford the labor intensiveness of detailed analysis of state or municipal level credits, let alone of individual utilities or projects. Unfortunately, though, the risks of sovereign credits do not correlate well with state, local or project risks. As Enron learned first-hand when its Dabhol, India, project was stopped after a change in state government, an individual project stoppage – or even expropriation – can occur without being reflected at all in the host country's sovereign credit standing at the federal level. There is no automatic or predictable correlation.

Thus, the hurdle which must be overcome in order to begin using credit derivatives sensibly to handle customized risks like contract frustration is that some middle ground must be found. The trigger for the derivative must be something on which portfolio investors can readily obtain and evaluate sufficient information, yet not be so far removed from the project and contracts for which the risk protection is being sought that there is no correlation between them.

In larger countries, such as Brazil and India, one possibility may be to use a state or province's credit as the trigger. In theory, there would be at least some correlation between problems at the project level and at the state government level, since the projects' customers are utilities owned or controlled by the state. If the state ran into economic problems, one could anticipate problems with payment obligations at the project level. Likewise, if a major project within a state were stopped or expropriated, one could anticipate that that would loom large enough to affect the state's credit standing. At least the correlation would be greater than between the individual project level and the national level. Also, at least for major states in larger countries, credit information is increasingly readily available for portfolio investors to assess. With this information availability, a derivatives trigger (or reference asset) structured at the state level may be feasible for portfolio investors to evaluate and accept. For other (smaller) countries, potential solutions remain to be devised.

Despite these difficulties, credit derivatives (for both customized and standardized risks) as well worth the effort to develop them further. They can offer wide flexibility for use in as targeted a fashion as desired, and can provide the liquidity which is lacking in insurance arrangements.

For example, credit derivatives can be structured to use any specified event as the default trigger, and to cover any number of years desired – and even to cover only specified years (e.g., years 3–5 of a project's life). More importantly, such credit derivatives offer a way to move in and out of coverage positions whenever desired – not by unwinding positions (akin to canceling an insurance policy), with all the costs and difficulties that entails, but simply by entering into additional derivatives transactions which offset the original ones. Credit derivatives – like some of the other capital markets instruments (e.g., CAT bonds), mentioned earlier – can also provide an avenue for a whole new class of capital markets players to become involved in the political risk arena, players who may ultimately bring even more capacity to bear than insurance companies can. For all of these reasons, credit derivatives are attracting a lot of interest, and a lot of experimentation is under way to figure out how best to make use of them in all sorts of emerging markets projects, including infrastructure projects.

Another avenue for introducing both new players and liquidity into the realm of political risk is the Catastrophe Risk Exchange, or "CATEX." CATEX is an electronic trading forum that was originally designed to handle only hurricane and earthquake risks. In the course of several particularly bad occurrences (Hurricanes Andrew and Hugo), the losses went far beyond the ability of traditional primary insurers and reinsurers to handle them. New players and new methods of distributing the risks were needed.

As the process of organizing CATEX proceeded, starting in 1996, the founders quite sensibly began to realize that other categories of exposure besides hurricane and earthquake risk were very much in need of new outlets for coverage, too. Enron, among others, argued for the inclusion of political risks – which, after all, are similar to hurricane and earthquake risks, in that they are infrequent, highly severe when they do occur, and not susceptible to actuarial or other standard predictive modeling techniques. Ultimately, the CATEX founders decided to allow all types of risks to be posted and traded on CATEX. I am pleased to say that Enron is now one of the early subscribers to CATEX, and recently became the first party to post units of political risk on CATEX for placement through that electronic exchange.

Enron is quite excited about CATEX's potential for trading political risks for several reasons. CATEX provides a neutral, supervised electronic trading floor for two-way trades of "bite-size" ($1 million) units of risks. By breaking risks down into $1 million units, it becomes possible for many more players to participate. Insurance companies who are interested in taking on some political risk exposure for their portfolios, but who are not large companies, or who, regardless of their size, only want to "stick their toe in the water," can readily do so via CATEX. Each insurer can take on as many or as few units of risk as it wishes, regardless of the size of the project to which the risk relates, and many different insurers can take on limited pieces of the same project. This structure enables a lot of insurance companies who would otherwise be too small – or too reluctant due to lack of prior experience – to help provide some of the political risk coverage needed for infrastructure projects.

Furthermore, CATEX introduces liquidity: it provides a forum for *continuous two-way* trading of units of risk, thereby enabling companies to move in and out of coverage positions at will. As with derivatives, this need not be done by unwinding a coverage previously put in place (via CATEX or otherwise), but can simply be done by entering into additional trades which offset the original trades.

To date, CATEX has only allowed insurance companies, self-insured parties (captive insurance companies) and some insurance brokers to trade on its electronic exchange. However, CATEX will soon begin allowing capital markets players to begin trading on its exchange, too (as soon as certain legislative and regulatory changes are completed). This should add tremendous additional capacity. Moreover, the costs of trading through CATEX are quite modest, and we at Enron would strongly encourage anyone concerned about (or interested in) political risks to consider participating in CATEX.

Finally, a last example of new avenues for bringing in more capacity and more liquidity for political risk coverages is something Enron is working on in-house: the launch of a political risk trading book, much like our gas and electricity trading books. Enron pioneered the development of gas trading in the early nineties, began leading the development of electricity trading in the mid-nineties, and today is one of the market leaders, with large trading floors in both Houston and London. Enron is now studying the feasibility of setting up a political risk trading book similar to our gas and electricity trading books. This is a very labor intensive process and requires breaking considerable new ground – creating a proprietary database and proprietary methodology for risk analysis and pricing, as well as making maximum use of all potential new avenues for syndicating risks (CAT bonds, derivatives, MIGA CUP and other insurance, CATEX, etc.). Enron is quite hopeful that it will prove to be feasible to build a political risk trading book.

Conclusions

Based on the lessons we have learned, and continue to learn, in the marketplace, it is clear that new approaches to handling political risks – especially approaches that improve capacity, flexibility, and liquidity – are sorely needed. This need will be an ongoing one, and will be with us as long as market conditions continue to change and evolve. It will continue to take on increasing importance as project economics become ever more squeezed, leaving less and less room for any cushion against unexpected problems, while political risks remain as complex and vexing as ever. In short, project sponsors like Enron will continue to need all the help they can get from private lenders, multilateral and bilateral agencies, academics and others in devising new types of creative, cost-effective mechanisms for handling these risks.

III
Political Risk Insurance as a Tool to Manage International Political Risk

Theodore H. Moran

Overview

The international political risk insurance industry has undergone a transformation over the past decade.

Initially, as Malcolm Stephens, Secretary-General of the International Union of Credit and Investment Insurers (Berne Union), points out, coverage of political risks was largely considered a task for the public sector. The lumpiness, unpredictability, and duration of political risk makes it difficult to submit such business to actuarial analysis and pricing. Exposure could build up quickly and take a considerable period to subside, so that private insurers could not take their normal approach of breaking risky business into pieces and assuming only a small share of any large case. There was a general feeling that salvage or recovery could better be carried out by governments.

For many years the vast bulk of insurance against political risk, observes Stephens, has in fact been issued under export credit arrangements. Investment insurance was largely limited to expropriation, war or insurrection, and an inability to remit profits and dividends. Some insurers were prepared to provide coverage only if there was an investment protection agreement between the home country of the investor and the host, further supporting the view that political risk insurance was a public sector activity. Private sector underwriters did not want to be subject to political direction. There was little practical cooperation between public and private sector participants.

In the 1990s this began to change in fundamental ways.

Complementary Roles for Public and Private Sector Insurers

In 1990 private political risk insurers were few in number, the options they provided were limited, and the coverage they offered was short.[1] Even by 1994 the maximum periods of private sector cover for confiscation and for contract frustration still averaged around three years. By 1997, however, the number of participants was growing, capacity was rising, and maximum periods of private sector cover for contract frustration had been extended to five years and for confiscation to ten years.

The expansion of private sector participation in insuring political risks grew, in part, according to Charles Berry, Chairman of Berry, Palmer & Lyle, from the realization that high levels of uncertainty and the lack of a statistical base for calculating the exact probability of loss were not necessarily an insurmountable obstacle to the creation of an insurance market for a particular class of risk. Coverage for oil rigs in the North Sea and for satellites are examples, according to Berry, where insurance became available before a loss history could be firmly established. All that was fundamentally needed was a price at which buyers and sellers agreed to exchange a defined risk.

A second reason for private sector expansion came from the confirmation that adequate profits were available in the industry. When insurers like AIG (American International Group) can show a consistent track record of writing political risk coverage with a loss ratio under 40 percent, points out Berry, the possibilities for others "begin to attract some attention."

Finally, the problem of aggregation has become more manageable. A Tokyo earthquake or a major US East Coast windstorm can pose aggregation risks in the tens of billions of dollars, dwarfing political risk exposures, but the careful spreading of exposure among direct writers and reinsurers can make such aggregates digestible.

John Salinger, President of American International Group's Global Trade and Political Risk Insurance Company, estimates that there were 23 companies and 43 syndicates at Lloyd's underwriting political risk insurance in late 1997, and that it is possible to arrange as much as $1 billion in coverage on a single risk.

Looking to the future, Stephens and Berry agree, the growing willingness of the reinsurance market to take on significant amounts of risk is likely to reinforce the participation of the private sector, since this offers the possibility of breaking large transactions into relative small portions and spreading them over a large number of underwriters.

Rather than finding that private sector political risk insurers will simply replace public sector insurers, however, the two are likely to grow in tandem since they have distinctive and complementary roles to play.

These distinctive and complementary roles can be captured, according to Gerald West,[2] in an analogy derived from property insurance: "if both groups were property insurers, it could be said that one group installs lightning rods (i.e., provides service to mitigate the effects of a loss) and the other both installs lightning rods and seeks to influence the weather (i.e., to reduce the frequency of lightning strikes on the building)." In short, to the role of providing possible compensation when disaster strikes must be added the role of deterring the disaster from occurring in the first place.

In this context, the need for the continuing presence of public sector political risk insurers – national and multilateral – is likely to grow over time. As Stephens points out, like national and multilateral financial institutions, they represent a channel for potential leverage over host government actions via aid, trade, finance, and other political relationships that cannot be matched by private insurers.

Private insurers, argues West, are usually constrained from even revealing their presence by considerations of moral hazard: to the extent that the host authorities realize that the investor is insured, the more reckless various actors in the host country may potentially behave and the weaker the bargaining position of the investor against them may become. In many instances, therefore, even the existence of private insurance coverage must remain secret.

Public sector political risk insurers moreover have been adding a new dimension to their role of deterring unfavorable treatment of investors; namely, facilitating mutually acceptable settlement of host/foreign investor disputes. Out of four notifications of a potential claim at one large national insurer, for example, only one progressed as far as an actual claims payment, reports West; the other three were quietly settled before there was any loss.

The largest national investment insurance programs are located in Japan (the Export-Import Insurance Department/Ministry of International Trade and Industry, or EID/MITI), Germany (TREUARBEIT), the United States (OPIC), the UK (ECGD), France, and Canada. The Berne Union counts among its membership twenty-two national investment insurers. In some countries trade and investment insurance are provided via a single agency (e.g. the Export Credits Guarantee Department, or ECGD, in the United Kingdom, and Compagnie Francaise d'Assurance pour le Commerce Exterieur, or COFACE, in France). In other countries there are separate agencies for trade and finance, whose missions partly overlap (e.g. in the United States, the Overseas Private Investment Corporation, or OPIC, for investment, and the Export-Import Bank for trade and some project finance-related investment promotion as well).

These national programs offer long-term (15 to 20 years), non-cancelable coverage. They usually have eligibility restrictions as to national ownership and/or project attributes (e.g. that insured projects not displace jobs in the home economy). There may also be limitations as to country eligibility on human rights, nuclear non-proliferation, or other policy grounds.

A Growing Role for Multilateral Investment Guarantees and Political Risk Insurance

The multilateral financial institutions, led by the Multilateral Investment Guarantee Agency (MIGA) of the World Bank Group, provide political risk insurance with fewer restrictions on eligibility of projects or counties than many national programs.[3] MIGA fulfills this function by issuing guarantees to investors against losses resulting from four kinds of non-commercial risk:

1) Currency Transfer (inconvertibility). MIGA guarantees investors that they will be able to convert their local currency earnings into foreign exchange and that they will be able to export the foreign exchange from the country;

2) Expropriation. MIGA insures investors against the risk that they will be deprived of their property due to host government actions directed against the investors or due to a series of such actions that produce a similar cumulative outcome;
3) War and Civil Disturbance. MIGA insures investors against losses resulting from military operations or civil upheaval in the host country;
4) Breach of Contract. MIGA insures investors against breaches of contract on the part of the host authorities if the investor also is denied access to an appropriate adjudicative forum within a reasonable period of time or is otherwise denied the ability to enforce a favorable judgment regarding the breach.

MIGA only insures investments in countries that are members of MIGA. In addition, MIGA obtains the consent of the host government before issuing any insurance for an investment in the country. As in the case of the participation of World Bank group members in the financing of investment projects, the involvement of MIGA in any investment dispute provides a channel for the influence of fellow World Bank agencies (IBRD, IFC, and IDA) on host country behavior. In this context, even a relatively small amount of coverage can act as a "trip wire" to generate a disproportionate amount of disapproval toward host country damage to foreign investors.

Indicative of the synergies inherent in the intimate relationship among the members of the World Bank group is an experimental program in which the IBRD would provide a contingent loan to a host country to fund the host's obligations under coverage administered by MIGA. The World Bank would disburse funds under the contingent loan only if and when needed by MIGA to finance payments of claims by the investor. The country would be obligated to repay to the World Bank all amounts withdrawn under the contingent loan, or be in default to the Bank.

New Forms of Cooperation
Between Public and Private Sector Insurers

Public and private sector insurers/guarantee agencies have begun collaborating in novel ways that benefit each other. Beginning in 1997, for example, MIGA and ACE Limited, one of the largest private sector excess liability insurers, signed an agreement in which ACE will reinsure MIGA contracts of guarantee written for amounts exceeding $5 million. This relationship provides additional capacity for MIGA's clients without increasing MIGA's retained liability, and reduces MIGA's exposure to specific projects. It simultaneously extends the participation of private sector coverage up to 20 years, and adds the deterrent ingredients of the World Bank Group to that coverage.

In the same vein, MIGA has launched a cooperative underwriting program (CUP) in which MIGA issues a contract of guarantee for the amount of insurance requested by an investor, remains the insurer-of-record vis-a-vis both the investor and the host government, but retains only a portion of the amount for its own account. The remainder is assumed by one or more private insurers, using the wording of the MIGA contract.

The CUP approach allows private insurers to participate under the risk mitigating umbrella of MIGA (and its association with the broader World Bank Group) and enables them to benefit from MIGA's claims and recovery procedures and subrogation rights. The CUP format reduces administrative requirements since only one insurance contract is issued; it provides comfort to all parties that the project will meet World Bank enviornmental and developmental criteria. Finally, the CUP initiative offers some investors the possibility of allowing their own captive insurance companies to participate under the MIGA logo.

This cooperative impetus builds up capacity for expanded political risk coverage. It also, according to Charles Berry, provides stability and balance to the industry. If most national (or even multilateral) insurers had to pay a total loss on their largest policies, suggests Berry, the claim would exceed their annual premium income by a large multiple. A private sector syndicate such as Lloyds, in contrast, with a $50 million line for a particular political risk policy might well after reinsurance be retaining a net line of $2.5 million in the midst of annual premium income across all lines of $200-$300 million. A total loss on the $50 million policy might therefore affect the bottom line profit for the syndicate by less than one percent.

The Use of Political Risk Insurance by Banks and Other International Lenders

Many of the bank lenders who underwrite a substantial portion of the burgeoning amounts of project debt have an on-going need for political risk insurance, according to Robert Malleck, Vice President for Structured Finance at Citibank. The great majority of the 50 to 90 commercial banks who involve themselves in project finance are located in Europe. They face strict regulatory requirements with respect to provisioning their cross-border exposure. If a UK bank wishes to participate in the Lihir gold mine in Papua New Guinea, via a $20 million 12-year loan, for example, the Bank of England, in examining that bank's exposure in various classes of assets, might insist that the bank set aside funds to cover possible defaults, lowering its prospective returns. The easiest way to avoid direct provisioning is to purchase political risk insurance.

Political risk insurance also helps in leveraging available financing. Political risk insurance is often available for countries whose risk profile would otherwise not support large amounts of capital. The presence of political risk insurance supports longer maturities than might be impossible without it. Political risk insurance may in fact even be provided at rates subsidized either by the host or by various developed countries for strategic reasons. The multi-billion dollar Alumbrera mine in the Catamarca Province of Argentina, in an example provided by Malleck, received subsidized coverage from underwriters whose governments saw the importation of copper concentrate as a strategic interest for their economies.

In the petroleum, gas, and mining sectors, however, there may be a movement away from traditional commercial bank underwriting with political risk insurance to bonds and securitization of export receivables without political risk insurance. Building on the earlier analysis by Patrice Jordan of Standard & Poor's, Robert Malleck argues that where there are marketable, tradable, hedgeable commodities, with a contractor whose track record suggests building the plant to industry standards, on time, and within budget, with an operator who can manage the plant according to normal prudential guidelines for the industry, with an OECD creditworthy off-taker, and with the monies deposited into escrow accounts under the domain and control of the lenders, the contracts represent predictable obligations to pay and take and can be securitized in the form of project bonds. Such was the case in the financing of an Alcoa project in Brazil that Citibank led in 1996 where a $400 million issue of securitized export receivables with a 12-year maturity received a BBB rating from Standard & Poor's.

These project bonds and securitized off-takes may be structured with backloaded amortizations, so the net present values compare favorably to more traditional loan structures. They are increasingly appealing to high-yield bond dealers in the United States (where they satisfy 144-A requirements), in Europe, and in specialized markets such as among Islamic institutions in the Gulf.

The project bond markets and markets for securitized export receivables are able to absorb a good deal of political risk. If the lenders are not concerned about political violence in the country where the operation is located, or about old fashioned expropriation of the facility, then those lenders, according to Malleck, might well "get comfortable" proceeding without political risk insurance.

Finally, Citibank, like Enron, has been devoting a great deal of attention to the possibility of creating political risk derivatives. There are investors, in Robert Malleck's estimation, who would like to be "long" in exposure in one country and "short" in exposure in another country. Just as Linda Powers argued in Section Eight, this would add both liquidity and flexibility to political risk coverage. If political risk coverage could be standardized in some fashion and broken into pieces, large numbers of participants could acquire manageable bits of exposure as is already done for catastrophic natural risks like hurricanes and earthquakes. Simultaneously underwriters and insured parties could move into or out of paying for coverage as the circumstances surrounding long-term projects changes, and the price for coverage could fluctuate. Such flexibility is not available today. Instead the terms and conditions of political risk coverage are set for quite long-term projects at the moment the project is launched, without much possibility of adjustment thereafter.

Political Risk and Political Risk Insurance in the Future

"I think that those who dismiss political risk as a diminishing threat," argues John Salinger, "will reevaluate their assessment."

"Political risks are not a thing of the past," asserts Malcolm Stephens. "The next ten years are unlikely to be like the last ten years. In my view, they will be far more risky for investors and lenders."

In particular, points out Salinger, while project finance is not an entirely new concept, it represents "unfamiliar territory" for most political risk insurers and reinsurers. There are complicated new types of exposure, over unprecedentedly lengthy periods of time.

The three-year barrier for private investment insurance coverage was breached only recently, and many underwriters, according to Salinger, appear to have made adjustments no more profound than crossing out the number "three" on their slips and writing "ten" years or longer in its place.

In the midst of this expansion and innovation in the political risk investment insurance field, a number of questions and concerns have arisen. Three of the most crucial involve the targeting of political risk coverage, the utilization of insurance for breach of contract, and the provision for inactions as well as actions on the part of sub-national and national authorities.

Questions and Concerns for the Future

First, can political risk coverage be appropriately defined and targeted in ways that meet the needs of both insurers and investors?

Charles Berry points out the potential difficulty of distinguishing between the good faith and the good credit of a government. Some of the commitments that hosts make to project sponsors are regulatory in nature (e.g., to set certain tariffs or to grant certain tax reliefs) and as such involve only the good faith of the government. Other commitments that hosts make to project sponsors, he argues, might better be considered a blend of political and commercial obligations (e.g., to supply power or to maintain transport services), and as such involve the good judgment of government not to over-commit itself.

Over 90 percent of the more than 120 paid political risk losses at Berry, Palmer & Lyle, since 1993, he reports, have arisen from public sector "insolvency," where a government buyer or supplier was unable to meet all of its obligations in full and on time, defaulting because of over-commitment on the part of the authorities. The insurer needs to assess just how extensive his exposure is to economic misjudgment when he writes a policy ostensibly focused on political risk.

Andrea MacDonald of Exxon poses a variant of the same difficulty of targeting coverage, suggesting that the definition of political risks is liable to be too narrow or too broad to provide effective protection for the buyer.

Political risk insurance contracts, in her assessment, are built around "but-for clauses" – "but for this political event" the operation of the project would be proceeding smoothly. If a disruption is caused by events in which the actors claim to be motivated by environmental concerns, on the one hand, or by labor grievances, on the other, however, the coverage may not be triggered.

This leads some project sponsors to despair that political risk insurance will be of much use for them, she observes, because either they must purchase coverage for all conceivable eventualities or else they must face a substantial likelihood that their claims will be denied.

Clearly issues of defining contingencies and targeting coverage will continue to preoccupy both buyers and sellers of political risk insurance.

Second, how can political risk coverage be focused in the most useful way on the issue of breach of contract?

MIGA coverage for breach of contract, for example, hinges on whether the investor is denied access to a forum for arbitration within a reasonable period of time and/or denied the ability to enforce a favorable arbitral judgment.

John Salinger argues that this indirect approach is the most promising path for private sector coverage of breach of contract and contract frustration as well: the key issues in breach of contract and contract frustration are the creditworthiness of the counter-party, the enforceability of the contract, and the path of remedy; if private insurers cannot achieve recoveries of losses they pay out, they do not have a viable business. The model of simply insuring a contract that stipulates ten cents per kilowatt hour against renegotiation to nine cents per kilowatt hour, he asserts, is not a viable proposal.

But, counters Andrea MacDonald of Exxon, the most frequent cases of breach of contract involve something like arbitrarily raising a royalty rate from 5 percent to 10 percent, which may not destroy the viability of the project, but which may indeed reduce the internal rate of return substantially. Going through arbitration, losing, and then turning the project over to the insurers for recovery, she asserts, is simply not a viable path for the investor to try to cope with such a risk (especially since the insurance coverage is likely to be only a small fraction of the value of the entire operation).

Moreover, adds Linda Powers of Enron, the negotiating position of a host government that tampers with the operating arrangements of an investor who is sitting on top of a capital intensive project with large fixed costs may be quite strong. The pressure on the investor to keep the operation going by giving in to some "compromise" on new contractual conditions, rather than standing pat on principle as operating losses pile up, is intense. By the time arbitration has been sought and remedy secured, the accumulation of red ink can be formidable.

Thus there are doubts that the predominant model for insuring against breach of contract is in fact appropriate for dealing with any but the most egregious scenarios of contract frustration.

Perhaps Robert Shanks has identified the key ingredient that may make coverage of breach of contract more effective, namely, progress in streamlining the arbitral process itself via speedy and reliable mediation or dispute resolution mechanisms.

Third, can political risk insurance be effectively written to cover inactions as well as actions, and be extended to include actions and inactions of subnational entities?

Malcolm Stephens points out that the viability of a project can depend on insuring against inactions as well as actions taken by host authorities: tax breaks not being allowed to lapse, export or import duties being waived (not being applied), licenses being routinely granted (not being scrutinized or questioned). This illustrates a much more complicated environment of uncertainty about public sector actions/inactions than merely having the government as seller of the input to an investor buyer or an output from an investor.

John Salinger points out that the principal interlocutor in many infrastructure projects is likely to be a sub-sovereign entity. The underwriter has to consider what leverage he has to enforce performance, and, if he pays a claim, what rights of subrogation he enjoys and how valuable they are, at the state or municipal as well as national levels.

What authority, then, asks Malcolm Stephens, can make a commitment to abstain from both actions and inactions on both the national and sub-national level? Who can sign a letter "committing" the entire array of host authorities to certain behavior in all relevant contexts?

Related to this, add Stephens, is the non-trivial issue of "documentation risk." Who among the insurers, financial intermediaries, and sponsors, will assume responsibility for the writing of such complicated coverage under a complex set of contingencies? If a claim arises because a document is faulty or not enforceable who is liable?

Since documents in project financings can be a meter or so high, Stephens points out, and since in some countries key aspects of the "new" legal framework may not be clear or have not been tested, whether or not every insurer and every financial actor will vet every single document of all other parties is an important question for the speed and effectiveness of the process.

Yet if political risk insurance, project finance, and foreign direct investment in natural resource and private infrastructure projects are to continue to grow together in the future, as they have in the past, procedures will have to be worked out to apportion risk and responsibility among the parties themselves who are attempting to launch these important and promising new ventures.

Notes

[1] Kit Brownlees, "A Private Market Comes of Age," *Reinsurance* (June 1997).
[2] Gerald T. West, "Managing Project Political Risk; The Role of Investment Insurance," *The Journal of Project Finance* (Winter 1996).
[3] Benoit, op. cit.

9
A Perspective on Political Risk Insurance
Malcolm Stephens[*]

Introduction

The first section of this paper will try briefly to set out the present position and how and why we have reached it. The second section will try to describe some of the changes which are taking place. The third section will attempt to assess the importance of these changes and how they might develop over the next few years.

Four Key Points

My four main general points are:

(i) Political risks are not a thing of the past.
(ii) Political risks are themselves undergoing great changes.
(iii) There is now an uncomfortably wide gray area between political risks and commercial risks – what, for example, is the risk of a Government entity breaking an "undertaking" which may have been a crucial part of the security package for a project financing?
(iv) The next ten years are unlikely to be like the last ten years. In my view, they will be far more risky for investors and lenders.

These may well not be thought to be surprising coming from an insurer!

_____

  [*] *Malcolm Stephens is the Secretary General, Berne International Union of Credit and Investment Insurers. The views in this paper are personal and are not intended to reflect the position of the Berne Union or any or all of its Members.*

The Past

Political Risks: General

With a few exceptions, it is almost certainly not a gross distortion to say that the conventional wisdom has been that political risks – and especially those outside the area of short-term trade finance – have been seen as an area for government and the Public Sector rather than for private sector insurers and, especially, reinsurers.

It is, perhaps, less easy to say why this has been the case, but there are probably ten main reasons:

(i)   The risks were felt to be unpredictable and thus not subject to commercial/actuarial analysis (and pricing).

(ii)   The risks often come in very large lumps (i.e. high-value contracts or projects or investments).

(iii)   These risks frequently had very long tails (i.e. the period of cover sought from insurers could spread over 15 years if both the construction/manufacturing and the credit periods were included).

(iv)   The cases often arose in very difficult/high-risk developing country markets where the private insurance market had both little experience and little risk appetite.

(v)   There was felt to be an unacceptable level of aggregation risk (i.e. that overall exposure could both build up "too quickly" on a buying country and also take "too long" to run off).

(vi)   The belief (quite wrong in my view) that, if a buying country had problems, then all business done in that country would go into default of various kinds and so lead to claims.

(vii) Taken together, these factors could produce unbalanced portfolios.

(viii) As another generalization, there was perhaps also some feeling that the nature of the major risks involved probably mean that salvage or recovery was better carried out by governments (either bilaterally or as part of a formal inter-governmental group) rather than by private loss adjusters.

(ix)   Finally, the few insurers in the market and the almost total absence of any kind of substantial or credible reinsurance market meant that private insurers could not apply their normal approach (i.e. breaking into pieces and only taking a "small" share of any large case).

(x)   Arguably, the point that this kind of underwriting was increasingly done in the public sector and/or the fact that some of the key decisions (including on premium) were taken by governments probably made the view that such risks were, somehow, inherently not "commercial" and so not "appropriate" to the private sector – a self-fulfilling belief and thus a fact.

The main result of these factors was the establishment and spread of Export Credit Agencies and Investment Insurers which were either government/public sector bodies or who wrote the business on behalf of, or on the account of, their governments.

To this extent, export credit and investment insurance underwriting decisions were increasingly seen as being taken for political reasons of various kinds. As noted, this inevitably led to this class of risk business being regarded as unsuitable or inappropriate for the private sector and so, effectively, to no real competition from the private sector.

Investment Insurance

It is important to make clear at the outset that investment insurance and political risk insurance are NOT the same. In crude terms, investment insurance is one form of political risk insurance. It is not so much that investment insurance and political risk insurance are different but that the former is but one form of the latter.

Traditionally, there has been felt to be a clear difference between investment insurance and, on the other hand, export credit insurance.

Export credit insurance was associated with the sale of goods and services or loans to finance such sales. Thus there were clear repayment dates and the risks covered by Export Credit Agencies normally embraced both commercial risks and political risks.

In the last 20 years, the terms of export credit support for medium- and long-term credit have been subject to the terms of the OECD Consensus which sets out, for example, the maximum length of credit, the minimum down payment, the profile of repayments, the starting point for credit and the minimum interest rate which can be "supported."

For investment insurance, on the other hand, the cover was applied to equity investments where there were no fixed repayment schedules and where the risks covered were both limited and political only.

In other words, not only were commercial risks excluded, but the political risks covered were normally restricted to three, i.e.:

(i)   Nationalization or expropriation without compensation;
(ii)   War or civil war; and
(iii)   Inability to transfer or remit profits and dividends.

One "organizational" result of this was that either investment insurance and export credit insurance were done in different organizations, (e.g. OPIC and US EXIMBANK in the United States) or the insurance cover was subject to totally different facilities within the same organization and were managed and operated by separate underwriters, often in separate "units."

Investment insurance has not been subject to the OECD Consensus and, for so long as it was restricted to equity investment, this did not matter.

However, as explained in the next section, some investment insurers are now prepared to look at providing investment insurance cover or investment insurance-type cover for loans as well as equity and to look at covering political risks which go rather wider than those set out above (e.g. breaches of host government undertakings or other political events leading to non-payment of an insured loan into a project).

One result of this has been the development of a gray area between investment insurance and export credit insurance.

In addition, it has also led to some confusion by people who use the phrase "political risk insurance" to refer only to Investment Insurance, when, in practice, the vast bulk of insurance against political risks has, in the past, been issued under export credit arrangements.

For various reasons – some of which are not immediately obvious – the level of business done by investment insurance has, with one or two exceptions, been rather lower than might have been expected. This is, perhaps, partly due to the fact that in many OECD countries the bulk of direct investment in the past has tended to go to other OECD countries, rather than to developing countries.

But this also suggests that, in the past, the existence of investment insurance has not been a major factor in the decisions of investors on whether or not to make an investment. No doubt this is partly because investment insurance cover, as noted above, still leaves the investor with the whole range of commercial risks and, in many developing countries, these risks were felt to have been unacceptable.

In addition, a number of investment insurers have only been prepared to provide cover if there is in existence an Investment Protection Agreement between the investing country and the host country. *Inter alia*, this tended to enhance the view that the insurance was, inherently, a public sector activity.

In summary, I suppose that the main points from the sections above are: first, that there has, traditionally, been little appetite for political risks in the private sector. Second, a fairly clear distinction existed between export credit insurance and investment insurance. Third, little practical cooperation existed between insurers in the private sector and the public sector, essentially, in my view, because the public sector underwriters felt that this business was not really of interest to the private sector, whilst private sector underwriters tended to feel that the public sector underwriters either did not do it "properly" or were too subject to political direction or interference.

All of these factors are now subject to significant change and challenge.

The Present

Short-Term Trade Finance

One of the most interesting and important developments of the recent past has been the increasing willingness of private sector insurers and, particularly, reinsurers to cover political risks in relation to short-term trade finance type business. The maximum exposure has been six months and there has been some tendency for insurers seeking reinsurance to put together the political and commercial risks and to seek a combined reinsurance package for the two. The main motivation for this action has probably been two-fold:

First, the view of a number of governments that, generally, they want to reduce their activities and the consequent feeling that, if an activity could be carried out in the private sector, then it should not be carried out in the public sector and that the public sector should not somehow crowd out or even compete with the private sector. This trend was given impetus by developments within the European Union and also by the decision in the UK to privatize the short-term business of its export credit agency, ECGD. Within the European Union, these developments led to the development of the concept of "Marketable Risks" which were felt to be those risks which were acceptable to the private sector insurers/reinsurers and "Non-Marketable Risks" which were felt to be appropriate to governments on the basis that they were not acceptable to the private sector. One of the difficulties has, in my view, been that these concepts, if they are to be of any value, cannot be static and must reflect the evolution of the private sector. They should not stultify or inhibit the development of the private sector. In addition, it is one thing for the European Commission to say what cannot be done by or in the private sector, but it is simply not the way that markets work for the European Commission to purport to say what will be done in the private sector. These are business decisions which will be taken by private sector parties themselves, namely in this context whether or not they (as insurers or reinsurers) find certain risks acceptable or not.

Secondly, the development of export credit insurers who operate outside their own borders and who want to offer to customers – and especially large multinational companies – facilities to embrace both domestic trade and exports from any country to any country. Such arrangements could hardly be structured on the basis of government or public sector reinsurance (which is available only for "national" exports of goods and services) and so there have been strong marketing reasons for the development of totally private insurance arrangements with no government involvement of any sort. It is, for example, now estimated that up to 20 underwriters or underwriting institutions are offering this kind of cover in the London market alone and, more importantly, that 85 percent of short-term export credit insurance within and out of the European Union is carried out by the private sector.

Project Business

Because, *inter alia*, of the international debt crisis of the eighties, there has been significant disenchantment with sovereign guarantees, both from those who gave them and those who received them or regarded them as the main security for their activities. In addition, more and more governments are being encouraged by the international financial institutions and others to privatize and decentralize and to disengage from industrial and commercial activities.

This had led to the rapid development of project financing. Put simply, the main difference between a project financing and a more conventional financing for a project is that, in the latter, the lender or insurer looks primarily to the strength of the buyer/borrower/guarantor for security whilst, in the former, the main security are the cash flows and viability of the project itself.

Thus, an increasingly large percentage of project business coming forward is primarily on a private sector or privatized basis and this has produced significant challenges for all parties, including both export credit insurers and investment insurers.

Another aspect of this development has been that the "political risks" involved have changed.

It is not only a question of what might be thought of as the "traditional" political risks including those referred to earlier, but also a range of new political risks which could impact on the ability of borrowers in a project financing to generate sufficient income to repay loans.

For example, in many projects, a key point in the security package will be the willingness of the host government to allow tariffs (e.g. for telecommunications or electricity or water projects) to be adjusted to whatever level is necessary to repay foreign creditors. When, for example, in a country there is a shortage of foreign exchange for whatever reason and where there is then a significant depreciation in the local currency and where a project may earn no foreign currency, there may be some doubt about the willingness of host governments, in practice, to see tariffs for sensitive items like water or power increase substantially for domestic consumers (who are also voters) simply in order to repay foreign creditors.

These questions come into sharper focus following recent events in South East Asia where exchange rate depreciations have exceeded 40 percent. Thus projects which have income in local currency and debts in foreign exchange are uncomfortably vulnerable to the consequences of liberalized and open economies and especially to flexible exchange rates.

For more detailed comments on project financing and the export credit agencies/investment insurers, see Appendix A to this paper.

Investment Insurance

As noted earlier, one of the most interesting recent developments has been the willingness of investment insurers to look at covering some new or additional risks in project financing and also to give cover to loans as well as on equity investments. But this is not the whole or even, probably, the most important development. There is an increasing willingness on the part of private sector underwriters to give cover on a growing range of political risks.

Traditional inhibitions against large exposures or long horizons of risks or to underwriting certain risks such as war risks or transfer risks have been softened, not least since the belief has grown among private sector insurers that investment insurance has been quite good business for public sector insurers in the past and this makes it even more attractive to private sector institutions who are actively looking for new sources of premium income.

It is important to note that the percentage of foreign direct investment which is insured is rather low. For example, a high level of investment insurance by Berne Union investment insurers (see Appendix B) would be $20 billion in one year. No doubt this is partly because commercial risks are not covered.

In summary, the main points which flow from these developments are the cluster of reasons which have led the private sector to take an increasing interest in underwriting political risks, the evolution of new financing structures for project business in particular and the underlying fact that, for most insurers and reinsurers, the last three or four years have been rather good ones for those who have underwritten political risks.

One of the key and most fascinating questions which this produces is how effectively the private sector and the public sector insurers can cooperate and to what extent they will – or will be allowed to – compete.

In addition, there must be a question about whether or not in a world of overlap between investment insurance and export credit insurance, the former can much longer be excluded from the requirements/rigors of the OECD Consensus relating to repayment terms.

Collaboration in terms of business actually signed, remains at a rather low level, but is a key area for the future. Common wording or a willingness to accept the wording of others is a vital area, but so are premium rates and "respect" for the underwriting of others.

One other key point is that there are serious risks of host governments or public sector bodies breaking "undertakings" which may have been of central importance in project financing. Whether or not these are political or commercial risks is, in my view, of considerably less importance than whether insurers are prepared to underwrite such risks or not.

The Future

A Basic Question

I suppose that some people would say that one of the most important questions for the future is why the private sector apparently now feels able to underwrite political risks on some scale when this has not been the case in the past. However, in my view, the much more important question is why it has taken the private sector so long to come into this area!

It has, as noted above, traditionally been the case that political risks have been said to be "too unpredictable" for the private sector. But, are political risks really any more unpredictable than earthquakes or hurricanes or two jumbo jets crashing over New York? I would argue that many political risks are indeed more predictable than such events.

The fundamental change seems to me to be that not only are private insurers now prepared to look at these risks but, very importantly, there is a growing capacity and willingness in the reinsurance market to take such risks. This offers the possibility of breaking large transactions into relatively small packets and spreading them over a large number of underwriters, both insurance and reinsurance.

A key point for the future is what happens with regard to these risks. If there are no problems, investors may want little or no insurance and so demand will fall and so will supply. If, however, there are serious problems and large claims then the effect on the private insurers and their reinsurers could be swift and significant. This, perhaps obvious, point really demonstrates the importance of risk and uncertainty.

It may well be true that old style expropriation will not quickly reoccur. But I believe strongly that "squeezing" of various sorts will grow. Whether or not this will be seen as creeping expropriation by insurers is a good – and far from academic – question.

A Watershed?

If I am right in this view, then what is taking place represents some kind of watershed or sea change in the way in which political risk business is done. I do not myself subscribe to the view that, as soon as there are any claims, then the insurers and reinsurers from the private sector will disappear. This is surely a misreading of the nature of insurance and the business sense of those in the private sector who carry out the activity.

In other words, insurers and reinsurers know that a business which never gives rise to claims is a business which will constantly be at risk either to other insurers offering lower premium rates or, probably more dangerously, to insured parties engaging in "self insurance" – in other words, not seeking insurance cover from anyone. Thus insurers and reinsurers expect to pay claims – the key point is that claims should not, regularly, exceed premium income.

In addition, and very importantly, there is now a clear sign of the capital markets being willing to finance/fund quite substantial projects via bonds without seeking traditional or, indeed, any insurance facilities.

This is of course one form of "self insurance," but the fact that so many bond market investors are no longer afraid of lending into "Emerging Markets," must have some effect on the position of political risk underwriters both in the private sector and in the public sector. The capital markets are now willing not only to take project risks, but also to take the pre-completion or pre-credit risks which arise before a project is completed and comes on stream.

Two very important advantages for the capital markets are first that – unlike the export credit agencies – they are not interested in the source of the goods and services used in the construction of the projects and, second, that the finance will not be subject to the restrictions on credit terms and the profile of repayment imposed on the export credit agencies by the OECD Consensus. Thus, the capital markets could, if they were happy with the credit, do, say, 15-year bullet payments.

However, I sometimes have the feeling that some capital market lenders and bond holders believe that if countries get into difficulties or run short of foreign exchange, then they will get a free ride and other creditors – especially banks and official creditors – will take the strain. This seems to be grounded on the view that we shall all see turmoil in the capital markets as unacceptable. I believe they are wrong and that if – as I think is certain – some countries do get into foreign exchange difficulties in future, then all creditors will be expected/required to share in the pain and grief.

This is an especially relevant point as the composition of the external debt of many countries changes and, in particular, as bank debt falls and bond debt and linked outflows on investment rise.

I cannot resist noting, in passing, that these kind of developments pose important questions, not only for the export credit agencies but also for the international financial institutions and for the World Bank in particular. In other words, what is their role in a world where so many projects are handled on a private or privatized basis?

Another interesting development has been the soon to be finalized agreement within the OECD on minimum premium rates. Depending on where these are set, they will offer the possibility for private sector insurers – who, unlike export credit agencies, are not subject to the OECD Consensus – to undercut the premium rates being offered by official insurers for business in "low risk" countries. They could also make the cost of "uninsured" funding from the capital markets more attractive to borrowers/buyers.

For official insurers, one of the key issues is that they no longer have a monopoly product. This leads on to the – no longer academic or theoretical question – of whether they are happy to be the insurer of last resort taking only business or risks that no one else wants?

A Dilemma for Export Credit Agencies

For many official insurers, their "mandates" from their governments are likely to be under strain. In other words, many have the dual objective of breaking even over time, but not competing with the private sector and, in some ways, being the "insurer" of last resort. In particular, if official insurers are to break even, then they, like any insurers, need a spread of risk and so it is very difficult for them both to break even and also not to seek to do any business if the private sector is prepared to do it. Thus, one of the interesting questions will inevitably be the extent to which the private sector and the public sector can both cooperate and compete.

In the area of investment insurance, there are already clear signs of a much greater willingness on both the part of private insurers and public insurers to cooperate. Most substantial Berne Union members are also engaged in cooperation with each other and have actually reached the stage of issued countries.

A rather striking – and potentially very significant – example of cooperation between public and private sectors was the recent Quota Share Treaty Reinsurance Agreement between MIGA and the ACE Insurance Company of Bermuda. ACE will reinsure the full terms extended by MIGA both with respect to the spread of risks covered and horizon of risk.

However, I think it is difficult to work on the basis that private sector insurers can somehow require or expect that, if they are willing to do certain cases or certain categories of business, then the public sector insurers must, unilaterally, withdraw from these areas. This is one of the key constraints on collaboration and cooperation. In other words, if the private insurers see the role and objective of the public insurers to "cooperate" themselves out of business so as to leave the whole area for only the private sector, it is scarcely surprising that there is some tension and some hesitancy on the part of public insurers in full and unfettered cooperation!

This may, in turn, throw emphasis not only on what is and what is not fair competition, but on what competition between a private and a public insurer really means or involves. For example, private sector insurers are required to pay taxes and are subject to "Insurance Regulators." Many public insurers are not subject to these requirements. Many public insurers have facilities which attract "zero weighting" or nil provisioning from banks who lend on the basis of their facilities.

Conclusion

It is, I think, by no means certain how some of these questions will be answered or some of these problems solved. But, in my view, they cannot simply be ignored or swept under the carpet. Personally, I believe that it is a very good thing that new underwriters – especially from the private sector – have begun to underwrite political risks. But I also believe in competition and not the simple exchange of one kind of monopoly for another.

Who could ever oppose cooperation; it ranks with motherhood and apple pie! But cooperation needs trust on both sides and some degree of shared objectives. Who does it really help for public insurers to be reduced to the status of last resort insurers doing only business that no other underwriter will do?

In other words, cooperation, to be real, must mean more than one party withdrawing when the other party appears. Cooperation must, in my view, be a continuing relationship. It must extend well beyond the issue of an insurance policy document, in a particular case. There needs, for example, to be shared views on claims and salvage.

If it really happened that official insurers withdrew automatically when others appeared, then official insurers and their owners (e.g. governments and taxpayers) would almost be certain to face losses and thus face closure by finance ministries not looking for new ways to spend (or lose) taxpayers' money. The level of business public insurers did and so the level of their premium income could be so low as to make it impossible for them to keep in place the basic "infrastructure" of skills and expertise and resources so as both to give a good or acceptable level of service to customers or to be able to handle any upturn in demand if the level of business grew especially if, for whatever reason, private sector underwriters became less willing to do the business.

Put starkly, if official insurers simply withdrew because some other insurer was prepared to write the business, a number of consequences would follow. For example:

(a) Customer choice would disappear or be reduced.
(b) Official insurers would have little or no spread of risk and horrible concentration of risk and exposure.
(c) Sooner or later, starved of premium income, official insurers would not have the income to keep a basic infrastructure of staff and expertise in place. This would not easily or quickly be re-created or re-established.

I am not sure that I agree with the popular view that the more insurers or lenders (including the international financial institutions) which are involved in a case the better. Large numbers of insurers, lenders and the various international financial institutions would inevitably mean that there would be complexity of almost geometric progression proportions and it would, in my view, be very difficult to keep creditors together, especially if some claimed "preferred" status of various kinds.

Overall, I think that the one certainty is that, in terms of the Chinese proverb, all of us who work in this area will certainly be living in interesting times!

APPENDIX A:
How Different Export Credit Agencies (ECAs) Approach Project Risk

This Appendix tries to cover four main areas:

1. Very short background on Export Credit Agencies (this includes Eximbanks).
2. Some comments on the export credit/political risk and export/project finance world or at least this world as seen from the Export Credit Agencies.
3. Some general comments on some developing trends in the financing of projects.
4. Cofinancing between Export Credit Agencies and the international financial institutions/multilaterals.

Export Credit Agencies: General

It is important to stress at the outset – there is no such thing as a typical export credit agency. They come in all shapes and sizes: some are parts of government and some are private companies. It is, therefore, very dangerous to generalize about them. However, they are involved in very substantial activities, by any standards. Each year the more than 46 ECAs who belong to the Berne Union:

(a) support exports with a value of about $420 billion.
(b) insure or finance projects in non OECD countries of over $100 billion.
(c) insure outward direct investment of $15–20 billion.

Thus their role in world trade as a whole is vital and especially in the financing of projects in East Europe and in non-OECD countries where it is of quite central importance.

Export Credit Agencies (ECA) traditionally give insurance or guarantees to either or both of exporters who are supplying or constructing projects or to the banks who are providing the loans to finance the projects. Traditionally the ECA cover embraces both political and commercial risks. This insuring activity would, for example, typically be that of COFACE of France, HERMES of Germany, SACE of Italy, ECGD of the UK, EID/MITI of Japan, and CESCE of Spain. However, some ECAs are also direct lenders (e.g. US Eximbank, EDC of Canada and EFIC of Australia) and some like OeKB of Austria refinance lending for medium- and long-term credits already made by commercial banks.

The one generalization I can safely make in this area is that medium- and long-term political risks insured by the ECAs are invariably taken, ultimately by their governments. In the past, this has not been an area in which private sector insurers or reinsurers were really interested – although many ECAs would welcome some competition or someone with whom to share the burden/risks. However, this may now be changing.

Many Export Credit Agencies also provide investment insurance against the main political risks (e.g. transfer of profits and dividends, expropriation/nationalization, and war/civil war).

Some Relevant Background Features/Factors

The export credit world has been a changing one for as long as I can remember! However, it is probably true that the changes have in recent years seemed more rapid and more significant. Four strands seem especially significant.

The first strand concerns the debt crisis. Many ECAs have suffered the consequences of the series of debt crises. This has meant that for some years they have paid claims which are in excess of their premium income and most of them – at least in respect of their medium and long-term credit activities – have accumulated deficits. In addition, in recent years as there has been some tendency towards "debt forgiveness" under Toronto and Trinidad and Naples terms, the recoverability of some claims they have paid has worsened/disappeared with a consequent impact on the finances and balance sheets of the ECAs.

Against this background, most ECAs have had to review both the level of their premium rates and the amount of new cover they have been able to provide.

The second strand concerns what might be called "International Discipline." There has for some time been – more or less – general agreement that a credit war or international export credit subsidy war is not a great idea, especially from the point of view of tax payers of exporting countries.

Thus, largely in the forum of the OECD, there has been a pretty consistent trend – using the vehicle of the OECD Consensus – to squeeze interest rate subsidies out of the system. Thus, the special fixed export credit interest rates for credits of more than two years have been brought closer and closer to market rates. This trend continues.

However, as blanket subsidies were squeezed out, the temptation was to introduce selective subsidies, largely through the use of blending aid and export credit in, so called "Mixed Credits." But these too are now subject to increasing scrutiny, prior notification, reporting and control/discipline. This trend also continues.

The new development is the recognition of the importance of the difference between premium rates for medium- and long-term credit and the "distortion" which the disparities between premium rates causes. While these developments are not likely to produce "harmonized" premium rates, there will be minimum or floor premium rates and thus much greater similarity between premium rates from different ECAs.

The third "strand" concerns competition. In the past, ECAs tended to be "national" and competition was between countries. However, especially in the area of short-term export credit, the role of governments is being reviewed in many countries and one result is increased competition for business between insurers and thus between ECAs. Contrary to some popular beliefs, the phenomenon is not restricted to the UK in particular or the European Union in general. It goes far wider than this.

Fourthly, the private sector (both insurers and reinsurers) is – at long last some would say! – now showing increasing interest and activity in the area of political project/investment risks. This, coupled with the risk-taking appetite of the banks and capital market lenders, mean that the ECAs are not the only "show in town."

General Trends in Financing Projects

The traditional security for ECAs in projects in non-OECD countries has been government or sovereign guarantees.

However, one important background trend as noted above has been the large number of buying/borrowing countries who have defaulted and have gone to the Paris Club to reschedule their debts. This, and the trend to debt reduction and debt forgiveness, has meant that ECAs have paid huge claims ($150 billion over the last ten years or so) and most have suffered substantial losses.

The impact of this on ECAs and their governments remains substantial. ECAs are not, I stress, aid agencies – they are expected by GATT/WTO and their Ministries of Finance and Parliaments to break even. And thus inevitable disenchantment and poor experience with sovereign guarantees has coincided with the shift in a very large number of countries to privatization.

Privatization in its many manifestations has, in my view, had a major impact on how projects are financed. With increasing frequency, the host government is no longer willing to be the borrower or guarantor of repayment for lending into projects.

Together, these factors have resulted in much greater interest in project financing, or limited recourse financing, where the main security for the insurer or lender is the cash flow of the project rather than the financial strength of the buyer or guarantor. However, like many things in life, this is easier said than done.

Project financing present a whole new range of challenges and problems not only to ECAs and banks, but also to exporters/contractors and lawyers.

Political Risks: General

As a general rule, it is in the area of political risks that ECAs are most experienced. However, that is very far from the same thing as saying that there are a clearly defined set of risks which are universally accepted as political risks.

I should also note in passing that it is misleading to think or work in terms of political risks arising only in developing or non-OECD countries – what about the risks stemming from radical new environment laws or requirements in California on a half-completed power project?

At this point, I should stress a significant difference between Export Credit Agencies. There are, perhaps, two main approaches: (a) the UK, US, Japan, and Canada who (either lend directly or) usually give 100 percent and unconditional guarantees to lending banks; and (b) the French, Germans, Italians who give conditional insurance and less than 100 percent cover. But in the case of insurance and, especially where risk sharing is involved, it is necessary to be as clear as possible as to which risks are covered; and here, as in so many contexts, it is not a good idea to wait for a default and a claim to find out if a risk is insured/covered.

It may help to demonstrate the point if I caricature it. The banks would probably prefer an approach which specifies the risks which are not covered and to regard them as commercial risks and then for all other risks to be political and thus for the Export Credit Agencies to cover. The Export Credit Agencies, on the other hand, would prefer the political risks covered to be listed and all other risks to be commercial and for the banks to bear.

Political Risks: Specific Examples

Let me take two points, again to illustrate some of the problems:

(a) Who takes the documentation risk – is all or any part of this a political risk?
(b) Is any action or inaction of a government by definition a political risk?

"Documentation" Risk. For many Export Credit Agencies the traditional policy has been that the banks and exporters are responsible for their own documents and thus, if a claim arises because a document is faulty or not enforceable, this is not an insured risk. Thus, if an ECA stipulates a particular kind of guarantee, it will not "vet" or approve the guarantee from a bank or borrower at the time it is obtained. The key stage is then the claims stage.

Obviously, for project financing this is a very important issue, not only since the documents can be a meter or so high but because in some buying countries – especially in East and Central Europe – key aspects of the new legal framework may not be clear or have been tested.

Export Credit Agencies are naturally worried that, if they inspect the documents e.g. a take or pay contract, it will be very hard for them to "disown" all or any of them if a claim arises.

This is like so many issues in this area in that it is very dangerous to generalize between Export Credit Agencies or even between cases and thus the one truth about the question "Who Takes the Documentation Risk" is that it would be seen by most Export Credit Agencies as being in the category of a good question!

Actions/Inactions by Governments. My second point about actions or inactions of government is also much more difficult in project financing. This is especially true of infrastructure projects.

This is essentially because in such projects different bits and levels of the government of buying countries can play so many roles.

The viability of a project can depend on certain tax breaks and thus on these are not being changed by government or on an export licence for the output being approved or on certain export or import duties being waived or set at a fixed level. Government can be the supplier of feedstock or fuel or raw materials for a project. Government can be the purchaser of output from a project. Government can be the supreme/ultimate decision taker on tariffs or output prices from a project. Government can be the party which sanctions the transfer of repayments or profits or dividends.

This is not of course an exhaustive list, but it demonstrates that it is much more complicated than simply being the buyer. Actions or inactions in any of these contexts could be followed by problems for the project and by a default in payment or by a failure of the project to earn income/profits which it might otherwise have made.

This links back of course to the documentation risk if one tries to catalogue all the things government will and will not do in a single undertaking or letter. Apart from the clear risk of missing something out – who should sign such a letter and is it clear that the person(s) or entity(ies) signing the letter can commit the government in all of the contexts? And very importantly, should this letter contain any kind of "penalty" on the government if there is some breach of any of the undertakings?

Infrastructure projects present special problems as indeed do any projects which do not earn foreign currency which can be held offshore in an escrow account.

Infrastructure Projects: General

Infrastructure projects can present particular difficulties, especially in relation to developing a security package which is acceptable to lenders/investors/insurers. Oil or raw material projects can, for example, produce output which can be – easily sold – relatively on the international market and which can thus generate foreign exchange income/earnings, part of which can be retained in escrow accounts offshore and used to repay foreign borrowings.

This kind of approach can be much more difficult for infrastructure projects which usually earn local currency rather than foreign currency and can thus leave lenders/investors/insurers exposed to the risks of an inability to convert funds from local currency into foreign exchange and thus to transfer repayments, profits, etc.

There is also the point that the viability of infrastructure projects – even "privatized ones" often depend crucially on government decisions/permissions – especially in relation to tariffs.

As noted earlier, there are two main vehicles for ECA involvement:

(a) Export credit insurance and associated funding.
(b) Investment insurance.

Here are two main kinds of risk:

(a) Political risk.
(b) Commercial risk.

There is, however, a third and in many ways more important category, namely risks which do not fall neatly into one of these two categories.

The Changing Role of the Export Credit Agencies

Two important points in this contexts are:

1 "Privatized" needs to be in quotation marks. Host governments keep being dragged back into the area in these buying countries, supplying countries and funding countries.
2 Many of the traditional mechanisms are not ideally suited for project financing and privatized projects.

These points apply to the facilities of the Export Credit Agencies but also, in my view, to the "regulatory framework" of the OECD – the so called Consensus – which limits length of credit and, particularly, the profile of repayments. However, it also applies to other parties involved in funding such projects including the World Bank.

Most of the present funding and insurance infrastructure is based on government buyers or government borrowers or government guarantees in respect of medium and long term credit for projects.

In some ways, some ECAs have become "born again project financiers" with varying degrees of fervor. But in my own experience this is concentrated heavily on foreign currency generating projects with a consequent possibility of escrow accounts. Few infrastructure projects offer this possibility.

The main constraints on ECAs in this whole area are:

(a) Expertise – ECAs cannot have experts in all sectors.
(b) Analytical capacity – how many projects can an ECA examine at the same time. Projects which need a six- or seven-year period to structure financing (e.g. Hub River in Pakistan) are a dubious model for anybody or anything.
(c) The effects of the debt crisis – ECAs bear the scars and also have lost reserves etc. This has also led to parliamentary and Ministry of Finance scrutiny at unprecedented levels in most countries.
(d) The over-enthusiasm of some project sponsors and advisors who simply clog up the system by lodging too many "no hope" applications to be examined.
(e) The difficulty of progressing and implementing risk-sharing arrangements.
(f) The continuing misunderstanding in the World Bank and other places over the role of ECAs. ECAs are not sources of aid. ECAs are not sources of untied finance. ECAs are not simply vehicles for the industrial or foreign policy of their own governments.

The fact is, given not least the vast accumulated debts of the ECAs, it is simply not the proper role of ECAs to encourage or support exports to countries or on projects or buyers who will not pay.

It should be stressed that, in their medium-term and long-term and investment insurance activities, the ECAs are acting as, or for, or on the account of their governments and so questions of what is the proper role of governments have to bear this in mind in relation to privatized projects.

Projects Which Do Not Happen

Projects which are brought to closure are, in some ways, the easy ones since those involved will, hopefully, recover their costs from the project. Much more difficult are projects which do not happen; for any export credit agency this can be seven out of eight prospects.

A key question is who should/will/could bear the costs of working on these projects (e.g. all the costs of analysis, specialist advice, etc.)? There is no common policy on this amongst the ECAs but I would guess that it will be a question of increasing importance and difficulty. The temptation is, of course, always to see this as a problem for someone else or the costs to be met by someone else.

Pre-Completion Risks

This, too, is a difficult area, i.e. who takes the risks of non-completion and what is the "proper" role of the ECAs in this area. This has been an area of some change over the last year or so. Initially, some ECAs did not wish to take risks or cover any risks until after the commissioning of a project, feeling that the contractors and project sponsors should take the "completion risks." However, there has been some movement as more ECAs have become willing to take pre-completion political risks and others will look at a wider spectrum of risks. In this area, as in some other areas, there has been some development of a more common and consistent approach between the ECAs.

Cofinancing Between the Export Credit Agencies and the International Financial Institutions/Multilaterals

It is much easier to talk about this kind of cofinancing than actually to do it.

The basic point is that ECAs are primarily engaged in supporting/providing tied finance (i.e. finance tied to the procurement of goods and services from the country of the export credit agency) while the international financial institutions are involved with the provision of untied finance.

Thus the problem is often one of procurement. As a general rule, the international financial institutions look for International Competitive Bidding (ICB). Obviously the ECAs do not want to prevent or impede competition, but their own support will not be linked to a project, whoever tenders for it or wins the tender, but to suppliers from or contracts won by their own nationals.

This is an area of real significance since the ECAs are major players in the area of providing finance for projects in non-OECD countries. The facilities they provide/support are far larger than the facilities provided by all the international financial institutions combined.

The ECAs are in may ways, therefore, the natural cofinancing partners for the international financial institutions.

Cofinancing can take various forms, e.g.:

(1) Joint Financing
(2) Parallel Financing

Some are more straightforward than others and some projects do not easily lend themselves to breaking into separate parts and thus separate contracts for parallel financing.

An area worthy of further study, especially in relation to the recent arrangement by the World Bank of the "mainstreaming" of its guarantee authority, is risk sharing. This is particularly relevant in the context of "privatized" projects and, especially, such projects in the infrastructure area. This reflects the fact that no party is likely to be happy to take all the risks in a project, e.g.:

(i)   Construction
(ii) Completion
(iii) Political
(iv) Commercial

Thus arrangements which allow risks to be shared would be of increasing interest to most parties involved. Much work has still to be done in this area not only to produce cooperative arrangements of the kind which fully meet the needs of the project world in which we are all now operating.

Multi-Sourcing: Cooperation Between Export Credit Agencies

Commercial and industrial factors mean that it is now unlikely that a project of any size can be sourced from one single country. Thus, multi-sourcing is inevitable.

Arrangements have existed for some time for ECAs to cover goods and services supplied from outside their own countries and even more liberal arrangements exist within the European Union. However, there is strong pressure for ECAs to work even more closely together not only in "co-insurance/reinsurance"-type arrangements but also to avoid each ECA doing its own "due diligence" with costs and delays rising steeply. Some real progress has been in this area with bilateral arrangements (e.g. between COFACE and ECGD and EID/MITI and JEXIM). However, more remains to be done and the need is an urgent one.

Summary and Conclusions

My personal view – and I stress that – is that the consequences of these complex and inter-related factors are probably:

1 The sheer scale of financing required for infrastructure projects means that there is an important gap to be filled and a vital role for the ECAs in helping to fill this gap. It is not, however, a gap which the ECAs can fill totally.
2 Most ECAs have significantly reviewed and restructured their facilities in the project financing area. Most are now heavily engaged in project financing and have brought a growing number to financial closure.

3 Even better multi-sourcing arrangements and improved cooperation between the ECAs are required. This is largely for the ECAs themselves to sort out. But it is not an easy question.

4 More flexible repayment terms are needed under the OECD consensus, particularly in regard to the profile of repayments – especially the early repayments – since under the current structure the largest repayments are due immediately following commissioning when the cash flows of a project are likely to be at their most sensitive/delicate.

5 All parties producing or advising on projects should make conscious efforts not to clog the system with a mass of imaginary projects or involve ECAs at too early a stage.

6 The World Bank needs to review their priorities and practices to give much more emphasis to the role and views/practices of ECAs. In many ways the ECAs, not the commercial banks, are the natural co-financing partners for the World Bank and the other international financial institutions.

7 A key problem for the ECAs is to define the risks they can sensibly and properly cover. Blanket terms like "political risks" are unlikely to be helpful. It is preferable to define the risks which will be covered. It is very dangerous to work on the basis either that it will "be all right on the night" or to wait until a default and claim arise before knowing if a risk is covered.

A basic example of some of these points is in Russia and some other East European countries. The countries have been told to decentralize, privatize, withdraw governments from the industrial and commercial sectors, to relax regulations and deregulate, etc. However, at the same time, they are not only being told that, whereas they used to be creditworthy, now they are no longer creditworthy but also that the World Bank, for example, will require a counter guarantee from the host government if it issues any guarantees. These are two very difficult things to do and say at the same time!

One also has to beware of "fashion." An ECA nightmare is probably that nationalization is not so much a stage between privatization and privatization, but that, if the private sector is "oversold," then privatization may well be a stage between nationalization and nationalization!

Golden Rules

These are fascinating times for all involved with projects and if I could try to summarize my main point in this context, this would be in three "Golden Rules":

1. Do not generalize – the case by case approach is of fundamental importance.
2. Do not go into this area if you expect quick results. Every project will need considerable resources and time to develop.
3. Do talk to the export credit agency at the earliest possible time and do not work on the basis of either assumption or precedent or simply transferring models from other cases or countries.

Appendix B

The Berne Union

The Berne Union has a total of forty-one Members and five Observers: forty-five Members and Observers from thirty-eight countries and locations, and one "multilateral" institution (Multilateral Investment Guarantee Agency).

Argentina	CASC	Mexico	BANCOMEXT
Australia	EFIC	Netherlands	NCM
Austria	OeKB	New Zealand	EXGO
Belgium	OND	Norway	GIEK
Canada	EDC	Poland	KUKE
China	PICC	Portugal	COSEC
Cyprus	ECIS	Singapore	ECICS
Czech Republic	EGAP	South Africa	CGIC
Denmark	EKF	Spain	CESCE
Finland	FGB	Spain	CESSC
France	COFACE	Sri Lanka	SLECIC
Germany	HERMES	Sweden	EKN
Germany	C & L	Switzerland	ERG
Hong Kong	HKEC	Switzerland	FEDERAL
India	ECGC	Chinese Taipei	TEBC
Indonesia	ASEI	Turkey	TURKEXIMBANK
Israel	IFTRIC	United Kingdom	ECGD
Italy	SACE	United Kingdom	TI
Italy	SIAC	United States	EXIMBANK
Jamaica	EXIMJ	United States	FCIA
Japan	EID/MITI	United States	OPIC
Republic of Korea	KEIC	Zimbabwe	CREDSURE
Malaysia	MECIB		

International Organisation – MIGA (World Bank Group, Washington)

The Berne Union Secretary-General has also established cooperation arrangements with the new Export Credit Agencies in the Slovak Republic, Hungary, Romania, Slovenia, Latvia, Russia, and Uzbekistan.

10

The Future of Private
Political Risk Insurance

John J. Salinger[*]

I think we may be at a significant turning point in the life of the political risk markets.

For most of the recent past my thoughts about the market brought to mind a line from a song in the musical *Evita*, "When the money keeps rolling in you don't ask how." Now, however, I am reminded of Shakespeare's more enduring line from *The Tempest*, "What is past is prologue."

To address the topic in a more orderly way, I will organize my thoughts, as Malcolm Stephens has done in terms of the past, the present and the future.

In the early 1980s the insurance industry was awash with capacity. Insurance is a cyclical industry. Excessive capacity led to an expansion of coverage terms and a reduction in rates. As property/casualty rates plummeted, insurers searched for new business to write. Some decided to enter the field of political risk insurance. I am sure they reasoned that if AIG and Lloyd's of London could do this business, they could too. In any event, the wisdom of the day was, "Countries don't go broke." And the money came rolling in.

Unfortunately, the timing was not very good. At the same time that capacity increased conditions in the developing world were changing dramatically. It soon became clear that, while countries didn't go broke, a lot of them had acquired more obligations than they could service.

This led to a great deal of red ink. Those affected re-evaluated their strategy. In the banking sector, many regional banks had been lured into the sovereign debt syndication market in search of higher spreads. Most of them concluded that international lending was not part of their core business and abandoned the market.

There was a similar response from the insurance sector. Underwriters were surprised by the size of the losses. Most did not have the resources to devise and

[*] *John J. Salinger is President, Global Trade and Political Risk Insurance Company, American International Group.*

execute recovery strategies. Underwriters withdrew from the market. Reinsurance capacity melted like snow in the noonday sun. The industry came very close to disappearing.

To illustrate the severity of the situation. AIG experienced 137 claims in our 1982–5 programs. We paid losses of nearly $400 million against premiums of only $186 million. Fortunately, AIG had the deep pockets, as well as the resources and the determination to pursue recoveries aggressively. Today recoveries of those losses stand at more than $220 million, and we are still counting.

At the nadir of the cyle, total private sector capacity dropped to $150 million per risk for a three-year Confiscation policy. If Currency Inconvertibility risk was required, worldwide market capacity was no more than $25 million.

This brings us to the present day. For most of 1997, virtually every financial market has been characterized by high liquidity and large capital inflows. This is certainly true of the current insurance market.

Just as they did in the 1980s new entrants have jumped into the political risk market. By our count there are 23 companies and 43 syndicates at Lloyd's that underwrite political risk insurance. We believe it is possible to arrange as much as $1 billion in coverage on a single risk. Much of this capacity is medium to long term and includes both Confiscation and Currency Inconvertibility cover.

And the money keeps rolling in. Despite the problems in Asia, there are market rumors that more companies, fearful of missing out on a good thing, are poised to enter the market. On top of that, we understand that the huge European credit reinsurers, that have historically eschewed political risk, are reconsidering their position.

And why not? For the past several years I have heard that political risk has significantly diminished. The reasoning is:

1. The Cold War is over. Therefore military threat is very low.
2. Emerging market governments are privatizing and seeking foreign investment. Therefore, the risk of confiscation is practically non-existent.
3. Communism is discredited. There is near universal acceptance of the economic formula that includes a market economy, lower tariffs, decreased barriers to foreign investment, and the free movement of capital. Therefore the risk of Currency Inconvertibility is, if not zero, at least very low.

In short, political risks are significantly diminished. Anyone looking carefully at the banking, capital, and insurance markets during the past two years would certainly conclude exactly that.

But remember Shakespeare's line about the past and the future. In the early 1980s new capacity rolling into the insurance markets coincided with significant changes in the risk markets.

I think the same thing is happening today. We have to be mindful that privatization of infrastructure is a radical, new concept. Historically governments, generally national governments, took responsibility for power, communications, transportation, and water. Today they are turning to the private sector to finance and operate these politically sensitive sectors of the economy. While there is a consensus that this is a necessary step, it has not yet been subjected to a stress test. We do not know how governments will react when trouble comes.

Secondly, keep in mind that, while project finance is not a new field, it is unfamiliar territory for most political risk insurers and reinsurers. We have been a short-term market for 20 years. The three-year barrier was breached only recently. How many underwriters have made fundamental changes in their approach? How many have just crossed out the number "three" on the slip and replaced it with "five," "seven," or "ten?"

Finally, it is important to recall that this is an industry that is characterized by adverse selection. That is, the market is taken up with bad risks only; good risks do not tend to buy insurance. This makes it much more difficult to fulfil the insurance principle which is to take a little bit of revenue from a whole lot of participants to cover the problems of the unfortunate few.

I would argue that the state of global economic affairs today is dramatically different from the state of global political affairs. While the economic system is becoming more globalized, the political system, especially since the end of the Cold War, is becoming more localized. When the global economic system does not deliver the prosperity it promises, there will be a local political backlash. Politicians do not like taking responsibility for bad news. It is easier to place the blame elsewhere. When it comes to scapegoats, "foreign devils" are a time-tested, effective choice.

I am asked to make a few predictions about the future state of the market and, with some trepidation, will do so.

First, I think that those who dismissed political risk as a diminishing threat will re-evaluate their assessment. To the extent that projects go forward, demand for coverage will increase.

Second, I think there will continue to be downward pressure on rates. In the early 1980s it took insurers longer to recognize the severity of the risk than other financial markets. This may happen again. As long as new capacity rolls in, rates will be soft.

Third, I think some markets will explore new areas of coverage. Two possibilities come to mind: breach of contract performance and guarantees of performance by sub-sovereign entities.

Demand for these coverages will be strong. They also present considerable risk. Before underwriters accept this kind of risk, they should ask a few questions: Is the guarantor or counterparty credit worthy? What leverage does the underwriter have to enforce performance? Finally, if we pay a claim, what are our rights of subrogation and how valuable are they?

Last but not least, I want to comment on the relationship between the government and private sector underwriters. The historical relationship has been poor. The private sector regarded the government underwriters as the big elephant in the forest. The government underwriters saw the private sector as either irrelevant or as undesired competition. Fortunately, I think we are beginning to move beyond that. In recent months we have concluded major transactions with both OPIC and MIGA. After years of negotiation, we have finally agreed on documentation for a Cooperative Underwriting Program with MIGA. It would be more beneficial if this were a common occurrence rather than a noteworthy development. However, it is progress.

I think this is happening for two reasons. First, private sector capacity has grown and broadened dramatically since 1996. The private sector can no longer be dismissed as irrelevant by anyone. The second is the changing circumstances of the government underwriters themselves. Many have been instructed to withdraw from markets, such as short-term export credit insurance, that can clearly be fully served by the private sector. Others are in the process of being privatized, or they are fearful of being put out of business. It may be that the two sectors are beginning to see mutual advantage in cooperating with each other.

I would also like to comment on the practice of government underwriters purchasing reinsurance from the private sector. On the one hand, it is a way for government underwriters to augment their capacity without relying entirely on their government. One the other hand, there are some potential pitfalls.

The most obvious is that government underwriters issue long-term contracts. When those contracts have a 20-year tenor, the insurer has accepted a 20-year credit risk on the reinsurer. If a loss occurs in the distant future, the insolvency of the reinsurer does not relieve the insurer of the obligation to pay a claim.

A second problem is the potential limitation of action that the government insurer accepts when it enters into a reinsurance contract. In addition to their responsibility to their government sponsor, the insurer accepts a fiduciary responsibility for the reinsurers. It has to safeguard their interests in a loss/recovery situation. After the Gulf War, the US government led a Paris Club decision to forgive a large part of the rescheduled official obligations of the government of Egypt. Had a government been acting on behalf of reinsurers, they would have been obliged to refuse the debt forgiveness. Governments who purchase commercial reinsurance must be prepared to subordinate political considerations under certain circumstances.

Finally, reinsurers commit fewer resources to understand the risks underwritten than do insurers. This can lead to a phenomenon known as "innocent capacity." The problem with innocent capacity is that it has no staying power. When losses roll in, that capacity tends to withdraw. If government underwriters want to work with the private sector, it would be preferable to work with structures that create knowledgeable, professional underwriting capacity.

Nevertheless, anything that fosters more cooperation between the government and private sectors is a positive development.

The primary beneficiaries will be investors and financiers who need the insurance to manage their risk, to increase business, or to have a partner to assist in the event of difficulty down the road. They will be best served by a market with depth, competitiveness, and a measure of stability that has been absent. Meeting the development needs of the emerging markets and spreading the inherent risks of infrastructure development with require expertise and capacity from both sectors.

I agree with Malcolm Stephens that we live in interesting times. I would add that those who fail to understand their history are doomed to repeat it.

11

Political Risk Insurance, International Banks, and Other International Lenders

*Robert H. Malleck**

I shall try to address the subject of political risk protection from the perspective of diverse debt sources, not banks exclusively. When we talk about the debt side of the equation and the role of political risk in arranging financing facilities, we really need to talk about the full range of where the money comes from.

Where a lot of the cutting edge activity, if you will, is occurring right now, is how to find ways not simply to load up the universe of potential commercial bank lenders with project risks, including political risk, but to uncover new pools of investors, mutual funds, pension funds, and interesting regional pockets of investment money that are willing to take on these risks.

Having said that, let me begin by discussing the traditional reasons why the banks who have been the underwriters of so much project debt have turned to political risk insurance. Of the 50 to 90 traditional commercial bank investors in project finance, the overwhelming majority are European. And banks in many European countries face very strict regulatory requirements with respect to provisioning their cross-border exposure.

The easiest way to get out of this provisioning is simply to layer on political risk insurance. Thus there is a regulatory reason why in today's market, with finite capital, we would turn to a traditional source of political risk insurance such as a MIGA or an OPIC or the political risk insurance policies out of the European export credit agencies.

What we mean by mandatory provisioning is the following: if for instance a UK bank that wishes to participate in the Lihir gold mine in Papua New Guinea wants to take a $20 million piece of a 12-year amortizing loan, the Bank of England might come along at the end of the quarter and ask what is your exposure in such and such a class of assets, and the UK banker will have to come forward and say, well, I have got $20 million lent to the Lihir gold mine in Papua New Guinea with a tenor of 12

Robert H. Malleck is Vice President, Global Project and Structured Trade Finance, Citicorp Securities, Inc.

years. What do you think about that? This is a rather crude description of the process, but I think what the Bank of England regulator will probably say is, well, we think you are going to have to provision for that risk. The banker may have promised his credit committee a particular return and he did not forecast he was going to face a mandate to write down his returns by some percent (which could theoretically be quite high).

Here in the United States the US banks are not under quite the same degree of regulation in terms of a mandatory requirement as far as I am aware. While there might be great levels of scrutiny from the Federal Reserve, and various levels of other regulatory oversight, there is not a mandatory requirement to provision against these exposures *per se*.

The US banks utilize political risk insurance, therefore, not because their hand is forced so much as because they have a leveraging of capital issue that they would like to get over with their credit committees.

Political risk insurance can be used to leverage capacity. There is a finite amount of risk capital, with an incredible demand for risk capital to be invested in emerging markets. This is dollar-based finance or hard currency-based finance very often, on relatively attractive fixed or floating interest rates, on terms up to 12 years. You can do it through a credit agency that has the support of its national treasury. You could do it through swap markets. You could do it through options. You can do it through the bond markets. We turn to political risk insurance because we need to leverage scarce risk capital.

We use political risk insurance for all sorts of project finance simply because it is very adaptable. The risk of inconvertibility is the risk I think most underwriters are concerned about these days. There is a trend toward privatization and a trend away from expropriation. Creeping expropriation remains a very big concern, but at least outright expropriation is not really the concern most bankers are worried about these days.

And political violence, yes and no. I would contend that in today's marketplace if I were a savvy sponsor, and my bankers came to me and said you absolutely must have political risk insurance in order to get this deal, I might say, well, just how much political risk insurance do I need, because as you know, the traditional coverages of political risk insurance are political violence, expropriation, and inconvertibility risk. How much political violence are we concerned about in Trinidad? So if I were a savvy sponsor, maybe I could pare down 30 basis points per annum, which is a very material number to my overall project economics.

Political risk insurance can help support very large fund-raising exercises. When we are doing multi-billion dollar projects, there is just no way one single source is going to raise all that money. We invariably have to come up with a financial plan that optimizes the sources and minimizes the weighted average cost of debt.

Very often political risk insurance providers or guarantors offer a rate that is subsidized for various reasons. When we were looking at Alumbrera, a multibillion dollar gold/copper mine in Catamarca Province, Argentina, many political risk underwriters saw the importation of copper concentrate as a strategic opportunity for their economies. So they were willing to provide some subsidized coverage in order to secure long-term sources of copper concentrate.

In short, political risk insurance can support the large sums that need to be raised, and is very often subsidized. Furthermore, it is available in countries considered to have a high amount of risk. When we are looking at long-term project finance or even a sovereign-related or parastatal financing in the emerging Turkic republics, places like Uzbekistan, Tajikistan, and Kazakhstan, we will often turn to various sources of political risk insurance in order to provide complementary financing to the arrangement, for instance, of export credits.

Finally, political risk insurance allows us to extend credit to bond investors or traditional commercial bank lenders at tenors that are what we call "off market." That is, for example, without political risk insurance I may only be comfortable making a five-year loan in Argentina. With the political risk insurance I may be comfortable in making a ten-year loan in Argentina. Since a more patient amortization will help improve the overall project economics, ten is better than five, and so we go to political risk insurance.

Traditional political risk insurance of the kind that the debt underwriters get would not protect against devaluation. A legal market-driven force is not a political risk that is underwritten. I cannot go to MIGA or OPIC if suddenly the cost of debt in local terms from my borrower has skyrocketed. If they default, that is a commercial risk, and I just have to eat that.

So what we really need to do in cases of currency devaluation is factor in adequate cushions and reserves in projects, as well as adequate hedges and pass-throughs of the costs of potential devaluations into pricing formulas for power or other outputs.

Now let me turn to the mining, oil, and gas industries. I do not purport to be an expert *per se*, although I have had involvement in some fairly large transactions and have participated in the formative discussions among the lending groups, the lead arrangers and underwriters, and the sponsors as well, discussions concerning why we would recommend one financing plan versus another. What I have seen over the last three years or so is an evolution away from traditional political risk insurance and toward the capital markets, plain and simple.

That is, three years ago when sitting down with project finance colleagues at Citicorp to think about ways to finance investments in the oil, gas, and mining sectors in Latin America, you would never not consider going to the OPICs, the ExIm Banks, the Hermes, and so on. These days, except for very risky countries, there has been a remarkable transformation in perspective, a decided shift toward providing capital without political risk cover.

When we got to doing Petrozuata, a several billion dollar, heavy oil upgrade project involving Conoco and Maravan in Port Jose in Venezuela that closed in 1997, we were successful at tapping about a billion dollars of project bonds in the capital markets. The bank underwriters who were there were scaled back significantly. I feel somewhat sorry for them. They came into the deal with high expectations of owning a much larger share of a marquee project and ended up owning a much smaller share of that project at the same rates. So word of caution to all bank lenders.

The sizing of the capital structure happens when the bonds are launched. If we could have gotten $1.5 billion, maybe we would have scaled the commercial bank lenders entirely out of the transaction, except that that would have made a lot of important relationships very, very unhappy. So we have seen this evolution away from traditional commercial bank underwriting with political risk insurance to an upsurge of capital market activity without it.

On the other hand, the vulnerability of executing any project and mitigating cross-border risk by underwriting in the bond markets is that they may not be there when you need them. Or if they are there, they might be there at a price that is unacceptable. I have to tell you that out of the blocks, for instance, on the Petrozuata transaction, which was pre-Southeast Asia contagion, a bond was, as I indicated earlier, very much at the forefront of the mix of sources we were expecting to tap. If that project were midstream today, in 1998, or just starting out, I have to believe that if I were the sponsor, despite my desire to get this thing done as quickly as possible, I might have put far more emphasis on corralling a committed bank group together lest I get to the finish line and discover that I could not get my bond done.

Now, with regard to mining, oil and gas projects, the important point is very simple from a funding perspective, namely that these involve a marketable, tradable, hedgeable commodity. What we are trying to do is interpose an OECD credit risk in the form of a creditworthy off-taker who is taking fixed quantities of the product, maybe at a market price, over a long period of time. Once we have that, and we believe in the ability of the contractor to build the plant, build it at cost, on specification, on time, and we believe in the operator to operate the plant according to normal prudential guidelines of the particular facility in the industry in question, if we believe in the supply of the basic raw material – looking at, for instance, Atlantic LNG, which is a billion dollar single train LNG facility in Trinidad with a supply of long-term gas coming into the project from Amoco – if we believe in all that, then we (as debt investors and risk takers) can really focus on where the cash flow to amortize the debt will come from, and that is from the off-take.

These contracts are scrutinized. They represent secure predictable obligations to take and pay. The monies are deposited into escrow accounts under the domain and control of the lenders. We have significantly, although not entirely, mitigated the cross-border risk of currency inconvertibility and inability to transfer.

If you do not have too much of a concern about political violence in that market and you do not have too much concern about the expropriation of that facility (which would be a spectacular reversal of government policy considering what Trinidad has stated it wants to do with its natural resources and how it wants to treat investors), then you probably can get fairly comfortable with this project. And that is what has happened. A market that really did not have too many precedents for long-term fixed rate or floating rate debt has been extended out 13 years for this project, and a large slug of it without any political risk insurance.

As it happens, we also have political risk insurance, too. But I must tell you that over the life of this project the sponsors became less and less convinced that it was required, but the insurance came with the deal and so we stuck with it. And that political risk insurance, I should say, was fairly finely priced, but when you looked at the cost of it compared to the cost of the "clean" debt, even without factoring the cross-subsidization, if you will, of the political risk insurance tranches to the clean tranche, the political risk insurance tranches all were more expensive than the clean tranches, so there is a bit of a paradox there. It means one of two things. Either the clean underwriters mispriced their loan, which is possible, or the export credit agencies and political risk insurance providers were overpricing the cost of that political risk, which is also possible. I shall leave it to others who have similar projects and experiences, or who have faced similar situations, to do that analysis and try to understand whether or not the pricing in any particular deal is the correct or fair pricing.

So my assessment on oil and mining and gas is that in many instances we have a securitizable off-take and, in fact, are moving from project bonds to the securitization of future receivables. An example I would give is the Alcoa Aluminum deal that Citibank led in 1996 in Brazil. At the time, Brazil was a B+ rated country. The issue got a BBB rating from S&P and Duff & Phelps; $400 million of securitized export receivables, 144-A format, 12 years with an eight-year average life, executed at Treasuries plus 140 basis points.

We are considering steel-making facilities in Venezuela, where there is extremely low basic cost to produce direct reduced iron. We are looking at the securitization of offtakes from these projects and expect that we can also achieve very attractive economics. It should be pointed out that many of the bonds in the market today can be bonds that have back-loaded amortizations – many bullet bonds – so when you compare the net present values of these structures versus the traditional amortizing loan structure, there is a very strong argument, if I were a sponsor, to take the bond alternative.

The traditional project bond markets have really blossomed for project finance, and these are markets that take political risk. The high yield markets in the United States now includes a tremendous amount of cross-over investment. I have colleagues who are traditional high-yield guys on Wall Street now off in the far corners of the world arranging sub-investment grade project debt.

There are also Euro-bonds, of course, and then there are instruments that are not formally called bonds as such, but which also get traded into the capital markets – things like forfait paper, which is a European type of non-recourse finance, utilizing bank guarantees, or avals, fixed rate paper, sold without recourse, as supplier credit. These structures have been utilized in projects and for good corporate credits in Latin America, sometimes for regulatory reasons. In Chile the Encaje – the reserve requirement for Chilean borrowers – can be gotten around if we use the supplier's credit structure.

What is interesting about the loan product these days is our ability to uncover unique investor pockets among the banks. The most distinct is the Islamic segment in the Gulf. We can raise very long-term attractively priced money out of a group of Gulf-based and Islamically-constituted institutions for projects in places like Bahrain, Kuwait, Saudi, Oman, and so on.

Looking to the future, I think that it is incumbent upon all the sponsors, developers, and institutions that want to allocate political risks in the capital markets to try to find ways to effectively trade instruments that bear such risks. With arbitrage among the total universe of players, developers, financiers, and other bearers of risk, we should be able to find opportunities to buy and sell these risks.

At Citicorp we have spent a fair amount of time trying to develop sovereign risk derivatives because, in fact, there are people who would like to be a little "long" in one country and a little "short" in another country, with adequate premiums to be had for all market participants using an instrument like that. The idea of having more players joining the trading system, as has happened for handling hurricanes, earthquakes, and other catastrophic risks, makes sense for political risk as well.

How do we register standardized political risk insurance contracts that can be bought and sold, creating liquidity outside of the traditional underwriting reinsurance industry? Political risk has traditionally been viewed very statically: there is a point in time in which everybody comes together, we sit at a table, we say we need this, and the participants decide we can or cannot do it, we can or cannot reinsure it and there is a price put on the coverage.

But, in fact, these are contracts that cover long periods of time. And there has been very little ability to get out of political risk insurance contracts, or to re-price them, either from an underwriter's perspective that the risk has gotten worse, or from the insured party's perspective that a situation has improved greatly and the coverage is not longer needed as much, or, if kept, should be reduced in cost.

Consider industries like the power sector, which rapidly are being commoditized. In this country, we can now turn to the Dow Jones and get a current price on an energy future, an electricity future. Even in emerging markets we are seeing the advent of merchant plants and the development of the free trade of electricity. So, I think that there is room for innovation here.

There are ideas like indexation in relation to an emerging market bond which might work for political risk insurance policies – where if you are over a number, one party gets compensated, if you are under that number, the other party receives a compensation – something similar to the instruments that we see in the options world.

12

The Challenges of Aggregation, Bad Faith/Bad Credit, and Public/Private Sector Cooperation

*Charles Berry**

There is little, if anything, in Malcolm Stephens's paper (Section 9) with which I can take issue without appearing to be quibbling. I basically agree with his views on where political risk insurance has been, and where it is now going.

I would therefore simply like to comment and build on three themes that are central to the paper:

- the private insurance market, and why its conventional wisdom of the past has changed, albeit slowly;
- the gray area that has developed between traditional investment and export credit insurance, with particular reference to breach of contract risk;
- cooperation between public and private insurers, and why it should be encouraged.

The Emergence of Private Sector Political Risk Insurers

All the reasons mentioned by Malcolm Stephens contributed to the conventional wisdom of 20 years ago that private insurers should not be involved in political risk. However, the principal reason was the unacceptable level of aggregation of risk presented by the class.

High risk and a lack of a statistical base for calculating the true probability of loss are not an obstacle to the creation of an insurance market for a particular class of risk. Oil rigs in the North Sea and satellites are two examples of high-risk assets where insurance was available long before any statistics become available on loss history. In Lloyd's and the other sectors of the insurance and reinsurance industry where you find true risk taking, all you need to place insurance is to find a price at

---

Charles Berry is Managing Director, Berry, Palmer & Lyle Ltd.

which the buyers and sellers agree to trade a defined risk; it is not necessary for the price to be actuarially correct.

It was not the level of risk and lack of predictability, but fear of aggregation that drove the industry-wide agreement of 1936 that banned all insurers from writing war risks on land. The industry looked at the effect of the bombing in the Spanish Civil War and concluded that the aggregation risk posed by modern weapons of mass destruction would undermine the financial soundness of the industry. This industry-wide ban on war risks on land was probably the main factor in forming the industry's conventional wisdom against insuring political risk.

That conventional wisdom has not basically changed. The industry still believes that war risk and other political risks should not form part of the general property insurance market. However a new consensus has emerged that political risks, including war, can be written in the private market on a financially sound basis as a specialist class. This new consensus has been driven by:

a) improved techniques in the industry for managing risk aggregation: an East Coast windstorm or a Californian or Tokyo earthquake would present huge aggregation risks to the industry. Yet through reinsurance and the careful monitoring of aggregates by direct writers and reinsurers alike, the industry is confident that it can manage a $50 billion plus insured loss to a major East Coast windstorm. The aggregations run by the industry in the political risk area are small in comparison.

b) track record: the insurance industry is very conservative. It does not react well to bright-eyed young men with new ideas. However, insurers like AIG can now show a 20-year track record of writing political risk with a loss ratio of under 40 percent. In an industry where any loss ratio of under 100 percent is greeted with delight and surprise, that type of track record begins to attract some attention.

By definition, a long-term track record takes time. Equally, as the aggregation risk that forms an integral part of political risk insurance must be very broadly spread around the industry before the class can be written soundly, it is not surprising that it has taken time for political risk business to permeate through the industry. However, over the last 20 years political risk insurance has taken root gradually in the private insurance market. The class was not sunk by the first wave of bad political risk losses that hit the market in the wake of the 1980s debt crisis. The new consensus will not be blown away by a new round of losses. In brief, I believe that political risk insurance is soundly and securely based in the private sector today. On the investment insurance side, it is probably more soundly based than it is in the government sector.

The Gray Area Between Traditional Investment and Export Credit Insurance

Malcolm Stephens is absolutely correct in pointing out that the clear distinction that used to exist between export credit insurance and investment insurance is becoming blurred. Many risks in the project area occupy the gray area to which he refers.

When looking at foreign government risk, many political risk insurers have, I believe, drawn a distinction between the sovereign or regulatory role of a government and the commercial activities of that government. Traditionally investment insurers have only been concerned with the actions or inactions of a host government as regulator. When dealing with a government buyer however, export credit insurers have mainly been concerned with the foreign government acting in a commercial role as buyer or borrower.

As a result, the risks under the two types of political risk cover have been very different. Investment insurers, in limiting cover to the sovereign or regulatory actions of the host government, have essentially run the risk of the good faith of the host government. While export credit insurances cover sovereign actions too (e.g., embargo), the main risk covered is non-payment and where the buyer is the foreign government the risk becomes not simply the good faith of the government, but its good credit. The main cause of political risk losses to both public and private sector underwriters has been foreign governments' bad credit rather than bad faith.

Though foreign governments cannot be subjected to the discipline of a bankruptcy procedure, they can and do over-commit themselves. Insolvency means being unable to meet all your commercial obligations in full and on time, and in this sense foreign governments can certainly become insolvent. Our experience at Berry, Palmer & Lyle since 1983 indicates that over 90 percent of our 120 plus paid political risk losses have arisen from such government "insolvency": a government buyer or supplier has been unable to meet all of its commercial obligations in full and on time and has defaulted because it is over-committed.

In some of the project business we see today the distinction between the regulatory and commercial function of the foreign government has become less clear. Some of the commitments that governments make to project sponsors remain undertakings that are regulatory in nature: obligations to maintain a local monopoly or oligopoly for a cellular telephone operator, to set certain tariffs, to grant certain tax reliefs, all of these are regulatory commitments and as such only involve the good faith of the government. As such they are more readily coverable by private investment insurer.

But not all commitments to projects are regulatory in nature. Take for example a mine in a remote location that needs to be linked to the national railway system by a spur line. Where the government grants a licence to the mine sponsors to build that spur, I believe that most investment insurers ought to agree that cancellation of that licence to build and operate the spur is the type of risk the insurers should accept. However if instead of granting a licence, the foreign government commits to build the railway spur, and then guarantees that the state railway authority will perform transport services for the mine, a different situation arises. The subsequent failure of the government to build the new line or ensure that the transport services are provided represents a failure by the government to honor commercial obligations. Such failure would not usually be covered by an investment insurance contract.

A commitment to buy all the output from a power project or, indeed to supply its raw material, is more than a regulatory commitment. In essence it introduces a risk that investment insurers have not traditionally been concerned with, namely that of over-commitment. The action of the Indonesian government in postponing and reviewing certain major projects, while arguably a sovereign act, has been prompted by the Indonesian government being over-committed or wishing to avoid over-commitment.

Different insurers may be willing in certain circumstances to cover breach of both commercial undertakings and regulatory undertakings by foreign governments. However, care needs to be taken to ensure that there is a meeting of the minds between policyholder and insurer as to what is covered under a particular policy and what is excluded.

Public/Private Sector Cooperation

From Berry, Palmer & Lyle's perspective, cooperation between the public and private sector while at an early stage, is increasing and should increase further.

From the policyholder's perspective, they need the capacity of both sources and they need the different benefits that both bring. They also need an element of competition between the sectors, and for that matter between private insurers.

While good for the policyholders, cooperation can also be good for both public and private insurers, I believe, because their capabilities are in a sense complementary. The public insurers still provide the best umbrella of deterrence; private insurers have considerable ability to absorb the losses that will inevitably arise from this new wave of infrastructure investment.

Through private market insurers now offer some form of umbrella for their policyholders, government agencies on the whole are more likely to have a deterrent effect on a foreign government and are more likely to recover losses following a claim.

However, the government investment schemes in particular are not well placed to pay losses without internal repercussions with their own government. Their ratio of premium income to their policy limits is simply unstable in many instances. If most government investment insurers had to pay a total loss on their largest policy limit, the claim would exceed their annual premium income by a large multiple.

This is usually not true in the private sector. A Lloyd's syndicate with a $50 million line size for expropriation risk might well, after reinsurance, only be running a net line of say $2.5 million. The syndicates' annual premium income across all lines might be $200–300 million. In other words a $50 million loss might only affect the bottom line profit for that syndicate by about 1 percent of its annual turnover.

Any insurance class needs losses. However, insurance only works by distributing these losses so that they fall lightly on the many rather than heavily on the few. An insurance class also only works if in the long run the premiums paid in exceed the claims paid out. Both conditions exist so far in the private market.

A natural structure for co-operation therefore is for government agencies to lead business with smaller participations, and for private insurers to provide supporting capacity. This is indeed beginning to happen, but as Malcolm Stephens's paper points out, this requires increased respect, trust, and understanding between the two sectors.

Index